THE McGRAW-HILL
HomeBook

THE McGRAW-HILL
HomeBook

HOME INFORMATION SERVICES, McGRAW-HILL INFORMATION SYSTEMS COMPANY

This first issue of The McGraw-Hill HomeBook is dedicated to Joseph A. D'Amelio whose early vision and creativity were responsible for the development of this new information service for the homeowner market.

ISBN 07-606612-6

Copyright © 1979 McGraw-Hill Inc. All rights Reserved
Published by Home Information Services,
McGraw-Hill Information Systems Company,
1221 Avenue of the Americas,
New York, New York 10020

Printed and Bound in the United States of America
Library of Congress ISSN 0162-8151
Library of Congress Cataloging in Publication Data
Main entry under title:

The McGraw-Hill HomeBook

Includes index.
1. Dwellings—Maintenance and repair.
2. Dwellings—Remodeling.
TH4817.M32   643.7   78-26658

McGraw-Hill Inc.

Harold W. McGraw, Jr.
Chief Executive Officer, Chairman of the Board

Paul F. McPherson
President, McGraw-Hill Information Systems Company

Richard B. Miller
Group Vice President, McGraw-Hill Information Systems Company

Rick Jannott
General Manager, McGraw-Hill Home Information Services

Philip Brown Sheehan
Editor

Jan V. White
Art Director/Design Consultant

Residential Architecture

Walter F. Wagner, Jr., AIA

Geoffrey Hindley

Remodeling, Building Products & Appliances

John H. Ingersoll

Ruth Greene

Home Furnishings & Interior Design

Carole Frankel

Jan Jessup

Energy in the Home

Elaine Hudson

John H. Ingersoll

William Houseman
Chairman, McGraw-Hill HomeBook National Editorial Advisory Board

Mary Kraft
Vice Chairman, Editorial Advisory Board

Maxine Livingston
Member, Editorial Advisory Board

Anna M. Halpin, FAIA, CSI
Member, Editorial Advisory Board

JoAnn Francis Spelman
Member, Editorial Advisory Board

Neil Kelly
Chairman, NHIC Contractors' Council, Member, Editorial Advisory Board

Hugh S. Donlan
Marketing Manager

Leslie Winters
District Manager (New York)

Joan A. Baehler
District Manager (Chicago)

Paul W. Stone
District Manager (Cleveland)

Rick Jannott
Publisher

Contents

Preface

Without the slightest exaggeration, we can say that The McGraw-Hill HomeBook has been years in the making just for you. Two things have been paramount in our minds in its preparation: *you* and *your home.*

Whether you recently moved into a modest dwelling, a lavish showplace or something somewhere in between, The HomeBook is ready to offer advice for your home improvement and decorating projects as well as generic product information.

It was designed for your use throughout the first year of your move, the time you'll have the most need for it. It was designed primarily as a "workbook" in the literal sense of the word. You'll find charts and graphs and other graphic aids which distinguish The HomeBook from other publications in the home improvement and decorating fields.

You'll find a section devoted to planning a workable kitchen, another on furniture selection and room arrangement. You'll be invited to take an energy inspection tour of your home and brought up to date on developments in residential solar applications. A section on color will show you the dramatic effects possible with just a can of paint. Another will review the myriad of serviceable and attractive floorcoverings available to you in today's marketplace. Still another will provide you with useful tips on window and wall treatments. Not content with solving problems *inside* your home, we went *outside* in a section devoted to making your living more enjoyable with decks and patios, greenhouses, gazebos and swimming pools.

Not only will The HomeBook help you with problems connected with your move, it will encourage you to make improvements in your home and by so doing improve the quality of your living, as well. We hope it helps you gain a deeper appreciation of how important your home is, not only to you and your family, but to society in general. The McGraw-Hill HomeBook is basically a celebration of the home as a shelter from the hostile elements of nature, as the depositum of all the values we cherish in the civilized world, and as the school where the animal in man is tamed, and the noble in man, nurtured.

We are honored that you have allowed us to share the delights of your home and we are pleased with the opportunity to help you make it an even more delightful place in which to live.

Philip Sheehan

Philip Brown Sheehan
Editor, The McGraw-Hill HomeBook

Why your house looks like it does: a review of architectural styles

Whenever it was built, your new home is part of a tradition centuries old. In 1907, architect Irving Gill was building futuristic homes for his clients in San Diego, California. The material was poured concrete, the technique followed contemporary European experimenters, yet Gill's inspiration was almost certainly the adobe missions built three hundred years before by the Spanish in California and these, in turn, owed something to the Pueblo Indians' houses.

Learning about your home can be an adventure into history. Foreign ideas of elegance, developments in building technology, the availability of natural building materials and the development of new materials, the ideas of Americans since colonial times about what a home should be, and simple changes in architectural fashion are all part of that history. In the twentieth century fashion has moved a long way from colonial and Victorian ideas, but even the most modern-looking home will show traces of its long ancestry. The first article in the *McGraw-Hill HomeBook* explores that ancestry to help you explore your home.

Early days

When he toured the Massachusetts Bay Colony in the 1650s, Edward Johnson blessed the "Wonder-Working Providence of Sions Savior that hath been pleased to turn all the wigwams, huts and hovels the English dwelt in at their first coming into orderly, fair and well-built houses." But it was not only the English. From very early in her history, America was settled by people from all parts of Europe.

The architecture of the South bears witness to French and Spanish presence there. The English settlers on the East Coast were soon joined by the Dutch along the Hudson River. Old stone houses in Albany, New York, with gables facing to the street, Dutch fashion, recall the time when the city was under Dutch influence. The brick courses might be laid in Flemish or English bonding. In southeast New York State, many old houses still have the flairing eaves known as "Flemish gutters," a feature still used for decorative effect by architects today. And it was the Scandinavians, settled on the banks of the Delaware from the 1630s, who introduced to America perhaps its most famous house style—the log cabin. In

the 18th century Scotch-Irish immigrants made it the ubiquitous home of frontiersmen in the northern regions of the country.

Early colonial

Early homes in Virginia and Maryland were built in the half-timbered technique of medieval and Tudor England. The spaces between the heavy wooden-frame timbers were filled with wattle and daub or sometimes brick nogging. The structure might be left exposed or clad in plaster or clapboarding, nailed to the posts and studs.

The quaint and attractive appearance of exposed half-timbering made it a popular decorative style in the later nineteenth and the twentieth centuries. But in these buildings the latticework of beams is often merely boards applied to a brick wall for purely decorative effect

and serves no structural function.

One of the most famous of these early colonial houses is that built by his parishioners for Parson Joseph Capen at Topsfield, Massachusetts. This stolid and imposing residence is clad in clapboarding and shows the overhang of the upper story over the ground floor characteristic of many early wooden

houses. Equally famous is the House of the Seven Gables in Salem, Massachusetts.

Williamsburg and Palladio

The painstaking and brilliant reconstruction at Williamsburg, Virginia gives the visitor a vivid encounter with late 17th-century America. Built in the 1690s, many houses survive, although the Governor's Palace and the Capitol are total reconstructions. It is possible that the buildings were to designs by Sir Christopher Wren, the master of English baroque—certainly his style was to influence many American homes during the coming half century.

It gave place to Palladianism, devised in England by Lord Burlington on the model of the Italian Renaissance architect Andrea Palladio. In America it took the form of Georgian elegance, embellished with restrained classical orders and porticos. It was especially fashionable in Virginia. Despite the relatively

small scale of the homes, the builders were able, by skill and a powerful sense of proportion, to attain an effect of dignity and size.

There were two basic styles. In one, both exterior and interior were neoclassical in the manner of the best houses of the English Palladian, William Kent. In the other, the exterior was in the unadorned Georgian mode and only the interiors were designed after Kent.

In the early 18th century, prosperous Americans modeled their homes on those of the English gentry. Thomas Hancock of Boston, building in 1740, commissioned a house with a classic Georgian frontage. Looking out over prosperous Boston harbor, it was four-square and symmetrical, built in brick and stone with multi-paned wooden

sash windows with restrained classical ornament flanking the door and central window. Even the balcony above the door seems to have been inspired by a London house, built a century earlier, possibly by Inigo Jones. The 'captain's walk' along the roof, a fine vantage for the merchant proprietor, is found in many later American shore houses. The house was demolished in 1863 but a replica was built at Ticonderoga, New York, as headquarters of the New York Historical Society.

Many other houses of the period, even the finest, were built of wood painted white. Few of the architects are known. Often the house was designed by the owner-client in consultation with the builder. Some knowledge of architecture was reckoned part of a gentleman's education. Architects' pattern books, first British, later by American authors, were drawn on for details of design.

Architecture of revolution

In the later 18th century the revived European interest in the classical past and the virtues of ancient republican Rome launched a neoclassical revival in the arts which squared well with the swell of republican sentiments in post-revolutionary America. Inaugurated by the imposing Virginia state capital, Richmond, it was established as the first

truly American style by Charles Bulfinch of Boston and the practical builders' handbooks published by his pupil Asher Benjamin.

Meanwhile, in Salem, Samuel H. McIntire was transforming a townscape with handsome brick, wood-trimmed houses embellished with slender columns and delicate classical mouldings and parapets. It was a light, graceful style which in many variants was to be found in the townhouses of America for the next two generations. In England the style came to be known as Regency, in America as Federal. It led to the Greek revival.

Greek revival

One of America's most popular styles from 1800 to mid-century, its characteristics are pillared door porches; flattened triangular or arched pediments over doors; porches and windows and, in larger houses, broad flights of stairs leading to impressive entrances. Some great houses were even designed as ancient Greek temples.

Drawing on ancient Roman as well as Greek models, the style of Romantic classicism was popular because it was elegant and because it was associated with the virtues of ancient republicanism. Cities all over the country commissioned capitals and civic buildings from architects trained in the style. Local homebuilders, using pattern books written by the professionals, produced their own variants. Absolute fidelity to classical architecture was not possible because most homebuilding was in wood. Knowing their market, the authors often modified or "Americanized" details of the classical masonry forms so that they could be worked in wood.

Picturesque

From the 1830s classical revival styles began to be challenged as American architects drew on the whole of Europe's past architecture to build their own ideal of the "picturesque."

In influential books the brilliant Andrew Jackson Downing attacked the use of Greek temple designs for everything from banks to houses and argued for a choice of architectural style to suit purpose and landscape. He built himself a Gothic cottage overlooking the Hudson River and, though he died tragically young in 1852, inspired the style known as Hudson River Bracketted.

The typical Downing house, built on a light wooden frame clad with vertical boards, had wide verandas, bay windows with Tudor-like carved detail on verge boards and veranda supports. Its interior foreshadowed open plan. Front and back parlours could be thrown into one large room by withdrawing sliding doors and, in some cases, the two rooms were made to interconnect with the hallway. Even houses of Greek reviv-

al pattern were given the Downing touch, the white painted clapboard and smooth Grecian trim being painted over in stony hues of gray and beige to give a more rustic effect.

Downing's *Architecture for Country Houses* also popularized Italianate villa designs which looked back to the Renaissance. Overhung roofs were supported by scrolled brackets; a square tower, campanile or observatory, rose from the center to give views over the surrounding country.

Mid-century saw some homes modeled on Swiss chalets with broad, low-pitched roofs, long outer galleries and ornate roof brackets. The theory behind picturesque was to fit the architectural style to the mood of the landscape. But in fact elements from various periods were often mixed in one building—the broad eaves of a Swiss chalet are found combined with a castle-like tower and bay windows from a Tudor-style parsonage.

The picturesque period was fertile in ideas like the tower and the veranda which long remained part of the American homebuilder's repertoire. Indeed, the veranda or porch has become almost standard.

In the North, the fashion for these open galleries was set by the Indian-style "Iranistan," built for Phineas Barnum at

Bridgeport, Connecticut in 1848. But southern plantation owners had been building them onto their houses for about a century, having no doubt learnt the idea from the British West Indies, where planters had introduced it from the East.

Gothic

"The style of architecture which belongs to Christianity, the sublime, the glorious Gothic." So wrote one enthusiast in 1836. He was ahead of the times, which still favored Greek revivalism.

But in America, as in Britain, the Victorian age was to be the age of Gothic and the neo-Gothic revival. The natural style for churches, it soon spread to domestic buildings. At first decoratively restrained, as in A.J. Davis' Gothic cottage built in 1844 at Rhine-

beck, New York, it soon blossomed into a riot of crockets and finials, lancet windows, pointed arches and carved decorations. Balloon frames were festooned with gables and steep-roofed porches.

As the style grew still more popular, wood-carving companies mass produced the decorative fretwork "carpenter's lace." Many carpenters designed their own houses too and drew on

handbooks by professional architects such as Calvert Vaux. The result was sometimes called "carpenter's Gothic," "American Gothic" or, as the fashion crept westwards, "Steamboat Goth-

ic." In the South, one of the finest and earliest examples of the so-called "Manorial Gothic" was the great mansion of Belmead, Powhatan County, Virginia.

Stick style

By the 1860s the craze for historical picturesque ornament was weakening in favor of a new American technique of timber building. The development of mass-produced machine-made nails made possible lightweight, timber "balloon frames," economical and quick to produce, which were clad in weather boarding.

The "stick style," using the balloon frame, often had imitation half-timbered panels as cladding and emphasized the structural function of the framing members, using simple timber beams to support the eaves of the porches. A carpenters' rather than an architects' idiom, it generally displaced older, heavy methods of framing. It was the ideal building method in the age of America's westward expansion. Whole towns went up almost overnight throughout the middle west and beyond.

Shingle style

Developed from the balloon frame construction technique, this style took its name from the tile-like wooden shingles used as cladding. This wraparound siding of the frame was in complete contrast to the exposed framing of the stick style.

The model was the slate-hung houses, built from the 17th century in eastern England. In shingle, the wooden tiles may be shell-shaped and gracefully molded over the roof in flowing curves.

Fine examples of the style were built by the McKim, Mead and White partnership in the 1870s and 1880s. With their houses, too, open-plan interiors, characteristic of modern American house design, first became fully developed.

The Philadelphia Exhibition of 1876 had awakened a new interest in colonial house styles and also in contemporary English house design. Particularly influential was the work of Norman Shaw, whose mansions showed a new freedom in planning with reception rooms opening widely off the entrance hall. American architects now applied this principle to the domestic interior. Living room, kitchen and dining room led off, through wide archways, from one another and the hall. The interior spaces were opened to the outside and further linked by carefully planned verandas and porches.

15

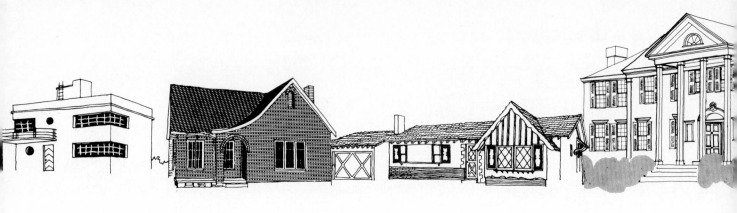

The modern age

It is difficult to trace a sequence of styles in the exciting experimentation and frequent return to historical designs which has characterized the twentieth century. The kind of house he or she lives in has always been up to the house owner. Over the last eighty years, new building materials and techniques and new living styles have opened up a more diverse range of possibilities than ever before.

The Proctor House, built by the brothers Henry and Charles Greene in Pasadena, California in 1909, demon-

strated an original but careful respect for the building material, in this case wood, which has inspired the best of modern building. A dozen years later

the Austrian-born architect Rudolf Schindler built a house on Sunset Boulevard which showed the same awareness for the possibilities of concrete. Like Le Corbusier, the great Swiss ar-

chitect, Schindler used it to develop a flexible living environment integrated into the landscape in a way which would have met with the approval of the picturesque movement of the previous century. It contrasted starkly with the austere geometry of such other European masters as Adolf Loos, who also had American parallels in the 1920s and 1930s. In the Schindler house, glass-sided rooms alternate with open-roofed courtyards to interrelate with the environment.

But the concept of house in landscape was most fully developed by Frank Lloyd Wright. In 1901 he published designs for "A Home in a Prairie" in the *Ladies Home Journal.* This house was never built, but the name was applied to many of Wright's later houses. In these, the brilliant, intuitive arrangement of rooms and space gave full play to the conflicting desires of modern people for intimacy, privacy and freedom of movement. In the Robie

Bettmann Archive

House of 1909 Chicago, Wright, as practical as he was creative, incorporated the garage into the overall design of the house, one of the first to do so.

The development of sophisticated heating and air conditioning systems has made it possible for architects to build houses in environments which earlier generations would have consid-

ered too hostile for domestic comfort. The Edgar Kauffman Desert House at Palm Springs, built by Richard Neutra,

expresses in its harsh horizontal lines a defiance of the rugged landscape and its shifting sands.

Simplicity of design, truth to materials and flexibility of interior space are the hallmarks of the best twentieth century houses. Open plan, in greater or lesser degree, has been a feature of American domestic experience for more than a century. It reached its ultimate expression in the house which Philip Johnson built for himself in 1949

at New Canaan, Connecticut. Standing among trees in private grounds, it is a stark and elegant box of steel and glass with a living area where only the bathroom is enclosed. Not perhaps to everyone's taste. But as this article has shown, the pattern of living has been almost infinitely varied and when a new owner enters an old house we can be sure the pattern of that house will change once again.

Let Wards be a part of your plans.

Suddenly, that new home of yours is no longer just a dream. You've worked hard to make it a reality. Now you want to make careful decisions about the kinds of things you need to make your home special—a reflection of your lifestyle, your good taste.

Montgomery Ward understands. We're in the business of providing a broad selection of the things you need and the looks you want. From paint to appliances, fencing to furniture, Wards can help you find what you're looking for—quickly, conveniently, affordably.

You can increase your buying power by applying for a Wards Charg-all account. Charg-all lets you purchase what you need without waiting—an important consideration as you move.

You may have a Wards catalog tucked amongst the boxes. It's likely there's a Montgomery Ward store nearby. Our experts are ready to give you free advice on decorating, help on installing new appliances, or professional assistance with other special services.

We want to help. And whichever way is most convenient, we can assure you of finding whatever you may need to create the home of your dreams.

Visit your local Montgomery Ward retail or catalog store. Or, for further information, contact: Mr. R. L. Abbott, Executive Vice President—Merchandising, Montgomery Ward, Post Office Box 8339, Chicago, Illinois 60680.

For more information circle 34 on the Reader's Service Card following the Index.

We've got what you want.

MONTGOMERY WARD

Keeping your house in good shape

A year-long detailed program for preventive maintenance and cleaning

With a little attention at the appropriate time, a house will last for decades, even centuries. Properly maintained homes just don't wear out quickly. True, they may look slightly dated or lack some modern conveniences, but they wear well.

In fact, an old house may actually be less of a risk. It has stood the test of time. And if it is healthy now, it probably will stay so via a *planned maintenance program.* Most maintenance is corrective—fixing something that went wrong. It's like shutting the barn door after the horse has escaped.

Preventive maintenance is merely the art of anticipating trouble. For example, the time to put a new roof on the house is *before* the old one starts to leak and ruins plaster and paint in the rooms below. Very few household disasters occur without warning signals. Learn to recognize them and you can save yourself some expensive repair bills.

Unfortunately, home maintenance tends to be both tedious and costly. However, it is less costly in the long run than dealing with major crises which require expensive solutions. *Plan on spending an amount equal to two percent of the cost of your home for maintenance and repairs each year.* If you have a $75,000 house, expect to spend about $1,500 a year in upkeep. Some years you'll spend less. And the year the house needs a new roof you'll spend more. In any case, be prepared to protect your investment.

Your own sharp eye is the best judge of when the paint on the outside of the house is growing thin, or where the carpeting is beginning to wear through. Your ear will pick up the banging in pipes or a strange sound in electric motors. It's encouraging to note that you need not be a Mr. Fix-it to be an expert in planned maintenance. Just know what needs doing, when and whom to call.

Repair or replace?

The expected life-span for various elements is listed on the following House Care Calendar. Keep a close watch on such equipment when it approaches a certain age and then budget for a possible replacement. The *actual life* depends on how well they were made initially, how well they have been maintained and the availability of replacement parts.

Repair costs will also affect useful life. As a rule of thumb, *when the cost of repairs is half the cost of a new piece of equipment (or more), junk it and invest in a new one.*

Saving on repairs

Breakdowns are annoying and service calls are expensive. Reduce them to a minimum with the following tips:

1. Buy household appliances and equipment from authorized dealers who will both install and service it. The few dollars saved by buying at a discount house may disappear with extra installation charges. Manufacturers' warranties will be voided by improper installation.

2. Check consumer reports, tests, performance and repair results before deciding on a specific brand or model. A little homework can save you money.

3. Be present when the equipment is being installed and hooked up. Ask questions about maintenance and read the manufacturer's instruction booklet cover to cover.

4. File all booklets and warranties in a manila folder for Household Appliances/Equipment. On the inside cover, keep a list of all essential information: manufacturer, model, serial number, date of purchase, dealer and serviceman. When repairs are needed, the critical data will be at hand, not hidden on a plate on the back of an inaccessible appliance.

5. Before putting in a panic call to a serviceman, look for obvious malfunctions that you can correct yourself: electric power failure, plug not tight in wall outlet or switch accidentally turned to "off". Some appliances have an overload protector switch that automatically turns the motor off if overheating. After it has cooled down, push the reset button to start again.

6. When you have tried all the obvious solutions, call for expert help. Have the model and serial numbers ready and ask to talk to the service manager, not just the operator. Given a brief description of the situation, a great many problems can be solved over the telephone at little or no cost to you.

7. Compile a list of good, experienced repairmen or services *before* they are needed. It will be invaluable when emergencies arise. (With an uncanny sense of timing, the sink only clogs up before parties or holiday dinners.) If you are new to the area, beg recommendations from friends, neighbors, the salespeople at a good hardware store, plumbing supply store or lumberyard. If the same name comes up more than twice, put a star by it.

8. Once you find good servicemen, stay with them. A repairman needs time to learn the eccentricities and mechanical system of your home. And in the meantime, his meter is running. You'll get more work per dollar spent from someone already familiar with the problem. Another important consideration is that servicemen who have worked with you before will be more inclined to rush out for emergency calls than someone you just picked out of the Yellow Pages.

"Domestic engineering"

One of the facts of life is that housekeeping isn't much fun unless you happen to be one of those gleeful souls who actually smiles at the reflection in the sink. And even then, it's hard to enjoy a sense of accomplishment when you realize that it will all have to be redone in a few hours or a few days. As the Red Queen remarked in *Through the Looking Glass,* it takes all the running you can do just to stay in the same place.

Somewhere between being a slave and a slob is the middle ground where most of us dwell, one jump ahead of the tide. The purpose of making light of housework is to free up time for the *really* important things in life—spending time with your children, your family, and pursuing personal interests. Ask yourself, *"Who am I keeping house for anyway?"*

The question seems simple enough, but it's easy to lose sight of the answer when you're shin deep in clutter, toys and dirty clothes. Certainly, it's not for your children. As the saying goes, you don't keep house for them, but in spite of them. Nor for friends and neighbors. They don't have to live in your home, and besides, they will enjoy a slight feeling of superiority if their windows are cleaner than yours.

A house should be kept for you and your mate according to whatever standards of order and cleanliness make you happy. A minimum of clutter and a modicum of order will see most people through life very nicely indeed. Here are some ways to achieve it:

1. *Put your house on a visual diet.* Clean out. Pare down. Simplify. One or two beautifully designed objects are more striking than a table full of bibelots. And less work to care for too.

2. *Re-examine everything that oc-*cupies space in your home. Have you used it in the past year? The past five years? Could you rent or borrow one if needed in the future?

3. *Does an object's care demand more time and attention than you wish to give?* Consider recovering, repainting, refinishing or replacing to reduce maintenance.

4. *When in doubt, throw it out.* Or better yet, sell it or give it away. Keep only those items that you really need or to which you have a strong emotional attachment.

5. *Before buying anything new, consider its upkeep.* Will it tarnish? Need professional care or cleaning? Soil easily? Buy accordingly.

6. *Remember that nothing looks new forever.* Just as age lines add character to a face, the worn spots and scratches on furnishings add a comfortable, well-lived feeling to a room. However, there is a definite difference between worn and worn-out! Retouch or recover when you've reached the latter stage.

7. *Children are generally capable of doing much more—at an earlier age—than asked.* Learn to delegate and enforce. Have patience and see that the job's done right. Stifle the thought that it would be easier to do it yourself. Things will stay a lot neater too, if kids know that no one will be picking up after them.

8. *Establish a clutter center.* It could be a cupboard, a basket, a large drawer, whatever. Find an out-of-sight locale for all those random objects that no one left behind, but here they are. Then there will be an obvious place to go to retrieve personal belongings.

9. As soon as they are old enough, *teach your children to work the washing machine and dryer, how to sort clothes and do the laundry.* And then take advantage of their newly-acquired expertise, reinforcing it with continual practice.

10. If a weekly visit from a housekeeper is beyond your budget, *consider a monthly or bimonthly cleaning service that will gladly do the scutwork you never seem to find time for*—waxing floors, cleaning ovens, washing windows perhaps. Being relieved of the monster jobs may make it easier to face the day-in, day-out little tasks.

11. *Get a telephone with a very long cord and have jacks installed in several rooms.* It's amazing how dishes seem to do themselves when you are visiting with friends or catching up on business.

12. *Whenever the urge to clean strikes, begin in a different part of the house.* Then if you are interrupted or simply wear out, you will eventually get to all of the rooms some of the time, instead of some of the rooms all of the time.

13. If you don't already have a self-cleaning oven, automatic dishwasher or self-defrosting refrigerator, consider their purchase as a worthy investment in your future happiness and mental health.

HOUSE CARE CALENDAR

HOW OFTEN?	LOOK FOR	EXPECTED LIFE SPAN	DATE	CONDITION
ONCE A MONTH				
Attic/attic crawl space	Water stains; condensation inside roof sheathing; presence of squirrels			
Basement	Dampness; cracks or leaks in walls and floors; termites			
Boilers Hot water heater	Drain sediment from bottom	20 years 10 years		
Radiators	Clean and check shut-off valve for leaks			

HOW OFTEN?	LOOK FOR	EXPECTED LIFE SPAN	DATE	CONDITION
Range/stove hood	Degrease from inside of hood and exhaust fan	15 years		
ONCE EVERY THREE MONTHS				
Hardwood floors	Remove old wax and dirt with hardwood floor cleaner; wax 2-4X/year	Indefinite		
Sump pump	Pour 2 buckets of water into pit to test motor and pump	15 years		
TWICE A YEAR				
Bathrooms	Caulking may need repairs along tub, wash basin and toilet base			
Electric motors	Clean and oil as needed; check belt	Indefinite with care		
Fire extinguisher	Check gauge to see if charged			
Refrigerator	Remove dust from condensor with vacuum. Door gasket should be replaced every 6 yrs	16 years		
Interior walls, ceilings	Damp spots, mildew, discolored areas due to leaks; condensation cracks around windows			
ONCE A YEAR				
Wood furniture	Wax once a year, don't polish	Indefinite		
Exterior window shutters	Secure laths and hinges			
Oil storage tank	Watch for leaks and water inside tank	15 years		
Water pump (for well)	Oil or grease; check belt	15 years		
Well water	Test for purity and quality			
ONCE A YEAR, SPRING				
Central air conditioning	Clean filter and replace. Remove garden debris from outside of condensor; trim back shrubbery near unit	15 years		
Concrete driveways, sidewalks	Repair cracks and holes. Resurface if flaking from salt damage	Indefinite		

HOW OFTEN?	LOOK FOR	EXPECTED LIFE SPAN	DATE	CONDITION
Fences	Loose posts, loose nails. Paint/stain may need attention			
Garages, outbuildings	Check foundations, roof, siding, doors, windows			
Interior paint	Wash walls and windows to retard discoloration by air pollution			
Retaining walls	Check for cracks caused by water buildup; unplug drainage holes			
Septic system	Professional service should inspect and clean when sludge is one-third depth of tank (every 2-5 years)			
Underground sewer lines	Look for greener vegetation over line; watch tree roots	Indefinite		
Vines	Keep away from walls of house			
Water storage tank	Insulate if "sweats" in warm weather			
Wood decks	Signs of termites, tunnels and decay in wood near soil			
Outside woodwork	Varnish on exposure with strong sun may check or flake	One year		

ONCE A YEAR, FALL

Brickwork	Look for cracks, loose mortar joints, repair efflorescence			
Caulking	Replace cracked, loose caulking in joints between siding and window/door frames	6 years		
Fireplace, chimney	Check damper and soot buildup inside flue. Clean if needed			
Furnace	Clean filter or replace; check blower belt tension	20 years		
Oil burners	Clean and adjust by serviceman			
Outdoor furniture	Clean and store under cover, iron in warm area, wicker in cool area			
Plumbing exposed to weather	Close shutoff valve and drain water from pipes and faucets			
Storm windows	Check for condensation inside glass; If present drill angled holes to outside to allow water to run-off outside			
Termites	Termites swarm in early fall before going underground			

HOW OFTEN?	LOOK FOR	EXPECTED LIFE SPAN	DATE	CONDITION
Weatherstripping	Check on doors and windows, replace as needed			
Trees	Check feeding schedule, spray for insects as needed, prune			

TWICE A YEAR, SPRING/FALL

HOW OFTEN?	LOOK FOR	EXPECTED LIFE SPAN	DATE	CONDITION
Areaways, basement windows	Clean, remove leaves, check for drainage. Check windows for rust. Cover before snow falls			
Asphalt driveway	Patch cracks and holes; coat with sealer			
Basement crawl space	Use flashlight to check for moisture, termites, rodents. Cover vents with screening			
Chimney cap	Use binoculars to inspect for cracks; flashing should be secure			
Exterior doors	Edges should be coated with paint or wood preservative			
Exterior house paint	Blistered, peeling or exposed areas should be primed. Repaint before temp. drops below 40°F	5-8 years		
Exterior siding	Repair cracked, loose shingles, boards; fill cracks in stucco and caulking; clear debris near wood			
Floor drains	Flush out with hose, clean if necessary			
Foundation walls	Inspect for cracks, termite tunnels, signs of moisture			
Gutters, downspouts	Remove debris; check for damage; d.s. should drain away from foundation	Up to 20 years		
Porches, wood steps	Inspect for decay, termites. Seal cracks and paint			
Roofs	Torn, loose shingles and flashing	20 years		
Windows	Loose/cracked putty; paint sash and frame if needed			

From start to finish, a good remodeling job needs a good contractor.

Pick an NHIC member– and be sure.

When you're starting a remodeling job, the last thing you want to worry about is the quality of the work.

Choose a contractor who is a member of the National Home Improvement Council, and you can be sure you'll be getting workmanship of the highest quality. And you'll get a lot more, too. Because every NHIC member is pledged to a Code of Ethics, for your protection. And with their years of experience and knowledge, they can help you get the most value from your remodeling budget.

Send for our free booklet "How to Start Your Home Improvement Project with the Help of a Reliable Contractor." It's full of good tips and thoughtful suggestions. Send a stamped self-addressed envelope to:
National Home Improvement Council
11 East 44th St.
New York,
New York 10017

MEMBER NHIC
Better Your Living
National Home Improvement Council

Remodeling

Some basic questions and answers

When to hire a contractor; when to do it yourself

How to begin a home improvement project with a contractor

Selecting a reputable contractor; examining the contract

nless you've been involved with a major home improvement project in the past, you undoubtedly will have a number of questions to ask. Fortunately, there are answers for them. Here are a few:

Should I find a contractor or should I try to do it myself?

On major projects most homeowners retain a contractor, for a number of reasons. Usually a substantial amount of money is involved, even without a contractor. Lacking confidence in his own ability, the average homeowner hesitates beginning something he feels he may not be able to finish or which will end up costing him more to correct.

Also, some lending institutions may not give loans unless a professional contractor is on the job. And some localities require a licensed contractor on major home improvement projects involving structural changes in the home. Under no circumstances should wiring or plumbing projects be attempted by anyone other than a professional.

Obviously, there are certain home improvement projects which are more appropriate than others for the do-it-yourselfer, such as installing floor tiles or applying wall paneling. In the last analysis, you've got to be very honest with yourself and ask some soul searching questions: Can I do it? Can I do it well? Do I want to spend the time and energy doing it myself will demand?

How do I finance my home improvement project?

There are several cash sources for your home improvements, some of which you may not have thought of. Naturally, you can apply for a loan at your local bank or savings and loan society, but if you do you'll be wise to inquire about an FHA loan at more favorable rates than those offered by the bank. You should also keep up with developments in Congress which more and more frequently favor the home-owner who makes energy-saving improvements to his home.

One of the least expensive ways to finance the renovation is to borrow against the cash value of your life insurance.

If you have a substantial savings account, it's possible for you to borrow up to the amount in the account at a very low interest rate, without touching your savings. This is called a bank passbook loan.

You or your spouse may have access to funds in a company credit union, which traditionally loans money at lower rates than those of a commercial bank.

Your equity in your home, if sizable, is an established asset to secure your loan, but there are other ways. One family found that valuables—gold and jewelry—had been accumulating for years in unopened dresser drawers. They were delighted to find the money for their home improvement project right under their noses.

Another solution, again not the most economical, is to pay for the project with a bank-based credit card.

Lastly, although it involves paying substantially higher interest rates, some homeowners prefer to borrow funds from finance companies. It's suspected that they are less intimidated dealing with them than with the less personal lending institutions.

How can I find a qualified professional home improvement contractor?

Since the most professional contractors have built their business on referrals from satisfied customers, word of mouth is still an excellent source for contractors. You should ask at home centers, lumberyards and hardware stores. If you plan to use the services of an architect or designer, he or she could advise you. There are some further safeguards. Be sure the contractor has an established place of business in your area. Beware the contractor working out of a pickup truck with out-of-state license plates. A call to your local Better Business Bureau is a good idea. They'll be able to tell you how long a firm has been doing business and whether or not they have a complaint file on it.

After you have made contact with a contractor don't hesitate to ask him for financial references. If he's on the up-and-up, he'll have nothing to hide.

Equally important are references from his customers in the area. You'll want to get in touch with them by phone, and perhaps follow up with an inspection of at least one of the projects.

Another good sign is a contractor's membership in professional associations such as the National Home Improvement Council or the National Remodelers' Association, which adhere to codes of ethics and standards approved by the Better Business Bureau. Some contractors display membership insignia in their offices and decals on their trucks. If your town doesn't have a Better Business Bureau, you might call the Chamber of Commerce, which often has a consumer affairs department.

Should I bother to get bids form more than one contractor?

Definitely. The important thing to remember is that the different contractors whom you have invited to submit bids should be bidding on *identical* jobs. Give to each one the same information, requesting that bids specify every detail of the project, total cost and completion date. Even with this precaution you'll discover that the bids will vary greatly. The lowest bidder is not always the one to go with, nor is the highest bidder necessarily the best contractor.

Is a contract necessary? If so, what should it contain?

A contract is a protection for both you and your contractor. Some homeowners regard it seriously enough to involve

their attorneys in its preparation. On an expensive renovation this would be economically justifiable and a sound move. The contract must be specific and written in simple, unambiguous language. Specify brand names, manufacturers' model numbers as well as color designations for all appliances and fixtures. This also applies for all building materials—brand names should be specified.

Make sure the contractor has a Certification of Insurance covering workmen's compensation, property damage and personal liability. Look for a cleanup clause in the contract. While the cost of cleanup may be reflected in his bid, most people prefer that he be responsible for this unpleasant chore.

Are permits necessary?

A building permit is generally necessary if any structural work is planned for your home. You will also have to seek zoning approval for your plans. Your building inspector can be of great assistance in determining if your plans meet the standards. A good contractor will handle the necessary paperwork. After the permit is granted you will be subjected to a number of inspections in the course of the project. Again, your contractor will be aware of the necessary scheduling and follow through on it.

Is there a suggested schedule of payments to the contractor?

Yes. In fact, this should be in the contract along with a guaranteed maximum price for the completed job. It is recommended that one third be paid at the signing of the contract, one third while the work is in progress and the final third when the project has been completed to your satisfaction.

Planning and budgeting

A plan for setting priorities and allocating funds for projects

After moving into a new house, there is a great temptation to rush into redecorating and remodeling projects to put your own personal stamp on the new home.

Some of these projects—which tend to be costly as well as semipermanent—should be postponed until you have carefully analyzed your home, its limitations, your furnishings and your goals as a family. You may be well aware of a problem area now. However, unless you are a professional with years of experience, the best solution usually dawns after you've lived with it for awhile. Putting a lot of time, energy and expense into decorative effects that will later have to be ripped out for structural or electrical improvements is heartbreaking to say the least.

Obviously, there are some structural defects, such as a leaky roof, that require little imagination and should be tackled immediately. But the decisions involved in redoing a house, or even a room, are so intertwined that long-range planning is not just desirable, it is critical; there is a logical order to making improvements and it is essential to work out priorities *first*.

Take a house survey

You probably took a close look at your new home before deciding to buy it. If not—or if you have moved into a newly built house and assume it's in mint condition—don't do anything else until you check out the house from chimneywork to foundation footings. It may seem like a rather boring exercise, but the answers will influence everything else you do, the order in which it's done, and the cost. It may also prevent some unexpected and unpleasant surprises when things go wrong.

If you don't know all the answers, call the previous owner, real estate broker, local building inspector, contractor who built it, servicemen and workmen familiar with the house, or even the next-door neighbors. Also try to get a copy of the *plot plan and blueprints* or working drawings used in construction of your home.

The plot plan will indicate the location of hidden items such as sewer lines, water mains or septic systems. And the working drawings will specify materials used in construction and show you the location of bearing and nonbearing walls. Depending on the age of the house, the city building department may have a copy on file.

If you feel inexperienced or less than capable of judging the condition of all aspects of your home, *call a home inspection service*. For a very reasonable fee ($50-100), an expert evaluator will give you a detailed report on the physical condition of your home—an

WHOLE HOUSE SURVEY

	TYPE	AGE AND CONDITION	REPAIR/REPLACEMENT NEEDED
Interior walls Plaster? gypsum board? paneling?			
Interior paint Latex? oil base?			
Flooring Wood? linoleum? vinyl? tile? vinyl asbestos?			
Electricity Capacity of service Fuse box? circuit breaker?			
Appliances Stove, oven			
Cooktop			

	TYPE	AGE AND CONDITION	REPAIR/REPLACEMENT NEEDED
Refrigerator			
Dishwasher			
Garbage disposer			
Trash compactor			
Fan/vent			
Washing machine			
Dryer			
Air conditioner			
Plumbing Copper? brass? galvanized iron? plastic?			
Sewer line Type of pipe? Location?			
Septic system Capacity? Location? Date last inspected? Date last drained?			
Heating system Forced warm air? gravity warm air? circulating hot water? steam? electric resistance? heat pump?			
Furnace or boiler			
Oil storage tank Capacity Location			
Water heater			
Water pump (well water)			
Sump pump			
Insulation			
Windows			
Storm windows/doors			
Foundation walls Poured concrete? masonry block? stone? brick? posts?			
Exterior paint Latex? oil base?			
Exterior siding wood? aluminum? vinyl? brick? stucco? composition material? steel?			
Roof Asphalt shingle? wood shingle? asbestos shingle? slate tile? metal?			
Flashing Aluminum? copper?			
Gutters and downspouts wood? aluminum? vinyl? galvanized iron?			

invaluable aid in budgeting for future needs.

Setting priorities

Now that you know what your house will be demanding in the way of attention, repairs and replacements during the next year or two, you can consider some of the less urgent improvements desired in the way of additions, remodeling and redecorating.

This is the time to reevaluate your life and your financial resources: *what is really important to you and your family?* Would a deck or garden room be preferable to new carpeting throughout the house? Would the addition of a skylight or a greenhouse mean more than new living room furniture? Would new bathroom fixtures come before new kitchen cabinets?

The purpose of this exercise is to help *fit your budget to your values.* Instead of spending money on impulse or compromise purchases, put it toward those areas that will truly and deeply enrich your life. Those items than rank higher on your personal priority list will require a larger chunk of your budget. And even though some less important areas may have to be sacrificed or compromised, it's worth it. The payoff is greater in such "cost effective" planning. The *cost,* although a major factor, is not as critical as the *effect* it has on you and your family.

Developing a plan

For anyone moving into a new house that is sorely or even mildly in need of redecorating, it pays to plan. People who shop aimlessly, hoping for divine inspiration on the furniture floor or among the wallpaper racks, are liable to be talked into something unsuited for the room. The risk of decorating in such piecemeal fashion is ending up with a room that looks confused and uncoordinated at best. Not to mention a drain on the budget! It's a sad fact that furniture, carpeting and draperies have a frustratingly long life-span when you have made a mistake.

Depending on the size of your new home, the size of your budget, the condition and quantity of furnishings, now put together a *one-year to five-year program* to help turn those priorities into reality. This is a long enough time to stretch your furnishing and decorating budget, but a short enough period to **realize your goals.**

Start by doing a room survey to focus on each room. This will not only help you realize what you have, but will also help you think ahead to visualize the final result. Under each item, fill in the appropriate information. Comment upon whether it is to be kept or replaced, repainted or recovered. Then begin to detail the possible changes and ideas that might work within the room. Decisions between walls, windows and floors are so interrelated that it's impossible to consider one without affecting the others.

Making up a chart for each room will help you organize a multitude of design elements into a unified whole. The process is similar to making brush strokes on a painting; each is less important than its relationship to the final work of art.

Putting it into practice

If you really intend to get organized, staple each page inside a manila file folder. On the facing side, staple a heavy kraft envelope to hold color samples, paint chips, sketches, brochures and receipts. Keep track of what you've spent on the outside of the envelope.

Decide first what is worth keeping. Does it need refinishing, reupholstering, slipcovering? Can it be put to another use? For example, a dining table might become a desk and a trunk might become an end table or coffee table. Each year's expenditures build upon the purchases made the previous year.

Professional tips

● Invest first in those items that are heavily used and not easily improvised, such as sofas and lounge chairs.
● Upholster or slipcover the major seating pieces in neutrals or naturals for the greatest flexibility.
● Use paint for color punch—it's inexpensive and easily changed.
● If you are short on furniture, pull it away from the walls and "float it" in the middle of the room.
● If a large discrepancy exists between your budget and the "must haves" on your priority list, either lower your sights or learn the art of creative shopping—at auctions, garage sales, flea markets and second-hand stores.
● Put inexpensive shades or bamboo blinds at the windows. Later, when the budget permits, add shirred drapery side panels, shutters or upholstered hinged panels on either side.

Splurge a little

One of the best reasons to develop a budget (and stick with it) is to be able to afford one absolutely marvelous find—an antique lacquered secretary, an oriental rug, an unusually handsome armoire, or a handstitched quilt. The presence of one striking object rubs off on the whole room, even when the other furnishings are rather ordinary. In fact, the other items in the room should *complement,* rather than compete with, your superlative piece.

Remodeling: a special challenge

An existing building is a more complex design assignment than a piece of land. It demands more ingenuity if the new construction is to marry and harmonize with the old. Architects are skilled space planners; if asked to solve one problem, they may derive a solution that takes care of four others.

Each remodeling project is unique although the factors in a decision to remodel remain the same.
● What is the present condition of the house?
● How long do you plan to live there?
● What is the estimated cost?
● Is the neighborhood improving?
● What are your other priorities?
● And can you recover the costs?

When does it pay?

Depending on what you have to start with, the improvements that add the greatest value to a house are a new family room, an extra bathroom (if only one), a new kitchen and modern bathrooms. A terrace or deck has become an increasingly valuable addition as well.

How to begin

Collect your thoughts. What should the remodeling accomplish? Let the family discuss where more space is needed and how it might best work. Take careful measurements and note plumbing, electrical or gas lines that might be present. Clip magazines, read books, go on house tours. Start a resource file.

Advice from a professional

● Study the design and structure of your existing home and be sure your new addition relates to it.
● Consider furniture arrangement and traffic patterns in your planning.
● An addition may block or remove

I chose some good reproductions.
And one original.

If necessary, hearing aid adapters are available from your telephone company.

It's nice to know there's one original everyone can afford. Genuine Bell.

You can choose from all kinds of colors, shapes and sizes. Plus a variety of convenient custom calling services.

So it's easy to match our styles with yours.

But no matter whether you choose a phone that's plain or fancy on the outside, you'll get genuine Bell quality on the inside.

So why settle for a reproduction, when it's just as easy to choose the original?

(🔔) **Bell System**

This isn't the phone.

This is.

BE CHOOSEY

some natural light. Add a window, skylight or clerestory windows to the existing structure for more natural light.

● Kitchen and bath additions should be planned with existing plumbing hookups in mind.

● The neighbors may object if your addition blocks a view, encroaches on their property or changes a drainage pattern in their yard.

● Your home may be located where it is because solid bedrock or loose fill exists beneath the site of your proposed addition. Preliminary soil tests are highly recommended.

Phased remodeling

If you can anticipate the future growth needs of your home, they can be effectively planned in affordable steps during the original design and remodeling. Extra bedrooms, studio, family room, and terraced deck or pool might appear on a master plan for your home. Tell your architect how you envision your home five and ten years hence. Allowing for your future needs now will lessen the difficulties, decrease the cost and maximize the success of improvements to come.

Why consult an architect?

Although building design is a job for a specialist, an architect is a generalist as well, and this makes him particularly valuable. Engineers will be enraptured with the mechanics of a space; interior designers or artists will underestimate the importance of engineering. An architect will generally have the fewest number of blind spots as well as the most imaginative solutions to offer.

An architect's work begins with an analysis of your family living patterns. Is it important to have a quiet place to listen to or practice music? Do you love to entertain with big parties? Should there be a mud room for dirty kids? Space for a workshop added to the garage?

The answers to these questions and dozens more will lead to a preliminary plan with improved arrangement of rooms and circulation. An architect may suggest that rooms be used differently; for example, moving the family room clutter and noise far away from the living room. Or a living room might become a downstairs bedroom, the dining room become the living room and a wall might come down to enlarge kitchen and family room plus a dining area. Generally, the house will be better planned, inside and out.

Room:	Comments	Changes	Budget	Purchase Plan
Walls				
Ceiling				
Floor				
Windows				
Window Treatment				
Furniture & Fabrics				
Color Plan				
Lighting				
Storage				
Accessories				

Meet the Wizard of Ahhs.

He's your Georgia-Pacific Registered Dealer. And he can help you get "oohs and ahhs" on all kinds of do-it-yourself projects. From building a bookcase or finishing a rec room to paneling your bedroom, or even adding on a whole new room.

Your G-P dealer is full of ideas and useful information. He'll help you select the right Georgia-Pacific materials and the right tools for nearly any home remodeling project. He's eager to lend a hand. So, why not take advantage of him.

You'll find your Georgia-Pacific Registered Dealer wherever you see our familiar blue and white sign.

Georgia-Pacific Corporation
Portland, Oregon 97204

Georgia·Pacific **GP**
REGISTERED DEALER
Home of quality building products and service

Planning your new kitchen

How to gain the kitchen you've always wanted— 8 pages of usable ideas

Planning a kitchen begins with you. Your wants. Your needs. The way you and your family live. When your new kitchen is finished, it ought to do more than please you. It should reflect your personality. A few examples:

• You are outgoing, convivial, enjoy entertaining and love to cook. Translated: a warm, friendly, open kitchen alongside a family room or eating area.

• You are a perfectionist, serious with a sense of humor, persistent. Translated: cooking is an art for you, and you need space, plenty of counters and a clear separation from living spaces.

• You are shy, intelligent and lean more to reading great literature than boiling potatoes. Translated: food is a means, not an end. A kitchen more functional than frilly, organized for quick meals. A window garden will please you.

The handsome kitchen at right, and all the ideas on the following pages are yours for the taking. Start by thinking about what you want. Put it in personal, not technical terms. Think, "I've got to have more space for china and glassware." Not, "We'll need two 18-inch wall cabinets."

You're not expected to be an expert. Put in personal terms, your needs are quickly converted to space and equipment by those who are expert: architect, designer or kitchen specialist.

That brings up other questions. Where do you turn for help? And should you? The answer to the second question is "Yes," unless you are an experienced designer. During the design conferences between you and the professional, your ideas—and perhaps some of your dreams—will get mixed into the new kitchen.

Help is easy to find. The cost ranges from nothing to mildly expensive. Design advice is available from kitchen dealers, many of whom have trained designers on staff, or on call. While CKD after a person's name (Certified Kitchen Designer) doesn't automatically imbue that person with talent, it's true this designation is given sparingly by the American Institute of Kitchen Dealers, itself a select group with demanding standards.

As a rule, there is no charge for design aid from a dealer. Or the charge for design conferences and preliminary plans is absorbed in the cost of the job when you sign a contract with that dealer. If you don't sign, then you pay a design fee.

Kitchen design breaks the buying rule—pay more, get more. Paying dearly for a well-known designer may win you namedropping points, but not always the ideal kitchen for you. On the other hand, a dealer, charging nothing for design, may deliver the kitchen of your dreams. The moral: shop around. Settle on the designer whose suggestions and past work best fit your vision of a superior kitchen. Interviews, by the way, cost nothing.

Before

When Dr. and Mrs. Maccaferri bought their house in San Marino, Calif., they were forced to cook in an old kitchen (left) with few counters and even less storage space. But the house was a good buy in a neighborhood they liked. Result: their first project was to remodel the kitchen. Since Mrs. Maccaferri enjoys cooking, she wanted a just-so kitchen, and turned to designer Chris Christiansen of Kitchen Design, Los Angeles, for help.

One of the most refreshing additions in their totally remodeled kitchen is the window garden (above) where moisture and sun nurture herbs and decorative plants. Natural cherry cabinets now proivde all the storage space needed by the Maccaferris, including a floor-to-ceiling unit (left). Separate refreshment area (below) features a bar sink and an ice maker. Opposite side of the kitchen (right) displays the cooking center plus a microwave oven.

Photos: George Szanik

Photos: Hedrich-Blessing

PLANNING

COOKING

Back to basics: here are time-tested steps to a step-saving floor plan

Frustration over your present kitchen may stem from a bad floor plan. A good one can rescue you from aggravation. The rules, which have long ago been proven, apply to new or remodeled kitchens.

A meal requires five steps from concept to clean dishes: planning, storage, preparation, cooking, cleanup. Each step influences design.

1. *Planning.* Organized space is needed for cookbooks, loose recipes, coupons, note pads, writing materials, a clock, telephone, perhaps a radio, and etc.

How much space? A desk 30 inches wide will do it. A width of 36 inches is better, and when space is at a premium, 24 inches is possible. Desk height from the floor is 30 inches. Easiest to build:

use the countertop material; install one large, or two small drawers beneath the desk top; have shelves built on the wall behind the desk. Position the desk out of the traffic flow.

2. *Storage.* This includes refrigerator and/or freezer plus room for dry foods and canned goods. Ideally, these three storage elements are positioned in one general area. Ideally, there is 18 inches of counter space alongside each element. Must the dry foods storage be near the refrigerator and freezer? No, but you'll find it more convenient if it is.

3. *Preparation.* Normally, items 3 and 5 are the same, calling for a good sink—preferably a double-compartment unit—dishwasher, garbage disposal, and possibly, a trash masher. If you have a choice of being generous here or elsewhere in the kitchen, spread out here. A counter 30 inches wide on both sides of the sink is about right. Less than that begins to crowd cleanup stacking, or food preparation. More than 30 inches is fine up to a point—that point when appliances are too far away from

the sink. A pleasurable extra would be a wood chopping block built in alongside the sink.

4. *Cooking.* A range top and oven are essential. A microwave oven is a useful addition. Some models combine all three. When the units are separate, they still should be grouped in the same area.

Allow 24 inches of counter space on either side of the range top and give yourself a bonus: a counter inset of heat-resistant material to take hot pots removed from the burner. This is needed alongside a wall oven, as well. A 12-inch-wide section of heat-resistant counter material will serve your needs adequately.

5. *Cleanup.* As mentioned in step 3, cleanup and food preparation spaces are identical, with one exception. In the *perfect* kitchen, a separate sink is used to wash and prepare food, a sink that often doubles as a bar sink. This unit features a gooseneck spout (easier to wash large heads of lettuce or cabbage), and a flexible hand-held spray attachment.

STORAGE

PREPARATION/CLEANUP

CHERRY PRESERVED

Fireside custom cabinets, a warm gathering of distinctively detailed, all wood construction and contemporary convenience by Quaker Maid. The softly eased, bevel edge batten style doors reflect the vibrant beauty of select knotty cherry, patiently hand crafted and hand finished into a look that rivals costly fine furniture. Beneath Fireside's country casual exterior, the easy-to-clean interior holds an array of Quaker Maid convenience features, all designed for pleasurable kitchen keeping. Quaker Maid also provides matching finishes to tables and chairs that harmonize with Fireside's natural beauty. Experience the charming warmth of Fireside at your local Quaker Maid showroom. They're listed in the Yellow Pages under "Kitchen Cabinets and Equipment".

Quaker Maid

a **TAPPAN** division· Serving the heart of the home
RT. 61, LEESPORT, PENNSYLVANIA 19533 215-926-3011

Countertop of DuPont's Corian®

Flooring . . . Primitive tile
by American Olean

For more information circle 11 on the Reader's Service Card following the Index.

ONE-WALL

CORRIDOR

The kitchen triangle is not eternal—just a way to help you plan for convenience. It is an imaginary line drawn between the three work areas of the kitchen: refrigeration/food storage, preparation/clean-up and cooking. When the triangle is just right, you save steps. When it isn't, you're either too crowded or set a distance record for indoor walking.

Picture lines connecting range, refrigerator and sink. For maximum efficiency, the lines should add up to no more than 22 feet, no less than 13 feet, and no leg of the triangle ought to be less than four feet.

Researchers have found that the path worn most lies between sink and range. It's logical to make this the shortest leg of the triangle—say from four to six feet. The same study uncovered the facts that the next most traveled path is between refrigerator and sink, the least trod between range and refrigerator. Plan accordingly.

This dandy triangle is a lot less efficient if traffic flows through it. That's one reason why the corridor kitchen,

open at both ends, is a poor plan.

Where does the built-in oven fit into the triangle? It doesn't, but that's not so serious. The range top is the workhorse of the kitchen. As long as the wall ovens aren't ridiculously far away, and do have a heat-resistant counter alongside, convenience is preserved.

Kitchen shape has much to do with your contentment. Not every worn kitchen can be transformed into the perfect shape, but many can, and you'll want to know the pluses and minuses of each.

The one-wall kitchen. *Plus:* the plan suits a small, tight space; is often a solution for a vacation cottage. *Minus:* rarely enough storage space; the "triangle" becomes a straight line. Convenience is saved by dividing range, refrigerator and sink with cabinets and counters.

The corridor kitchen. *Plus:* more packed into fewer square feet; a step saver; excellent for limited space. *Minus:* when open at both ends, it's a traffic jam waiting to happen. Two solu-

tions: close off one end, widen the aisle, (or both).

The L-shaped kitchen. *Plus:* often permits space for informal dining; adaptable to existing kitchen space; works well into a large kitchen. *Minus:* within the same square footage, has less counter and storage space than U or corridor kitchen; can produce traffic problems.

U-shaped kitchen. *Plus:* this plan is tops, say many kitchen designers; easily conforms to the "triangle"; good storage and counter space. *Minus:* not always adaptable to existing situations.

The island kitchen. *Plus:* an island immediately raises storage, counter space; is a good solution for a too-large kitchen. *Minus:* despite a touch of glamour, the island often impedes the work flow.

The peninsula kitchen. *Plus:* a fine way to expand kitchen functions; is often a means of separating kitchen and family or dining areas. *Minus:* it's a specialized plan that fits some kitchens, certainly not all.

U-SHAPE

ISLAND/PENINSULA

Karl Riek

Tappan à la mode.

After 30 years of electric ranges, this is our best ever.
A self-cleaning oven topped by a
Microwave with automatic temperature probe. Delicious.

TAPPAN
Appliances — Serving the heart of the home since 1881.

HAVE AN APPLIANCE PROBLEM? GENERAL ELECTRIC IS HERE TO HELP YOU SOLVE IT.

Darn! Your new house h◗ an old range. Does GE make a combination self-cleaning range and microwave oven?

Of course! Chances are, after move you'll need a new appliance of some sort. Well, don't worry. You've got a GE dealer here.

Just like back home, he h a whole range of the finest G◗ appliances with all the newes◗ features.

Like microwave ovens with code cooking. Dishwashe◗ with no-rust Perma-Tuf® tubs. Refrigerators with unique through-the-door ice, ice wat◗ and the exclusive crushed-ice◗ dispenser. Washers that come v◗ a Mini-Basket® for small load◗

In your new house, you should have things just the wa◗ you want them. And General Electric helps you do it.

Uh-oh! Your refrigerator clashes with the "new" house dishwasher. Does GE have a solution?

Certainly! If the dishwasher is a recent GE model, you'll have no problem. Because since 1973, they have come with easy-to-change color panels.

And the New Natural™ colors are designed to match or blend with all appliances, even other brands.

So match, blend or mix colors and enhance the beauty of your kitchen and laundry room.

Your home came with a GE washer/dryer as part of the deal. They look in good shape—but who knows?

GE does! Just look us up in the phone book under GE Customer Care® service.

One of our over 100 Factory Service Centers will make an appointment with you, morning or afternoon. And we'll send a trained serviceman with some 700 parts in his truck.

He will make a complete inspection and any adjustments or repairs that are needed.

In addition to our Factory Service Centers, there are over 5,000 franchised servicers to help you.

So whatever your appliance needs are, wherever you are, you don't need to feel like a stranger in town. You have General Electric here, too.

THE APPLIANCES AMERICA COMES HOME TO.

GENERAL ⓖⓔ ELECTRIC

A key to less work in your kitchen: organized storage

What is the recipe for smooth working conditions in the kitchen? A brand new range top? Only a minor advantage. An electric can opener? A mere pebble in an Everest of aids. If you guessed ''storage,'' you were close. The best recipe is *organized storage.*

Isn't it a hassle to pull out a saucepan from behind a bevy of other pots in a darkened base cabinet? Isn't it a joy to lift a saucepan from a hook on the wall near the range?

Therein lies the secret of organized storage. Assemble equipment and utensils near the spot where they will be used. A colander stores by the sink; food storage containers alongside the refrigerator; a spatula next to the stove.

Within each group of stored items, exercise rule number two: store the most used pots or spices or spoons near at hand. Put the next most important group in a more distant place, and those items seldom used (a lobster pot) ought to settle in an out-of-the-way place.

There's another good way to ease storage problems, and remodeling time is a perfect time to do it. Give away, throw away or sell the oddments you've stored but never used for years.

While on your clearing-out kick, ask yourself if something stored in the kitchen might logically go somewhere else. Perhaps special-occasion dinner ware would look smarter in a dining room corner cabinet with glass doors.

Make a decision now about the sof-fits—the space between the top of the wall cabinets and the ceiling. You have three choices: leave the space open (a sure dust catcher); close it off; or turn the space into long-term storage. Cabinet doors to match your wall and base cabinets can be mounted on the outer frame.

Cabinets. Widths, depths, types and specialties for cabinets are basic to your planning. Understand, first, that a kitchen cabinet can be built to suit the most demanding requirements. Custom cabinetmakers abound in areas around U.S. urban centers. For a price, these firms will produce what you want. What is discussed below are details of ready-made cabinets.

Wall cabinets. Widths of single-door cabinets run from 9 inches to 27 inches; double-door units from 24 inches to 48 inches. Heights range from 12 inches (good for the space over a refrigerator) to 48 inches. Four-door cabinets extend to 48 inches in width. Depth from face to wall is a standard 12 inches. Corner cabinets with a single door mounted diagonally across the corner are produced with fixed or revolving shelves.

Base cabinets. With countertop attached, base cabinets stand 36 inches from the floor. Widths of single-door units stretch from 9 inches to 27 inches; double-door cabinets from 24 inches to 48 inches. Depth from face to wall is a standard 24 inches. Base cabinets are produced with doors, with drawers and

Examples of prebuilt storage units offered by cabinet manufacturers: an organized cabinet (far left) for wines and liquors; easy-to-reach cup and saucer racks (left); a maple cutting board and drawer combination (below). And here's a decorative trend ering momentum—leaded glass doors (center) over wall cabinets displaying fine china.

Forget time, temperature, power and turning. Just remember to tap this control.

Now Panasonic makes microwave cooking so easy, even second and third graders (with their teacher's help) can cook a wide variety of foods. And did! To cook her roast beef medium, all Carolyn did was read the control panel. (That was the hard part for a third grader.) It instructed her to tap the auto sensor control three times. She did.

The Genius (NE-7910) did the rest. It automatically set the power, calculated moisture content, decided cooking time, cooked the roast, beeped to tell Carolyn it was done. And then shut itself off.

Carolyn, the other kids and the teacher were really impressed when they saw the new Panasonic Cook-A-Round™ magnetic turntable. It keeps rotating continuously so food cooks

Auto Sensor Control

evenly and thoroughly, without your touching it.

Charlie's red snapper, Erin's chicken, Zachary's ziti, Michele's vegetables and Judy's cupcakes were all cooked by The Genius. The kids just tapped the auto sensor control. Everything was delicious and looked it. Even most meats brown naturally.

Its extra-large 1.32 cu. ft. capacity is large enough to hold almost anything you want to cook. And you'll want to cook just about everything, because for so many recipes, The Genius does the calculating so you can concentrate on the creating. Of course, you can also create manually by time, with six different power settings to choose from.

The Panasonic Genius. Because it makes you one in the kitchen.

Introducing The Genius.™ The new Panasonic microwave oven.

Panasonic®
just slightly ahead of our time.

doors, or with only drawers. And you can select from among several drawer depths. Like their wall counterparts, base cabinets are available in corner units with fixed or revolving shelves.

Utility cabinets. Available in depths of 12 inches and 24 inches, these cabinets are a uniform 84 inches tall (which happens to be the working height of cabinet placement in the standard kitchen). Within, one tall space and an upper shelved space make room for brooms, mops, bags and cleaning supplies. Single-door units range from 15 inches to 24 inches wide; double-door cabinets from 24 inches to 48 inches. Various shelving arrangements are offered for the interior. A similar cabinet is produced to receive a wall oven, and a third for a built-in refrigerator.

Pantry cabinets. These units make life easier storing canned goods and dry foods. Most have heavily-hinged doors with one-can-deep shelving, top to bottom, on the inside of the doors. Others have ingenious swing-out shelving within. Cabinets are offered in wall and base cabinet heights, as well as the full 84-inch height.

Specialties. There are two paths to organized storage inside cabinets. One: buy standard units and fill them with portable racks, trays, revolving shelves and other organizers sold where housewares are displayed. Two: buy ready-built components offered by cabinetmakers. Though the second course is more expensive, add-ons produced by the cabinet manufacurer are designed to perfectly fit the cabinets.

What's offered? Nearly anything ever dreamed of for a kitchen. Here are just a few: glide-out vegetable storage; bottle drawers; wine racks; slide-out chopping blocks; silver storage drawers; cutlery racks; pot-lid holders (and what a convenience *that* is); tray storage panels; flour / sugar bins and sliding trays for linens.

Appearance may sway you before any of the preceding elements are considered. That's normal. The choices are many—from the most representative colonial wood style to sleek modern color in plastic. The cabinet door directs the show, and sets the style for the entire kitchen. There are raised-panel doors, "barn siding" doors, textured-surface doors, flush doors and framed decorative glass doors.

42

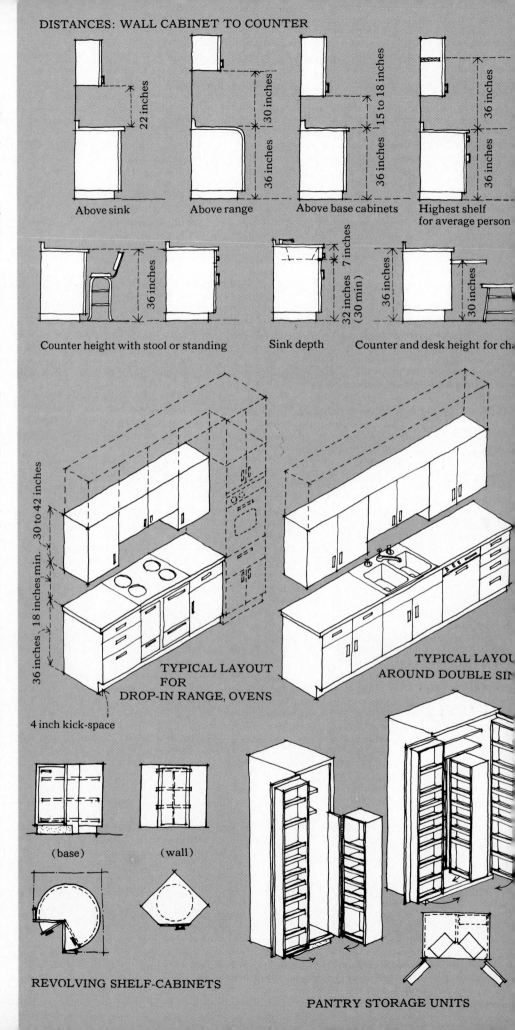

DISTANCES: WALL CABINET TO COUNTER

Above sink

Above range

Above base cabinets

Highest shelf for average person

Counter height with stool or standing

Sink depth

Counter and desk height for ch...

TYPICAL LAYOUT FOR DROP-IN RANGE, OVENS

4 inch kick-space

TYPICAL LAYOU AROUND DOUBLE SI...

(base)

(wall)

REVOLVING SHELF-CABINETS

PANTRY STORAGE UNITS

When you're building more than a kitchen.

We believe the best appliances should do more than look beautiful. So at Whirlpool we design new features into ours. And then build them to work hard, and to last.

That's why we make automatic washers and dryers with solid state controls that look simply beautiful. And are beautifully simple.

We give our touch control Microwave Ovens the look and the convenience of tomorrow.

To help hide fingerprints, we put textured steel doors on every kind of refrigerator we make. And one comes with a door-within-a-door you can open without opening the whole refrigerator.

And our Cook'N Counter™ ranges have brushed aluminum back panels, and black tempered glass counter space and oven doors.

We make our dishwashers with interchangeable panels. You can choose from four popular colors, select an optional black-glass look, or match your kitchen cabinet panels.

We even invented Trash Masher® compactors because they're a convenience we think no contemporary home should be without.

And we stand behind everything we make with fast, friendly service. And a toll-free telephone line open 24 hours a day to help with any problems or questions you might have.

We do all this because at Whirlpool we believe beauty is more than skin deep.

Whirlpool
Home **▲** Appliances

Quality. Our way of life.

Open storage above the island counter (left) is as much decorative as functional in this bright and open kitchen. Ceramic mosaic tile on the outward-facing side saves the island from looking dull. Stainless steel sink carries a certain elegance viewed from any angle; remains a popular choice throughout the U.S. Globe lamps above reflect a free and easy design scheme for the kitchen. Three-compartment, enameled cast-iron sink (upper right) is a blessing for the busy chef. Center-bowl drain is attached to a garbage disposal. Hand-held vegetable spray to the right of the single-handled faucet is a convenient extra. Such sinks are available in bright or muted colors and white. One-piece counter, double sink and backsplash (right) is 10 feet long and normal cabinet depth. This unique combination is produced of a new plastic that resembles marble, but unlike the original, resists impact damage and staining. This is available in white, as shown here, or a veined light beige. The 2" space between sinks is depressed slightly to allow water overflow.

Jessie Walker

A roundup of new advances that make kitchen equipment better than ever

Appliances. Faced with a decision to keep or replace old appliances, measure them in the same light as a car. Models five or more years old often begin to develop blips and quirks. Repairs may be small, but experience tells us once repairs begin, they seldom stop. Also, you may be shocked at the cost of even a small repair.

A second consideration will be pleasantly apparent to you in an appliance showroom. Compared to models five years ago, today's offerings are smarter, loaded with conveniences barely on the drawing board in 1974, and built with energy-saving qualities in tune with our times. There are also more choices. When microwave ovens first appeared, you could buy Brand A or Brand B. Now each manufacturer presents as many as a dozen variations on the theme.

No comment here on gas vs. electric appliances. That's decided by (1) a comparison of local rates and (2) personal preference. But sizes and features will help you plan. They begin below.

Range and oven. Freestanding ranges at 28" deep extend slightly beyond the cabinets. Standard widths are 30", 36" and 40". All have four burners, plus an oven and separate broiler below. Newer models feature a second oven above the range top. Some 36" models make room for a griddle between the burners. Pot and pan storage is part of the 40" models. There are smaller ranges (to 21"), and six-burner commercial ranges up to 48".

Drop-in ranges match counter depth, and feature a cooktop plus an oven with an integral broiler pan and grid. Available 27" and 30" wide. Drop-in cooktop calls for only 3½" clearance below the counter. Standard widths are 27", 30" and 36". Some units have a fixed, some an interchangeable griddle. And there are models with built-in grills, one with its own cooktop surface venting system.

Rough measurements for double wall ovens—one above the other—are 24" and 27" by 50". Single wall ovens are half as high.

Microwave ovens are made to be portable, wall mounted singly or doubled up with a conventional oven, and as part of a freestanding range (microwave above the cooktop). Measurements are slightly less than for standard ovens.

Among the best new features of ranges and ovens are: all-ceramic surface cooktops; instant-light gas ranges without pilot lights; digital read-outs on microwave ovens; self-cleaning electric and gas ovens; thermostatically-controlled top burners; automatic meat thermometers and keep-warm ovens.

Refrigerator. New models provide more storage space because of thin-wall insulation within the box. A number of models now feature ice water and ice cube dispensers on the outside of the door (preserving inside cool). Many units are on wheels; moved easily for cleaning. And frost-free operation is standard with better models. The latest wrinkle: a power-saver switch to cut down on electricity during periods of low humidity.

Nearly all upright refrigerators are 30" to 32" deep. Single-door refrigerators are as small as 24" by 56" (about 9 cu. ft.) Two-door units (freezer above) range from 28" by 61" to 32" by 66". Side-by-side refrigerator/freezers start at roughly 30" by 64" (19 cu. ft.) to 36" by 68" (25 cu. ft.).

Dishwasher. Energy savers that cut out drying or reduce hot water use are standard on nearly all models now. Nor, in most cases, do you need to hand scrub a crusted casserole dish. A super-power wash cycle will clean it. And a

And you thought we only sold great underwear.

Think JCPenney and you probably think underwear. Or sheets. Or workclothes. That's good. But that's not all. There's a lot more. And major appliances are a major part. Surprised? Then think about this.

For 77 years, we've had one goal: your complete satisfaction. So we've worked harder to make your life easier. By keeping up with the times without ever lowering our standards. With perfection guaranteed by the rigid requirements set at our Testing Center. So you can be assured of the quality.

It's what you've come to expect from JCPenney. Before you buy. And after. When you buy it from us, we keep it working. With at-home service by our staff of trained technicians. We're always just a phone call away.

And because we know a major appliance isn't as easy to budget as a good pair of briefs, there's our convenient Time Payment Plan, too. The result: Every JCPenney appliance comes with an extra that doesn't cost extra. Peace of mind.

This is JCPenney
We sell peace of mind, not just appliances.

45

Ernest Silva

A wood floor in the kitchen was normal during most of the 19th Century. Then linoleum, and later, vinyls, pushed the wood floor into obsolescence. Today, wood is back, strong as ever, protected by new polyurethane finishes (upper left). The revival offers you another dimension for decorating. In this kitchen, wood becomes a restful foil for red appliances. On the left wall is a pantry cabinet, one door of which is open. Note the pantry sketches earlier in this report. A fine U-shaped kitchen (lower left) packs everything into a relatively small space, yet does so without losing sight of the functional. In fact, this kitchen measures a perfect triangle between the refrigerator, range and sink (then back to the refrigerator). A maple chopping block in the foreground, and a stainless steel sheet alongside the range help smooth out the tribulations of any cook. Even a large kitchen (right) calls for careful design. Certainly this one, with its naturalbrick-surrounded grille and space for table and chairs meets that criteria.

Hedrich-Blessing

gentle setting safely cleans fine china and crystal.

Most washers are 24″ wide and measure the depth of the kitchen counter. Choose a built-in (generally positioned alongside the sink); an under-sink dishwasher (for a kitchen with a space problem); or a roll-around portable that connects to the sink faucet and drain for operation. Generally, the portable can be built in later.

Sinks. A dishwasher doesn't eliminate the need for a double-bowl sink, though single-bowl sinks often accompany a dishwasher installation. It's still pleasant to have one sink for soaking, one for vegetable washing. Three-compartment sinks? Yes, two standard sinks and a small round bowl attached to a disposer. A wood cutting board drops over one sink, fits around the disposer bowl. Two-handle and one-handle faucets with single swing-spouts are standard choices. Also available; a smaller bar sink with a gooseneck spout.

Traditional, long-lasting sink materials are stainless steel and porcelain on cast iron, the second of which is produced in a rainbow of colors. Also in colors: acrylic bar sinks. A new material, Corian, is offered as a one-piece counter and sink. Resembling marble, it is a plastic.

Ventilation. An HVI (Home Ventilating Institute) label on an exhaust fan assures you the unit meets strict industry standards. Range hoods enclosing fans are produced in enough variety to match any kitchen decor. They can adapt to inside or outside wall range installations, as well as island ranges. A special vent is made for a wall oven. Most units vent outdoors, but some are ventless, recirculating kitchen air through activated charcoal. The newest models offer a dual system: vented air for summer operation; ventless for cold weather, returning warm air to the kitchen.

Lighting. The rule: light over every work center. The reason: so you never work in your own shadow. The way: install general lighting overhead, shielded lighting beneath wall cabinets to illuminate the counters, light over the cooktop and sink. The means: fluorescent tubes offer more light per watt and last many times longer than incandescent bulbs. Select ''deluxe'' warm white or ''deluxe'' cool white tubes to more closely approximate the warm natural color of incandescent light. The obvious: use as much daylight as possible. It brightens and cheers the space— and it's free.

Surfacing. Your decorative statement

in the kitchen will be made as much b floor and wall colors and patterns as b anything else. It's well to keep counter white or light (but not glossy) for adde reflectivity. Materials must stand up t wear and repeated cleanings.

On *floors*, sheet vinyl coverings a moderate in cost and perform we ceramic or quarry tile wears like iror cleans easily; carpet, though soft unde foot, is more difficult to maintain; an wood floors protected by polyurethan coatings can stand kitchen wear.

On *walls*, nearly anything goe washable paint, vinyl-coated wallpape ceramic tile, or wood, hardboard plywood panelings protected by coa ings.

On *counters*, plastic laminates don nate the field, but are hardly alone Maple butcher block and ceramic ti are used for small areas or enti counters. And recently Corian, a ne plastic material, has entered the rac

Spacing. Dining in the kitchen convenient and cozy, but it takes spac Allow 2½ to three feet from a table edg to a permanent obstruction. This pe mits easy seating and rising. Allow least three and preferably four feet for passageway or a space between a tab and storage.

Free Information Center.
For products, planning, decorating and remodeling.

Many of the advertisers in the HomeBook are offering free full-color catalogs to HomeBook readers. Just turn to the back of the book and circle the catalogs you want on the postage-paid postcards. Drop your card in the mail, and we'll send back the catalogs you requested as soon as possible. Often as fast as three days of receiving your request. So that very quickly the information you need will be found right in your new mailbox.

More help from the HomeBook.

Planning your new bath

Aseptic decoration suits a bath of the past— remodel to please yourself

Your next new bath is going to be a smash hit. The ingredients for making it so are available in such profusion, you may have difficulty choosing, but certainly no trouble finding choices. It's a joy your parents probably didn't share. In their day, the bath for most was a no-nonsense collection of three white fixtures lined up like soldiers on white tile.

Ah yes, one thinks, but Dad could have done over the bath for $500. Now, we are lucky to get a bath remodeled for less than $5,000. Not true. There are still ways to redo a bath for under $500.

For example: leave the fixtures where they are. Change the color scheme with paint and new paper. Add mirrors. Buy a new toilet seat. Lay down fresh carpet. Build in more storage. You can even change the fixture color. Ask your paint dealer about new epoxy paints strong enough to coat and stick to worn vitreous china or cast iron.

Yet, why not have the bath you've always wanted? Paying the bills usually turns out to be a minor hurdle. As the pages here and those following attest, there are many ways to add dash and sparkle, comfort and convenience to an existing bath—within its four walls. And as many ideas for a new bath.

Putting your bath in its best light makes practical sense. If you were to add up all the time you and your family spend there, you'd be surprised. It's nearly always more than one suspects. That's reason enough to fix up the space. Add to that the pleasure of getting compliments from your friends, and the distinct advantage of gaining a house with more sales value (should that time come).

Practical also means staying within sensible boundaries. A custom-tiled tub the size of a small swimming pool may be perfect for potentates, but it's a costly nuisance in a home (unless you enjoy waiting an hour or so while the tub fills). There are ways discussed below to stay in bounds and be perfectly delighted with the results.

Begin planning your new bath with the guidance offered here. Personal help from professionals is readily available. Finding an architect or interior designer willing to spend time on a single bath may not be so easy. But it's possible. Bath design aid is also yours for the taking from bath specialty shops and remodeling contractors who concentrate on redos of baths (and kitchens, as a rule).

Who needs to spend bundles of money reviving a sorry bath? Answer: no one. The scene (lower left) shows an existing tub in a space rejuvenated with a few tiles, new wallpaper, clever storage and curtains. Or make the counter fit the bath (lower right)— easy with plastic laminates. Popular exposed lighting sheds a warm glow. A two-compartment bath divides shower toilet/basin (right). Mirrored door reflects stained glass over shower, ideal solution for light and privacy.

Lisanti

Photos: Dan Forer

You may have a bath with everything perfectly positioned and only want to replace the old fixtures with new. Fine. Further along is news of some improved fixtures on the market, one of which may capture your fancy.

If you're like most of us, though, there is something amiss with the present bath plan. It's too big, or too small. The window is in the wrong place. The fixtures are crowded together on one wall. There's too little privacy.

Now is the time to assess the plan. Try to focus on the source of your annoyance. Once you have it isolated, the solution rolls out with relative ease. Here are some typical problems and solutions:

The bath is too small. There are two ways to solve this dilemma. The first is to expand outward. Keep in mind that most small baths can be improved immeasurably by adding as little as six inches, rarely more than two feet. That should be enough to eliminate elbow-bumping (well, reduce it, at least).

The plumber will say, "You can't move that wall. The piping's in there." He's right, based on dollars. It's not impossible to move a "wet" wall (one in

which the piping is located), but it's costly. If the piping is ancient and must be replaced anyway, you can contemplate moving the "wet" wall.

However, there is usually one interior bath wall without piping. If it backs up to a closet or bedroom, a small shift in the bath wall won't seriously disturb the adjoining space. If it backs up to a hall, you'll need to study the move more carefully. (In one case, hall bookshelves the depth of the bath protrusion made the change natural.)

The second path to gaining more space is through fixture selection. A stall shower takes up about half the space of a standard bathtub. There are square tubs (with bathing space diagonally across the square) that use no more than 10 square feet, or corner tubs that extend a mere 4½ feet.

The bath is too big. Anyone who struggles every morning in a minuscule bath wonders why a big bath is a problem. But for those who bought a wonderful vintage house saddled with a bath converted from a bedroom years ago, the problem is real. It's difficult to keep the bath clean. There are drafts in winter. The floor creaks.

One solution is to give back some space to adjoining rooms. The restrictions over moving bath walls are the same as described above.

Another is to expand the use of the bath. Add a separate shower. Partition the space for private and communal areas. Convert one portion into a dressing room. Move the linen closet into the bath. Expand storage space. Set aside an exercise area. Install a sauna. Consider moving your laundry appliances to the bath. Or enjoy any combination of the above.

Or take a leaf from the plans of owners who have divided the space into two baths. For example, the bath opens to a hall and backs up to the master bedroom. A door is broken through to the master bedroom; a partition goes up; new fixtures are installed, and modern baths now serve smaller bedrooms off the hall and the master bedroom privately.

The window is badly placed. Have it moved, and/or buy a smaller window. Close it off entirely. Close it off and install a skylight. With proper ventilation, a windowless bath is comfortable, functional and private. A consideration:

A mini-solution for a too-small bath (above): use every square inch for some purpose. Shelving above toilet is functional and high enough for toilet-tank top removal. A need for privacy can sometimes be solved with a simple partition and a sliding pocket door (right). Tub is one of the new fiber glass varieties with a carved shape of its own. Vinyl-coated wallpaper behind tub is a satisfactory solution for a wet area without shower.

For more information circle 14 on the Reader's Service Card following the Index.

The Accent Is International.
The Quality Is Pure American-Standard.

From its International Group, American-Standard resents the Tilche Suite, a blend of European esign excellence and American versatility. esigned by Paolo Tilche, leading uropean designer, the suite consist- g of a pedestal lavatory and nique toilet, is a study in rves and angles to please e discerning eye. But see w the versatility of good esign makes it at home any decor. With our -foot oval pool, and the nderstated opulence of

Early American revisited. And e Tilche Suite goes right along. re, in new Bermuda Coral, it apts to the uncluttered Colonial od. Beautifully.

Oriental surroundings, the Tilche Suite in tranquil gold offers a bathroom that is sumptuous, yet easy to live with. We can only begin to show you the possibilities. The decors it inspires are endless. And the quality is always the expected excellence of American-Standard.

See the Tilche Suite, and other inspired American-Standard plumbing products for yourself. Call Toll Free **800-325-6400** for the location of the American-Standard showroom nearest you. In Missouri, call **800-342-6600**. Or write for our Bathroom Basics booklet. P.O. Box 2003, New Brunswick, N.J. 08903.

⬤ AMERICAN STANDARD

World's leading name in plumbing fixtures and fittings.

the contractor must match the exterior siding in the area where the window was located.

The fixtures are jammed on one wall. Move one fixture to another wall, and gain a bath that seems more spacious within the same space. The plumber may say, ''It's cheaper to put the new fixtures where the old ones were.'' He's right, because additional piping to accommodate the fixture in a new spot will cost more.

But balance the cost of new piping against a remodeled, yet not quite satisfying bath. Is it worth the initial saving?

Not enough privacy. Partitioning is the most straightforward solution. A sliding pocket door saves space. Or, a partial separation may be enough. That could take the form of shelving, or a floor-to-ceiling planter (with climbing ivy).

Some solutions seem more like options. Here's a trio of ideas that have become popular within the past decade.

The indoor/outdoor bath. Where structurally possible, a privately fenced garden or patio connected to the bath with glass doors is a delight.

An old window, too large and nothing but a nuisance in the shower area, was converted in this bath (below) to a clever assist. It now offers privacy for the bather, a discreet view outside and a modicum of natural daylight.

The bedroom vanity lavatory. An existing bath—too small—is off the master bedroom. One solution to ''two's a crowd'': a lavatory/vanity/dressing table on a wall in the bedroom adjacent to the bath.

Dan Forer

The sunken bathtub. Not sunken to the tub edge. That's almost never possible in an existing bath. But sunken in a platform built up from the bath floor and made accessible with steps.

Elyse Lewin

Drama in a bath is easier to obtain than you might imagine. The red and white scene (above) is elegant, to be sure. But note that the ''sunken'' tub is really not sunken at all, but surrounded by a platform—nothing more than conventional carpentry covered, in this case, by a white carpet. Room is oversized.

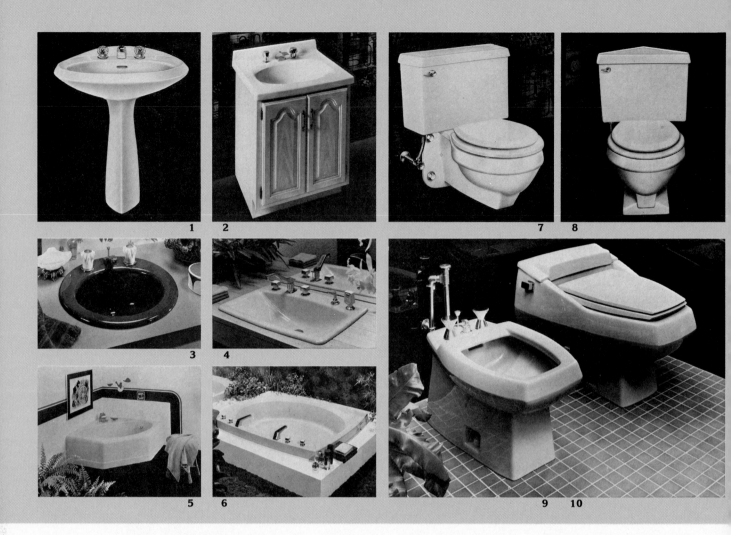

1   2   7   8

3   4

5   6   9   10

BATHS

The parts of a bath are as vital as the plan. Below are the important points to consider about each category, plus ideas for putting them to best use.

Fixtures. Color and shape are going to play a prominent part in your choice of fixtures, and for good reason. Manufacturers have outdone themselves capturing lively new colors and producing more realistic shapes. Yet, don't let them overshadow the practical elements—material and type.

Bathtubs are produced of fiber glass-reinforced plastic, enameled formed steel and enameled cast iron. If you seek durability, choose cast iron.

Bath/shower combinations are nearly always made of fiber glass-reinforced plastic. It is a material easily shaped into one-piece units, and given proper care (no abrasive cleansers), will last many years.

Tub shapes begin at a tiny 39″ square and range to a size nearly seven feet square. The most familiar tub is five feet long, 30″ wide and 16″ high. That rectangle also is available in 4½ foot lengths, and from one maker, seven feet long. Some run deeper and hold more water. One is modeled after a Japanese soaking bath—39″ square, 34″ deep with a seat at the 26″ mark. Most bath/shower combinations are five feet wide. Shower stalls begin at 34″ square and range to three by four feet. Some less expensive stalls are still produced of enameled sheet metal.

Shower fittings that hold the water temperature constant are worth considering. Also worthy: a flow-reducing shower head as a water saver. And take a look at the array of hand-held shower heads that substitute for or adapt to existing fittings.

Toilets (not including the seat) are made of vitreous china. China is long-lasting, noncorrosive and the surface is easily cleaned. To date, no other materials have been accepted by health codes for the toilet body in a residence. Elegance among toilets is identified with the one-piece, low-silhouette, silent-flush closet, a more comfortable and easier-to-clean unit. Some variations: a water-saving model using three to three-and-a-half gallons per flush instead of the usual five to seven gallons; a wall-hung, off-the-floor closet to facilitate floor cleaning; and from one maker, a closet with a triangle-shaped tank for a close fit in a powder room.

Plan a space of 30″ minimum in which the toilet is centered; 36″ is better. Allow 24″ from the front edge of the seat to the wall, tub or lavatory opposite.

Bidets are also made of vitreous china, and win honors as the most misunderstood fixture in America. Common in Europe, the bidet is about 12″ across, 26″ deep and 16″ high. It is a gentle cleansing apparatus meant for personal hygiene to be used by all members of the family.

Lavatories run the gamut of materials: fiber glass-reinforced plastic, plastic mixed with marble chips, enameled steel, enameled cast iron and vitreous china. Highest quality is vitreous china, followed closely by cast iron.

Most prominent among bath trends is the return of the pedestal lavatory, fashioned after European styles. But its return is still outnumbered by a wide variety of drop-in lavs for bath counters, and one-piece lavatory/vanities. Several models are longer than normal with a scooped basin designed for shampooing hair. They include a hand-held flexible spray.

12

13   **14**

11   **15**

1. Handsome pedestal lavatories are again in fashion. 2. Basin and vanity combinations—a quick way to make a change. 3. Tiny, but pretty, basins for small baths. 4. A large lavatory: space for a shampoo or baby bath. 5. Corner bath measures only 50″ from corner to front apron—ideal for the small bath. 6. Or, where space is generous, consider a bath big enough for two—5½ x 7 feet. 7. For clean-up ease, a wall-hung toilet is the perfect answer. 8. Then, there's the perfect toilet for tight corners. 9. A bidet on the left—the answer for personal hygiene. 10. And, on the right, one of the new, low-silhouette toilets with quiet flushing action. 11. A symphony in golden browns—very much in style at present, and all of long-lasting ceramic tile. 12. From the ceiling comes both light and heat, plus ventilation. 13. Aid for those who think of the bath as a library. 14. Weigh yourself; then, store the scales out of sight in the wall cavity. 15. A self-storing clothesline: what could be nicer over the tub?

When planning a counter with two lavatories, allow at least 24″ between them for elbow room, more if possible.

Lighting. Poor light is the bane of old baths, and an unfortunate condition of some new baths. Some basic guidelines:

Avoid glare. A current fad for bare theatrical-style bulbs around a mirror can be an annoyance if the light output is too high. Bulbs at 15 watts is enough; 25 watts is borderline unless controlled by a dimmer (a good idea by itself).

Model your face. Some form of shielded light overhead and on either side of a mirror delivers a shadowless glow correct for shaving or make-up.

Ceiling light. Install one for overall illumination.

Pleasant extras. A reading downlight over the toilet and a waterproof shower light for shaving legs are worthwhile considerations.

Incandescent bulbs always perform well. Go to fluorescents to save energy, but buy "deluxe" tubes to prevent you from looking ghostly in too-white light.

Accessories. Most important is ventilation. Install exhaust fans in windowless and windowed baths. A window alone never provides enough. In a house kept at an energy-saving 68° during winter, a bath heater is a low-cost luxury. Overhead fan-forced, radiant and infra-red heaters are available, along with wall-mounted radiant or fan-forced units.

In addition to such regulars as towel bars, rings, hooks, soap dishes and paper holders, there are some other niceties: glass or acrylic shelves, towel racks, built-in scales, recessed magazine and paper holders and various styles of over-the-tub clothes hangers (all of which retract).

Plan for ample storage for any bath redo: cabinets, shelves, even closets. Better than taking a chilly walk from a hot shower to a cold hall closet for a fresh towel.

Surfacing. Ceramic tile remains traditional for bath floors, walls and counters. It holds a commanding position for its long-and-hard-wearing qualities and the ease with which it's cleaned. Today, some makers have even conquered the grout-line problem with new

materials that shed dirt. Some notes on other materials:

On floors, vinyl sheet goods offer a huge choice of color and pattern; are easy to clean, generally cost less than ceramics, but don't last as long. Carpet is warm and soft underfoot, easy to install (there are inexpensive kits), but not so easy to keep clean.

On walls, nearly anything goes outside the shower enclosure: tile, paint, wallpaper (best buy is vinyl-coated) or even wood with a polyurethane coating. Hardboard, plywood and decorative gypsum board panelings are produced for bath walls. Inside the shower, fiber glass reinforced panels sold in tub-enclosure kits offer an alternative to tile.

On counters, plastic laminates are quite popular. Moving up are "cultured" marbles, chips and dust of real marble embedded in polyester to make a one-piece counter and basin.

Extras. Here's a shopping list to think about: sauna, whirlpool bath (also labeled hot tub), massage-action shower heads, ultraviolet tanning lamps, foot baths, steam bath, and from one firm, an enclosure for a sequential array of steam, dry heat and showers.

Laundries

Best of all locations for a remodeled laundry: the bedroom/bath wing

Including a page of laundry ideas immediately following baths was a purposeful sequence. Laundries in some new homes are still relegated to basements or "behind the kitchen." But where is the source of most soiled clothes? Right, the bedrooms and baths. More designers today are heeding this truism and positioning a laundry in the bedroom/bath area. They also do it because the slight but annoying odor of detergents and dirty clothes doesn't mix well with kitchen smells.

When adding laundry space, backing up to a bath is less costly because existing piping is used for the washer. A gas dryer requires a gas line, of course, and a means of venting outdoors, plus a 110/120-volt outlet. Except for the smallest units, electric dryers call for a 220/240-volt hookup, and generally are vented outdoors.

The smallest washers and dryers measure 24" wide and 22" deep. Most are designed to stack, dryer over washer in a 25" space. These units are the least utilitarian for a family. They can't handle large loads, and there is seldom extra space close by for storing laundry supplies or working with just-cleaned laundry.

A standard washer and dryer standing side by side take up a space about 60" wide and 28" deep. The units can fit snugly into a five-foot closet. Folding louvered doors are a practical closure. Wall cabinets to store laundry aids will fit above the equipment. This is an improvement over stacked units.

Better is a closet 96" wide, allowing washer, dryer, an 18"-wide clothes hamper and an 18" general storage cabinet. Above this can go a 36"-wide double-door wall cabinet, and alongside, a clothes rod to hang out just-dried permanent-press clothing. A counter over the floor cabinets offers ample space for folding clothes. Don't neglect good lighting.

Best is a laundry room. Now you can spread out, install such amenities as a drip-dry closet with a floor drain, a drop-in enameled cast-iron laundry sink (between 12" and 14" deep) for the counter, a built-in, fold-down ironing board and storage for all manner of things. In fact, with space to spare, a portion of the room could become a sewing center or, given the right orientation, a potting and planting center.

Venting for the dryer aside, a ceiling exhaust fan for excess moisture and heat during the summer is a wise addition. In winter, the same heat and moisture can help make the house comfortable.

Where space permits, nothing is quite so luxurious as a full laundry room. Cabinets store supplies and the sink facilitates special soakings. Through-wall air conditioner reduces humidity.

Shelves

Access panel

Dryer + Washer

Bi-fold door

Sewing cart Shelves

Greenhouse window Ironing board

Drip-dry Dryer Washer Storage

Plans (above) outline areas in the photos, and show, as well, a multipurpose laundry room which could substitute as a sewing room. Minimum-space laundry (right) still manages storage.

Free Information Center.
For products, planning, decorating and remodeling.

Many of the advertisers in the HomeBook are offering free full-color catalogs to HomeBook readers. Just turn to the back of the book and circle the catalogs you want on the postage-paid postcards. Drop your card in the mail, and we'll send back the catalogs you requested as soon as possible. Often as fast as three days of receiving your request. So that very quickly the information you need will be found right in your new mailbox.

More help from the HomeBook.

Basement Conversions

Lisanti

Since the 1940s, finishing a basement is probably an activity equal in popularity to buying a new car. What that means to you: almost every problem ever blocking a basement-finishing project has been met, and nearly all were overcome.

Ugly ducts and pipes showing? Cover them with a dropped ceiling. Basement floor uneven? Shim sleepers beneath a finished floor to level your walk. Object to masonry walls? Install what you wish over furring strips or studs attached to the masonry (and insulate behind the wall material).

Those are problems easily solved. The big hurdle is moisture (or just plain water). A finished basement is of little value if H_2O ruins the materials you carefully install. A hint of moisture seepage through the walls probably can be stopped with a coat of masonry sealant. But if water periodically appears on your basement floor, call in a waterproofing contractor for an estimate.

Rich-looking woodgrain paneling provides a boys'-room look to a basement doubling as bedroom and study. For quick entry, there's the fireman's pole with handy plop-on mattress for spills. Below: Abbe Darer designed this fuss-free, carefree family room. Brick-shaped ceramic tile, attractive paneling together with tough canvas cushions make it a durable room to take teen-age parties in stride.

A sense of privacy, without isolation, can be achieved with dividers. These prefinished storage units are on casters for easy movability. The brightly-painted plywood table provides space aplenty for play, projects and, in this case, for model trains.

Room design by Harlan Pomroy, A.S.I.D.

Man-made finish on real Masonite brand hardboard.

Lead a rich life without being rich. That's the beauty of Masonite brand paneling.

You can add a lot of living to your home by finishing that attic, basement, extra room or garage. And you can do it without finishing your budget.

For little more than the cost of redecorating a room, you can clothe your walls in warm, inviting BirchGrove™ hardboard paneling— creating a pleasant, yet highly affordable room.

In spite of its economy, tough Masonite brand paneling outlasts paint and paper, retaining its handsome appearance indefinitely. It's durable and easily maintained—stands up to bumps and dents, and wipes clean with a damp cloth.

When you're ready to add livability to your home, without bending the budget, see your Masonite brand dealer. He has some beautifully affordable ideas.

MASONITE
CORPORATION

Attic Conversions

Ernest Silva

In our culture, the attic was often a place of memories and romance, a hideaway and lookout. Maids, poets, children and family treasures are attic fixtures in fact and fiction.

An unfinished attic is also the most convertible space in a house. It is just as logical a resting place for youngsters (or anyone) today as it was in great-grandmother's day. In pre-1940 houses especially, enough attic room often exists to complete two bedrooms, a bath and a family/play/hobby area for the personal use of the under-roof inhabitants.

Before rushing up with nail, hammer and board in hand, consider some practical checkpoints on attic conversions:

Strength. In some older homes, attic joists will not bear the weight of finished floors, furniture and people. A seasoned carpenter can spot the problem quickly. Or measure the boards yourself, and the unsupported span. Take the measurements to a lumber dealer, who will have safe span charts for wood of various sizes. Can a weak floor be remedied professionally? Yes, with little trouble.

Top left: Attic bedroom with sloping ceiling and walls that angle in all directions might provide decorating nightmare to some... but Designer Ethel Samuels, NSID, accomplished transformation by "straightening out" the window wall to make storage compartments, and contrasting two wall panelings and boldly printed wallpaper with matching fabrics.

Walls and ceiling were covered with white paneling on one wall and ceiling; a rich looking woodgrain on other walls. Printed wallpaper was used in the recessed area above the bed. Bedspread, chair cover, window shades were in matching fabric and the white paneling formed window shutters with fluorescent lights to create a subtle tone. Houndstooth carpeting added further warmth to the room.

Left: Another romantic finish for a dull attic is the charming room that beckons warmly to visiting guests. Grandma's prize stove and attic junk have been tenderly restored to their earlier grandeur. The room exudes air of Early American warmth.

Height. Give yourself at least seven feet between floor and ceiling. Any measure less than that may prove claustrophobic. In many areas, building codes insist on a 7'6" ceiling. Check first.

As photographs on these pages show, ceilings at room edge are often slanted. This is acceptable under building codes, and cozy for the occupants.

Comfort. Before finishing the attic, remove insulation from what will be the attic room floor. New insulation must go *above* the rooms you're finishing. Insulate the walls before closing in the stud cavity with wallboard or paneling. Ventilate the space between ridge beam and the new attic room ceiling, if it isn't already ventilated.

A heating and air conditioning contractor may be able to tie in the attic rooms to your existing heating / cooling system. If not, consider electric baseboard heat or radiant ceiling heat—easy add-ons. And room-size air conditioners in a window, or installed through the wall can handle attic cooling.

Bath location. If possible, try to position a new attic bath directly over an existing bath below. In that way, new drain and supply piping is kept to a minimum.

Stairs. The ideal location for attic stairs is dead center in the house. Stairs entering an attic from either end will call for some juggling to squeeze out living areas and the halls to reach them. But it can be done.

Wiring. Almost surely, new wiring will be needed for a finished attic. Be sure your housepower is up to the job.

Dormers and skylights effectively open up the room at the top and the sunny, plant-filled dining area above with the skylight slashing dramatically into the roof is a good example of effective planning. Below left: Deft decorating by Lis King demonstrates how a dormer increases feeling of roominess. The dormer opens up so that sunlight spills across the room, bathing it with light and allowing privacy for luxurious sunbathing.

Garage Conversions

As the family car wheels into the heated garage, the portable dance floor squares are stacked neatly on their cart, for wheeling into storage. FAR LEFT: The bottom of the in-wall bed features an ancient game embroidered and painted on burlap. LEFT: Easy-to-open, the balanced mechanism permits the in-wall bed to slip down gently. Open, it reveals a comfortable double bed with sturdy headrest and rear alcove that hides indirect lighting.

Turning unused space into rooms for today's living: From grimy garage to gala guest room

A triple-purpose garage? Not impossible at all. Just sprinkle some imagination over a few space-age products, add do-it-yourself labors and some tried and true trappings. Three ingredients are at the base of this transformation:

1. A radiant ceiling panel with its own thermostat, which eliminates any need to tap into the house heating system.

2. Portable dance floor panels, normally a commercial ballroom product, but available to you, as well.

3. A pull-down hideaway bed that springs smoothly into a wall cavity.

What evolves? A garage during winter weather when cold is cruel to a car. Dressed in its living-space finery, this same garage becomes a den, workshop, hobby room, or, of course, a home ballroom. When the overnight guest list grows one too many, down comes the bed.

Except for installation of the radiant panel, nearly all conversions you see on these pages are grist for the home handyperson. The result is a saving in two ways. By exercising your own manual skills, you save the cost of hired labor. By stopping short of a complete garage conversion (a standard remodeling assignment for a contractor), you save an even larger sum, and gain the continued use of the existing garage.

Begin by insulating the walls before applying wallboard to the open studs. Leave access to the rafter space so you can insulate the ceiling after the ceiling panels are up. Ask your building-material dealer for advice on how much insulation to use.

The conversion shown here is in a country home north of New York City. Take and adapt the ideas to your own life-style.

The open bamboo screens reveal shelves with ample room for storage, hobby supplies, tools. The door-desk doubles as sewing table, desk, buffet for parties. Below: The closed screens display a woodlike-look created by wallpapering over bamboo shades with overall leaf pattern and then painting on trees.

Roofing and Siding

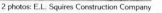
2 photos: E.L. Squires Construction Company

The before-and-after photos at left sh
how torn and lifted shingles were
replaced with strongly textured shing
that suit this rambling country house
Above and right: some of the many
colors and textures of asphalt shingle
available today to suit almost any ho
and any homeowner.

**Sooner or later you'll need to re-roof, or re-side.
Here are some of the things you'll need to know...**

You need a new roof. Yours is worn and it's leaking. What to do? Face it! It's not going to go away, it's not going to get better, and unless you undertake repairs or replacement, the water leaking in can lead to all kinds of expensive damage—to walls and to structure.

If yours is a tall house with a complex roof shape, you better plan on calling in a professional contractor. But, if you're the type and you've got a ranch house with a not-too-steep roof, you can consider doing the job yourself. No occult skills are required; but you do need to be in the "pretty-handy-with-tools" category and not afraid to climb ladders. If you're considering trying it yourself, buy one of the excellent step-by-step guides available in bookstores and from the home centers in your area (some of these are put out by trade associations). But probably most homeowners will opt to have the job done professionally. Be careful in your selection of a contractor for re-roofing or re-siding. It is a relative-

ly expensive operation, and the remodeling field abounds in shoddy and fly-by-night operators. Don't even talk to someone who knocks on the door offering a special price because "we happen to be working in the neighborhood." As in locating any professional, ask your realtor, builder, or a local architect.

There are a number of different materials available for re-roofing.

The most popular, by far (80 percent of all homes), is asphalt shingles. There are two basic types—the "organic," made by impregnating a mat of cellulose fibers with asphalt and surfacing it with ceramic-coated mineral granules; and the "inorganic," made the same way but with a base mat of fiber glass.

Both have advantages for different kinds of installations—best advice: take your contractor's recommendation. Both come in a wide variety of colors—and don't forget you'll have to live with the color you choose for as many as 25

years. Black is probably still the predominant color in the northern states, and white is extremely popular in the South (to reflect heat)—but you can get almost any color of the rainbow, with "earthtone" colors of brown, buff, olive and slate gray becoming popular lately. Also relatively new to the market and fast becoming popular are asphalt shingles with bolder textures, creating a richer-looking roof with deeper shadow lines—much as wood shakes do.

For some families, and some houses, there is still nothing but a wood shingle or shake roof. Shakes, with their thickness and strong texture, are especially popular in the West; the wood shingle is still popular in New England.

What to know when you're talking with your contractor...

Roofing is measured in "squares"—which simply means the amount of roofing required to cover a 10- by 10-foot area of roof surface. Another word

Today's aluminum siding is hard to tell from the original wood clapboard. Above, a handsome example; at right, a typical before-and-after proof of the pudding; below, new siding being applied over the wood surface. Factory-finished aluminum needs little maintenance.

3 photos: Asphalt Roofing Manufacturers Association   4 photos: Aluminum Association

you'll need to know is "exposure"—the distance between the butt edge of one course or line of shingles to the butt edge of the next. Since shingles overlap each other, the less the "exposure," the greater the "coverage"—the more thickness of shingle between you and the weather.

Shingles themselves come in different thicknesses or "weights"—and the greater the weight, the greater the life expectancy. So you'll have to decide whether it is worth paying for a more expensive shingle (labor costs the same) in return for a longer life. In general, you can count on an asphalt-shingle roof lasting from 15 to 25 years. Be sure your contractor is using shingles that meet any local codes as to fire resistance—they should carry the UL label on the bundle.

Can you re-roof over an old roof? The answer is sometimes...

No new roof will last its designed lifetime without a structurally sound base. Usually, you can apply a third layer of shingles before "tear off"—the removal of all shingles down to the wooden roof deck—is required. But if the roof is uneven or spongy or full of loose shingles, your contractor may suggest "tear off." If the wood deck, which may be boards or plywood nailed to the rafters, is questionable, it may even have to be replaced (that's the price of waiting too long to repair leaks). An asphalt-saturated roofer's felt goes over a new deck before the shingles are applied. And when you're re-roofing, be sure to check the attic ventilation underneath—the space beneath the roof should be well ventilated with louver vents or an exhaust fan in the attic.

New siding can cut down maintenance, save on fuel bills, improve appearance...

...but it is not a project to be undertaken lightly. If you are thinking of siding

as a major home improvement project, here are a few ideas to file away for future reference: The most popular siding material today is aluminum—formed into clapboards it is relatively easy to install, has a baked-on paint finish that may be guaranteed for 20 or more years, and when installed creates an insulated space that can cut your fuel bills. You can also get new siding of factory-finished steel, and of vinyl with molded-in color. And of course you could replace wood siding with any of the new plywood sidings, or new clapboards or shingles; though these would require removal of the old siding. Siding is in many ways more complicated than roofing since you have to handle—instead of a single great plane of roof—problems of fitting the new siding around doors and windows and under the eaves. Good advice, unless you *really* like working around the house: call in a professional and talk the problem over with him.

SOME COMMUNITIES LIKE TIMBERLINE® SO MUCH, IT'S THE ONLY ASPHALT ROOFING THEY USED.

Timberline was the original brand of asphalt shingle used to roof a number of neighborhoods around the country like Hidden Lakes, Norchester and College Park.

While we're honored, we're not surprised. Because there aren't any better asphalt shingles on the market.

Timberline shingles look great. Their unusual thickness and deep irregular shadow pattern give them the rustic look of wood. But they wear even better than they look.

Timberline shingles are composed of the highest quality, scientifically refined asphalt. So they repel water.

They also have a ceramic baked, granular surface that resists fire and reflects the harmful ultra-violet rays that eat away even the best of roofs.

And Timberline® shingles' self-sealing agent works with the sun to form a wind resistant one-piece roof. So your investment won't blow away.

They're virtually immune to manufacturing defects. At least for twenty-five years. We guarantee it.*

Timberline shingles come in six natural looking blends. To find out which one is right for your home, look in the Yellow Pages for your nearest GAF dealer. Or write GAF.

And put Timberline on your roof. If you don't, you may end up owning the only home in your community without it.

GAF® TIMBERLINE®
ASPHALT ROOFING
On top of the industry.

For more information circle 36 on the Reader's Service Card following the Index.

HIDDEN LAKES, KANSAS CITY

NORCHESTER, HOUSTON

COLLEGE PARK, DALLAS

Adding-on

Expanding your living by adding space to your home

Adding on to a house—like marriage—is not an undertaking to be taken lightly. Your best friend (if he were an architect) would tell you that the best advice to a new homeowner like you is "Wait a while. See how the house 'works in.' Make sure you *really* need more space, and find out how you're *really* going to live in your new house."

But let's assume that's not an option—that you bought a house because you just loved it and it's in a great neighborhood—but it only has two bedrooms and you've got four kids and twins on the way. Or you've got to and/or want to make room for a mother-in-law. In other words, you've got to add on—and you've got to do it as soon as possible. Where do you start?

The first thing you need to decide is just exactly what kind of space you need; if you need help get it from a professional.

The most common need for more space—as suggested above—is the need for more bedrooms. The same general principles apply no matter what you need to add, so let's use that as our example. Try to find a floor plan of your new house (or if you can't find one, do some measuring and make a good sketch). And then start thinking about the smartest place to make that addition.

What if you're just not good at "visualizing" the way to add on? What if you just can't read (much less make) drawings? Then...

You may want to start with a remodeling contractor or an architect.

Remodeling contractors of course have a lot of experience in the kind of work you have in mind, and many pride themselves on their skill in making design suggestions. How do you find the *right* one? Ask your new neighbors, ask the local realtors. Make a few phone calls or visit with a few. You'll find one that makes a good, sound impression—then check on him. Ask for the names of families for whom he's done work. Ask them if he completed the work more or less on the promised schedule, about the quality of the work, and about the way the job was managed. Any good remodeling contractor employs men who are not just good at their work as carpenters or plumbers or roofers or masons, but trains them in the special courtesy and care on the job required when remodeling—remember they'll be in and around the house with you from eight in the morning until four at night, and unless they work as neatly as possible (making every effort, for example, to contain sawdust, and cleaning up or at least straightening up the work place each night), the mess in the house may drive you insane.

How about an architect? There seems to be a reluctance on the part of families to call in an architect—and the reason given is usually "Architects will cost too much" or "I didn't know architects were interested in little jobs like this." Both are mistaken notions.

Not every architect *is* interested in home remodeling jobs—some firms specialize in larger jobs such as hospitals or office buildings. But many architects, especially younger ones, actively enjoy working on houses and will welcome your inquiry. How much will it cost? Ask them. Architects charge a fee most often based on the time that will be required to solve your design problem, to make the necessary drawings for a builder to follow, and to check on the work as it progresses. How much will that come to? Since fees vary among architects, the best advice is: simply ask them. Most architects will sit down with you in their office and discuss your problem—and then make a suggestion as to fee—that you are free to take or leave.

Most architects have about the same financial problems and needs as you—and you can expect them to want to make about as much money everyday as you do—unless of course you are a doctor or lawyer, in which case they will *not* expect to make as much money as you do. You should not look upon an architect's fee as an "extra"—architects can often save most of the cost of their fee by designing a more efficient space; or coming up with a "rearrangement" of existing space that avoids the need to add on at all; or by helping you contract the job yourself, eliminating a builder's overhead and profit. Talk about it with the architect...

The advantage of hiring an architect is his talent, skill, and experience—they study design for a minimum of five

Our neighbors recommended a HOWMET Plant-Playroom.™ For about half the cost of conventional construction...we're glad they did.

We simply needed more room for family activities.

A Howmet Plant-Playroom with its Temp-Trol™ * insulated roof solved our problems, quickly, at an affordable price. Now it's possible to heat or air condition a patio enclosure with minimal chance of roof condensation.

The Plant-Playroom is really a very ingenious system of traditional windows, doors and wall panels arranged in any combination you want.

The walls are load bearing, just like the walls of your home. Every unit is precision engineered and factory assembled for accurate, fast installation. A Plant-Playroom is completed in days rather than weeks because it's for recreational activity, and not a conventional room addition. The cost saving comes from the reduced assembly and erection time. It's sure a sensible solution to today's high construction costs.

For a free 24 page, full color brochure showing the features and benefits of the Howmet Plant-Playroom, call our toll free number today.   *Patent Pending

Call TOLL FREE
ask for Operator 74

1-800-241-8444

Except in Alaska and Hawaii
In Georgia 1-800-323-9123

HOWMET
Skylight Patio Covers

© Howmet Aluminum Corp. 1979

HOWMET ALUMINUM CORPORATION
A Member of The Pechiney Ugine Kuhlmann Group
BUILDING SPECIALTIES DIVISION   74
P.O. Box 163, Mesquite, Texas 75149
Where Ideas and Imagination Are Only The Beginning.

For more information circle 16 on the Reader's Service Card following the Index.

years, undergo a three-year "internship" in a practicing architect's office, and then must pass a state-administered examination which includes a difficult design examination before they can even begin to practice on their own. An architect will work closely with you—acting not just as designer but as your advisor. An architect—by the nature of his professional ethics—is always "on your side," just as your doctor or lawyer is.

How do you find an architect? The Yellow Pages (only recently have architects been permitted under their code of ethics to advertise, and most choose not to). How do you find a good architect? As suggested above, ask friends. Or you can call the local chapter of the American Institute of Architects—which will give you names (though not specific recommendations) of architects who are active in the residential field.

Back to our example of adding some new bedrooms: where do you start? Develop a plan.

First you need to consider your lot and eliminate the area you *can't* build. You can't build too close to any of the lot lines (restrictions vary: ask at town hall) and there may be other local code or planning restrictions. You can't build over the water or sewer lines or (farther out in the country) near the well or the septic tank. You'll need a set of the local building codes—and before you start you'll need permission to build from your local building inspector, who will check that your addition meets all local codes. Some other general advice:

First make sure you can't use some existing space...

Many houses built on sloping land have lower basement levels with windows on the downhill side—and this space is typically shown as a "rumpus room." Often, it is possible to excavate just a bit on the downhill side so that this space can open through big sliding glass doors to grade—and then you can partition the space off to create those new bedrooms. All the plumbing for a new bath will typically be nearby. The dampness problems (if there are any) are solvable.

If you have an attic, you can sometimes get that extra space inexpensively by building a long dormer at the rear,

letting in light and air and creating necessary headroom up there. The complication here is usually the stairs—

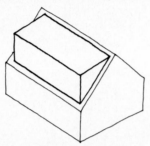

they take a chunk out of the floor in the attic and the floor below three feet wide and ten feet long, and it often is difficult to fit a new stairway into an existing plan. Some remodeling contractors specialize in adding a second floor to a one-story house. This is pretty major surgery—but you can consider the idea.

Many remodeling jobs involve converting the garage. If the garage happens to be on the side of the house where the addition logically wants to go, with some logical circulation path to the bathroom (or space for a new bathroom), this is a relatively simple add-on. You'll need a new floor, partitions, wall and ceiling finished off, a new wall and windows in place of the garage

Asphalt Roofing Manufacturers Association

doors (and *please* tear up at least part of the driveway leading up to the new wall and put in some plantings). With this solution, of course, what do you do with the car?

Finally, many relatively new houses come with both a living room and a family room. Ask yourself (it depends on your family life-style) whether you really need both. For example, you might consider dressing up the family room into a living room, remodeling the living room into a super-classy master bedroom suite (with its own fireplace!),

adding a new bath or (with luck) expanding the powder room into a proper master bath, and dividing the master bedroom into two smaller bedrooms for

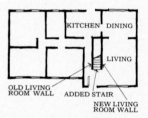

two children (again, don't assume the bedrooms will be too small for the children—most kids like small rooms). Which. example brings us to an often overlooked remodeling/adding-on idea:

Don't assume when you're adding on that rooms can't be changed in their use...and

that maybe instead of adding two new bedrooms, the better idea is, for example, to add a new living room and make the old living room into one or more bedrooms. (See "A Tale of One Old House".)

Or convert the old dark front dining room into a bedroom (again, assuming there's a bath reachable by a rational circulation path) and create a sunroom/dining room off the kitchen in the backyard.

Or divide the master bedroom into two smaller children's rooms (turning the whole upstairs, for example, into the children's department) and add on a new master bedroom downstairs—close to the kitchen for putting on the morning coffee, open to the backyard for the early morning stretch and a look at the weather, open to the best view and (someday, see another chapter) the swimming pool. Imagine rolling out of bed, sliding open the glass door, and plunging into the pool....

70

How to increase the value of your new home.

The Heatilator® EP Fireplace can help you save money now, and make money when you re-sell. It can lower your heating bills as well as add enjoyment to your home life. You can even install it yourself.

Just look at what you can have with your new Heatilator EP Fireplace:

Forced-Air Heating System
This "more heat for the money" fireplace takes in cooler air at the base and channels it around the firebox. As the heated air rises, built-in fans force the heat back into the room or into other rooms. You'll really appreciate this feature for fast warm-ups on chilly days.

Glass Doors to Keep Cold Out, Keep Warmth In
Our U.L. Listed glass doors increase heating efficiency and also protect against the danger of flying sparks. Open or closed, they let everyone enjoy the beauty of the fire.

Outside Air to Supply Oxygen for Fire
Instead of wasting heated house air for combustion, outside air can be channeled into the firebox. There's no longer a need to crack open a window or door—even in an air-tight home.

Installation is easier than you'd think.
All you need are a few basic tools. Simple instructions guide you every step of the way. Your Heatilator EP Fireplace was designed to make it easy for you. The insulated chimney sections just twist together and lock.

If it doesn't say "Heatilator Fireplace," it isn't.

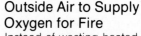

heatilator®
AMERICA'S LEADING FIREPLACE SYSTEMS

FOR INFORMATION: See your local dealer. Or write us: Heatilator Fireplace Division, P.O. Box 10360, Department 86259, Des Moines, IA 50306. In a hurry? Call toll free: (800) 247-6798. In Iowa, (515) 276-6400, collect.

For more information circle 37 on the Reader's Service Card following the Index.

When you're adding on to a two-story house, think two-story addition....

The reason for making a two-story addition is the same as the reason for building a two-story house—more space for the money. The reason is the cost of foundation and the enclosure of more space with fewer exterior walls and less roof.

For example, if you're building a new living room out back, you might want to build a loft at one end entered from the

upstairs hall, to serve as a sewing room or "family office" and occasional guest room.

Too often forgotten: you can't add on without working out a new circulation pattern....

To be obvious about it, and to pick up a warning given above, you can't add new bedrooms under a new dormer up in the attic without finding space to run a flight of stairs up there.

Or let's say that garage you want to expand into is on the living-room side of the house. You're not going to want to

use the living room as a corridor to that new space—so you'll have to carve out some space to use as a hallway.

If you add a new bedroom beyond the existing bedroom wing, you're going to have to give up space for a hall.

The same is true for a new living room out in the sideyard or backyard—you've got to make a rational connection between the existing circulation (hallways and entry) and the new room.

Once you've decided how the addition is going to work, the next step is to figure out what the new addition is going to look like.

Your first concern is what architects call *massing*—more simply the form and shape of that addition, which obviously must relate very skillfully to the existing house. This is another critical area where design skill is needed—and if you don't have it, make sure your remodeling contractor has it, or retain an architect. Nothing is sadder to see than a once handsome house pulled out of scale or otherwise rendered graceless by a clumsy addition.

It's difficult to give general rules (such decisions are what architects study for years) but there are a few general guidelines:

1. Start with the roof line. You can add on following the same roof pitch, or set

the roof at right angles, or roof the addition as a shed, or even make the addition flat-roofed (see photos below). One aesthetic almost-must: maintain the same roof pitch for the addition as the original house—if the main house has a steeply pitched roof, don't be tempted to save a few dollars by building the addition with a lower pitch—it will amost never look right.

2. The siding material of the addition should be either the same as the existing house, or contrast handsomely. And "the same" is less risky. And if the existing house has strong horizontal lines—clapboards or shingles—make every effort to line up the siding of the addition (as well as the window) with the horizontal lines of the house. A few inches off will bother a critical eye. The photos show some well-handled examples.

An architect can sometimes give you something really special.

The photos are examples of additions that are really quite beautiful and far from the everyday kind of add-on. In the house by architects Mayers & Schiff (photo right) a new and strikingly contemporary living room was, in effect, let into the corner of an existing colonial house. In the addition by architect Hugh Newell Jacobsen (photo upper right) an

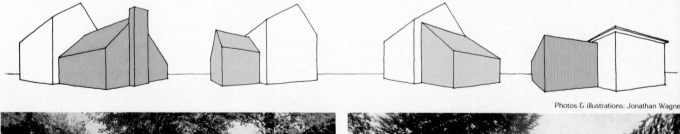

Photos & illustrations: Jonathan Wagner

addition was made to an existing Victorian house carrying out in contemporary terms the forms and decoration of the original (that's the addition on the left). Finally, while the house by architect Edward Larrabee Barnes (shown below) was built all at one time, it suggests another way to add on—build a separate building. For a vacation house (which this is) or for a house in a warm climate, making an addition separate from the existing house makes a lot of sense—the children's "mess" isolated, the guests have their own space and don't have to tiptoe around in the morning, the noisy laundry equipment or workshop is away from the living spaces.

But this kind of special work almost always takes an architect—and a good one.

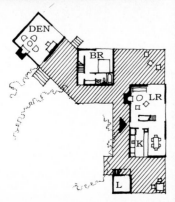

Tale of one old house

Photos and illustrations: Jonathan Wagner

The original house—built in the late 1700s—looked about like this (1). It was 16 by 20 feet—called a keeping house because it was the minimum size you needed to keep the land grant from King George.

Sometime way back when, a kitchen addition was made. That kept the cooking smoke out of the center of the house. And a shed was built along the back—probably for storage or as a barn (2). The plan probably was something like the one shown.

About 35 years ago, the house—fallen into disrepair (indeed, the great central chimney had fallen into the basement)—was purchased by a young couple with a lot of talent and energy. They patched the roof and floors where the original chimney had gone through and...(3)

A new plan was devised to meet their needs. The central front door was moved around to the side, so that when you entered, the living room (with a new chimney that served both the fireplace and the house's first furnace down in the basement) was straight ahead; the dining space was to the right, near the kitchen. The stairs were reversed to improve the circulation, and the upstairs was made into a master bedroom, a tiny children's bedroom (they had a tiny child at the time) and a bath.

The rear shed provided space for a powder room, a storage room, and a hallway leading to...

The first contemporary addition—a studio for the young couple—one a set designer, the other an interior decorator. It has a brick floor, corner fireplace, huge window for north light, French doors opening to the backyard. It was set back so that all of the windows of the existing house were unobstructed by the addition. The first young couple lived there happily for seven or eight years

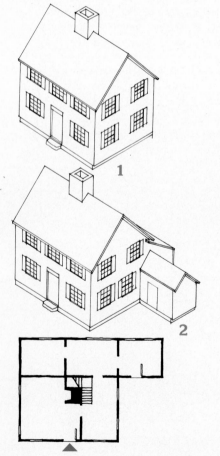

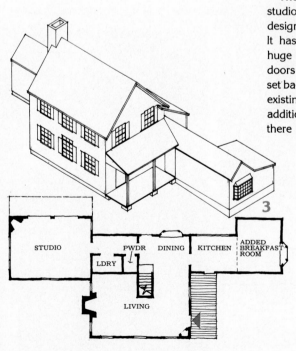

(making only a minor addition off the kitchen for storage) until they decided to build a larger house and sell the old house to a second young couple. The second young couple used the house as they found it for a number of years. Their first child went into the tiny bedroom. But then, enter second child.

The parents took over the brick-floored studio with its corner fireplace as the master bedroom, leaving the two upstairs bedrooms and bath for the children. The powder room was enlarged into a full bath (4). All went well for four years until child No. 3 arrived. Question: Move to a larger house, or add on? Answer: add on.

Solution (as faithful readers of the previous pages will guess): don't add more bedrooms, add a new living room and make the old living room (a bit small and dark) into a bedroom. The plan (5) shows how it worked. A new front hall was created by a storage wall that formed the bedroom. (Photos right). The living room was added just outside the dining area by window—indeed the opening into the living room is via the window framing. The former back door space was made into a wine rack. The child in the new bedroom did have to walk through the front hall to reach the bath—but then children don't seem to mind. Then...

In the L formed between the new living room and the master bedroom, a terrace was fitted in.

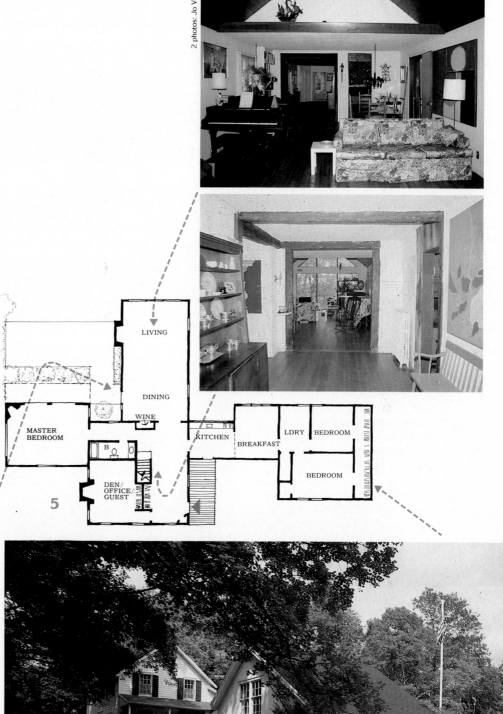

2 photos: Jo Voigt

Enter child No. 4 (this is the end). Solution (especially since there never was a garage): build a garage with two bedrooms over it. By artful excavation, the bedrooms are on the main-floor level, the garage cut into the hill below. The two boys moved into this space—and while again they had to walk a long way to the bath they were too young to know any better. The two girls took over the upstairs (privacy at last!). The front bedroom (which was still a little dark) was transformed into a home office/den/television room/guest bedroom (via a fold-out couch).

And so, a happy ending.

75

Booklets on heating and cooling. Information can be obtained most quickly by contacting local sources. But you may wish to write directly for some of the booklets illustrated. They are all excellent. (Allow 4–6 weeks for delivery.)

Home Heating Systems, Fuels, Controls,
Farmers' Bulletin No. 2235
U.S. Department of Agriculture
Office of Public Affairs Washington, D.C. 20250

Homeowners Guide to Residential Hydronic
Heating Systems
The Hydronics Institute
35 Russo Place, Berkeley Heights, N.J. 07922

Money to Burn? A Guide to Efficient
Use of Natural Gas in the Home
American Gas Association
1515 Wilson Boulevard, Arlington, Virginia 22209

How to Improve the Efficiency of
Your Oil-Fired Furnace
National Bureau of Standards
Public Information Office, Washington, D.C. 20234

Get the Most From Your Heating Oil Dollar:
Servicing Cuts Costs and Pollution
U.S. Environmental Protection Agency
Public Affairs Office, Washington, D.C. 20460

Guide to wise use of energy for electric
heating and cooling
Edison Electric Institute
90 Park Avenue, New York, N.Y. 10016

Heat Pumps for Heating and Cooling Homes,
Agriculture Information Bulletin No. 306
U.S. Department of Agriculture
Office of Public Affairs, Washington, D.C. 20250

Facts About Central Air Conditioning
Council of Better Business Bureaus
1150 17th Street, N.W., Washington, D.C. 20036

You have just moved into an older home. Even before you've finished unpacking, you should begin inspecting your heating and cooling systems to make sure that nothing is going to go wrong. Establish a preventive maintenance program so you won't be without heat or air conditioning when you need them most.

Adding more attic insulation, or a kitchen exhaust fan, or a new food freezer does not have to be a priority—unless you want it to be. The fine points of improving the energy efficiency, comfort, and conveniences of your home can wait a while. Heating cannot.

Get settled before making any major changes. Conduct continual inspections of your home, but don't do anything until you know what you're doing and you know what your needs are.

Don't wait for an emergency. Prepare a list of local dealers, contractors, service people, and repair people that you can call on. Ask your new neighbors for suggestions. Your local utilities, Better Business Bureau, Chamber of Commerce, and Consumer Protection Agency may also be able to help. And don't forget the previous owners of your home, if you can get in touch with them.

The previous owners may have names of service people who are already familiar with your home. They may also have warranties or service contracts that are transferable to you (not all are). If you haven't already obtained copies, get them now.

Every home, old or new, will have blemishes that need repair. But, with evaluation and planning, problems can be corrected at a leisurely pace—without costing you a fortune.

Here is what you need to know about making your home energy efficient, on a schedule that suits both your budget and the individual needs of your home.

Heating and cooling equipment.

Look for operating and maintenance instructions and for service records on or near your equipment. If you don't find any of these, try to contact the previous owners for information.

You can also jot down the makes and model numbers of your heating and cooling appliances and try to get owners' manuals from a local authorized dealer or from the manufacturer. But getting instruction booklets on your specific equipment may be difficult, particularly with older models.

On the other hand, good general information on the maintenance of different *types* of heating and cooling systems is readily available.

If your heating system operates on natural gas, electricity, or steam supplied by a local utility, ask their customer service department to send you information. If you have oil heat or bottled propane gas heat, contact the dealer that delivers it. Your electric utility is the most likely source for cooling system information, but you can also talk with your gas company if you have gas air conditioning.

Read the information you receive, and carefully follow the maintenance suggestions. Not only will your fuel bills be lower, but your heating and cooling equipment will last longer.

Your heating system.

Most likely your home already has central heating, in which the heating unit (boiler or furnace) is located in the basement or other out-of-the-way place, and heat is distributed to all parts of the house through ducts or pipes. Some homes have room unit heaters (such as plug-in electrical baseboard resistance heaters, or gas wall units). But central systems are the most efficient and economical method of heating, and most U.S. homes are centrally heated.

You will probably have a warm air, hot water, or steam heat system. Any of these systems can be fired with any fuel, which today is usually oil, gas, or electricity. A few systems still use such fuels as coal, coke, or wood.

Steam heat is generally found only in homes built before 1950. Homes built more recently will have either warm air or hot water systems, with warm air systems being more popular in the last few years because of their use for both heating and air conditioning.

Heating units on warm air systems are called furnaces, and hot water and steam heating units are called boilers (or sometimes, just to confuse us, boiler furnaces). Warm air heat is distributed to the house through ducting, and hot water or steam through pipes.

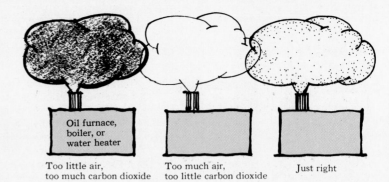

Oil furnace,
boiler, or
water heater

Too little air,
too much carbon dioxide

Too much air,
too little carbon dioxide

Just right

Yellow flame—
not burning cleanly

Flame dancing above burner—
needs adjustment

Just right

Oil heat. You can tell by looking if the oil burner on your burnace, boiler, or hot water heater goes out of adjustment between annual tune-ups. A pale gray smoke from your oil burner means that it's properly adjusted. Dark gray smoke coming from the burner means that the air/fuel ratio is too rich, and that your heating system is polluting the air. A white or colorless smoke means that your heating system may be running inefficiently and using too much fuel. Call a serviceman if the smoke is not pale gray.

Gas heat. If the burner on your gas furnace or boiler has a yellow flame, or if the flame dances above the burner, it's time to call a serviceman. Checking the burners on other gas appliances like water heaters and stoves is also a good idea.

If your home is less than 15 or 20 years old, you probably have the original heating equipment that was installed when the house was built. If your home is more than 20 years old, and the furnace or boiler looks old, you should consider replacing part or all of the system. It may be inefficient both because of its age and its old-fashioned design. It could also be unreliable, and replacement parts may be hard to get.

When you first move in, or well before the heating season, find a serviceman to come out and look at your heating system. All heating systems need periodic inspection, cleaning, and occasional adjustments. Unless there is a service record attached to the boiler or furnace, you have no way of knowing when your equipment was last inspected, or what work was performed.

As a general rule, oil systems should be tuned up every year before the start of the heating season. Even though gas equipment manufacturers recommend gas heat tune-ups every one to three years, a yearly tune-up of your gas heating system will help cut fuel costs and prolong equipment life. Electric heating equipment doesn't require a tune-up, but it will require periodic cleaning and occasional lubrication of some of the components.

When the serviceman arrives, watch what he does. Ask questions about your heating system, particularly about the maintenance chores you should be doing between service calls.

Ask the serviceman how you can

know that your heating system is operating properly. With gas heat, for instance, the appearance of the gas burner flame is one indicator. With oil heat, the color (or non-color) of the gases coming from the oil burner can indicate proper or improper adjustment. Noisy equipment of any kind probably means malfunctioning, and may require immediate servicing to avoid a breakdown.

A service contract on oil heat systems is an absolute necessity, and less expensive than paying for individual calls. Typically, an oil heat service contract costs $35 to $50, and pays for itself in fuel savings because it includes the annual tune-up. The company that delivers your oil usually provides your maintenance services too.

During the annual tune-up, the service technician should change the oil filter and replace the nozzle if it has become clogged. The nozzle, by the way, is what controls the amount of oil that reaches the burner. On many warm air or hot water (but *not* steam) heating systems, you can save both money and fuel, and *increase* the comfort of your home by having the service technician install a smaller-sized nozzle on your oil burner. This is called "down-firing" or "under-firing" and it works because most heating systems are too large (oversized) for the area they have to heat. An oversized heating system means both physical discomfort and higher fuel bills. (Many oil service technicians are now using the procedures for optimizing nozzle size

that are described in "A Service Manager's Guide to Saving Energy in Residential Oil Burners," developed by the National Bureau of Standards. Find out if your oil company has adopted these procedures as standard practice.)

To adjust your oil burner properly the service technician should be using special instruments during the annual tune-up. He needs these instruments to measure such things as the carbon dioxide (CO_2) level, the flue gas temperature just below the barometric damper, and the smoke number. Precise measurements cannot be made by "feel," so insist that your serviceman go back to his office for the proper equipment if he's neglected to bring it with him. Be sure to get a copy of the readings that are taken.

With warm air furnace systems, the service technician should vacuum the heat exchanger and change the air filter. On boiler systems, the boiler chamber should be partially or completely drained to remove any sediment, and then refilled. (This applies to gas and electric heat, as well as oil.)

With gas heat, it's often more economical to pay for service as needed. Gas utilities may provide some of your service requirements (such as answering emergency calls on gas leaks, or routine inspections when you suspect something is wrong) either free or for a nominal fee. But actual repairs and routine tune-ups may have to be done by a private dealer, so it might be advantageous for you to establish an

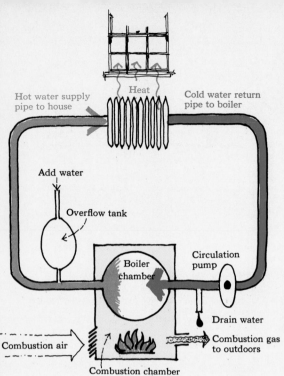

Hot water supply pipe to house

Heat

Cold water return pipe to boiler

Add water

Overflow tank

Boiler chamber

Circulation pump

Combustion air

Combustion chamber

Drain water

Combustion gas to outdoors

Hot water heat. Most systems have a circulating pump to make the water flow through the heating pipes. The overflow tank keeps the boiler chamber from overfilling. If your hot water heating system doesn't have controls that allow water to be added automatically, have controls installed. You will need to drain your boiler occasionally to prevent sediment build-up that can corrode the boiler. You can do this yourself once the service technician shows you how.

Steam heat. Steam circulates through the pipes by pressure. An elaborate network of pipes called the "Hartford loop" keeps the boiler chamber from overfilling. Like hot water systems, steam systems should have controls that add hot water automatically, and the boiler will have to be drained occasionally.

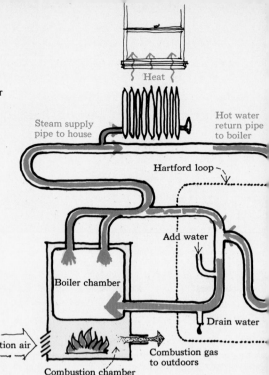

Heat

Steam supply pipe to house

Hot water return pipe to boiler

Hartford loop

Add water

Boiler chamber

Combustion air

Combustion chamber

Drain water

Combustion gas to outdoors

ongoing relationship with a local repair company so you can get service when you need it. Ask your local gas utility for advice on the local situation.

Gas-system tune-ups generally include checking the gas valve, blower, fan control, main burner, motor, pilot light and thermostat. Cleaning of the system is essential, and some adjustments may have to be made. Services vary in scope and complexity, and therefore in price. Make sure you know what you'll be getting for your tune-up dollar.

Service contracts on electric heating systems are not considered economical, but in some communities they may be the only assurance you have of getting prompt and reliable service. At the very least, find out how to get in touch with a repairman in case of an emergency. Plan ahead by asking your electric utility for suggestions.

Hydronic heating.
Hot water heat and steam heat are the two types of hydronic systems. Water is heated in a boiler, most often by a gas or oil burner located just below the boiler chamber. Alternatively, electric coils may be located in the water itself (just like an electric water heater).

Older boiler systems may still be burning wood, coke, or coal to heat the water. If this is your system, it will probably make economic sense for you to convert to gas or oil. A gas or oil conversion burner can be installed in the combustion chamber (where the wood,

coke or coal have been burned) without replacing the entire system (if the rest of the system is in good condition). In converting to gas, the gas lines will have to be run to the burner, but this is particularly economical if you already have gas service for cooking and other appliances. (Not long ago, the government was banning new gas line hookups for residential heating. However, the ban has been lifted in many communities, and you can now get gas.) With oil you will need a storage tank, which increases the installation cost.

You can often increase the efficiency of your boiler system economically by replacing the gas or oil burner. A burner that sits on a pedestal or platform in the combustion chamber means that you have an old-style conversion burner: it was installed a long time ago to convert your boiler from wood or coal, when burners were not as efficient as they are today. Newer conversion burners will be attached by flanges to the bottom side of the boiler chamber.

For safety reasons, new burner equipment should always be installed by a qualified service technician. When choosing a new oil burner ask for a carbon dioxide (CO_2) rating of eleven or twelve per cent—the higher the better. (Your present oil burner may not be able to operate much higher than at a 4%-5% CO_2 level without polluting the air.) When choosing a new gas burner, ask for the type that has an electronic ignition device instead of a pilot light.

The boiler chamber part of hydronic

systems is generally very sturdy, and shouldn't be replaced hastily. If it has been maintained properly (draining parts of the system to prevent sediment and rust buildup), its life-span can be indefinite. But keep an eye out for possible rust deterioration.

A few hydronic systems (in cities like Philadelphia, Denver, and San Francisco) still operate on "city steam," which is steam supplied directly by a utility, rather than being produced by a boiler in your basement. If you are using city steam, you may eventually have to install a boiler because utilities are gradually phasing out their steam services.

Warm air heating.
Especially if they are used year-round for both heating and cooling, warm air furnaces don't usually last as long as boiler furnaces. If you have an older warm air system, try to maintain your furnace by replacing components. Equipment life can often be prolonged by replacing the blower or by installing a new burner. Careful monitoring is preferable to spending $1500 on a new furnace.

When your furnace is more than 15 years old, be on the lookout for possible breakdowns. Visit your furnace every couple of weeks during the heating season and listen to the sounds it's making. An unusual noise is an indication that something might be going wrong—the same as with your automobile. If your warm air system also supplies air conditioning, monitor it in the summer too. Anticipating trouble can

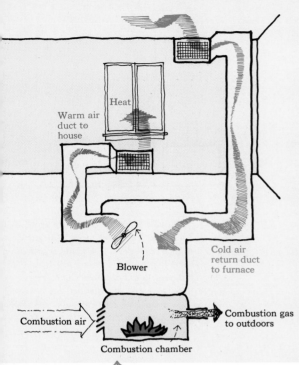

Warm air heat. Most systems are "forced" warm air in which a blower is used to circulate air through the heating ducts. Occasionally, older systems may circulate air by gravity (less efficient than with a blower). Heating registers are usually located near the floor and cold air return registers near the ceiling.

Steam radiator. Steam can enter and leave the radiator through the same pipe (one-pipe system, as shown) or enter the radiator through one pipe and leave through another (two-pipe system, not shown). The radiator valve must be entirely open when you want heat and entirely closed when you don't. The only way to control the temperature of a steam radiator is by replacing the air valve with a new air valve that has a thermostatic control.

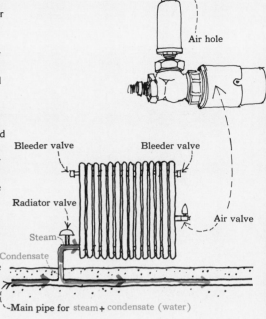

save you money.

No matter what the age of your warm air furnace, filters should be changed often. Air filters are very inexpensive (a dollar or two), but very important to the effectiveness of your furnace. Two types are generally available: the disposable glass fiber kind, and the spongy type that can be cleaned and reused. They are equally good.

Install new filters at the beginning of the heating season, and inspect them at least once a month. If the filter looks dirty when you hold it up to a light, it's time for a change. Air filters in some systems have to be replaced monthly.

Putting the heat where you want it.
Most homes have uneven heat distribution. You can expect your new home to have some parts that are too hot, others that are too cold. Was your previous home any different?

However, your home doesn't have to *remain* unevenly heated—if you know how to use the controls. Usually, simple adjustments to radiators or registers (where the heat enters the room) are all that's needed.

If you have a warm air system, start by inspecting (and vacuuming) all warm air registers. Warm air registers are located on or near the floor (cold air return ducts are near the ceiling). Each register should have an adjustable damper that allows you to open, partially open, or close the register by moving a lever. Most registers also have (and should have) vanes or fins (sometimes

adjustable) to direct heat into the room.

If you're not getting the heat distribution you want, consider replacing some of your warm air registers with the kind that have two sets of directional fins, both horizontal and vertical. Fin attachments for your existing registers may also be available at your local home center or hardware store.

Heating contractors can make further adjustments that will improve your warm air heat distribution. They can install an extra register in a cold room (so can you, if you know what you're doing). Dampers may be installed in a heating duct to slow the flow of heat into a warm room. Part of the warm air ducting might be replaced. But replacing *all* of your ducting system is expensive, so don't consider this unless you've tried the less costly approaches without success.

With hydronic heating systems, too, heat distribution control should begin where the heat enters the room—at the radiators. Dirt absorbs heat that should be going into the room, so remove the radiator covers and vacuum radiators thoroughly, inspecting them as you work. If you have baseboard or convector radiators with metal convector fins, use a pair of pliers to straighten any bent fins.

Hot water and steam radiators must be completely filled with water (or steam) to work properly. Unless you have metal fin radiators, you should bleed all radiators at least once a year (preferably in the fall when you first turn

on the boiler) to release unwanted air. If a radiator seems cooler than normal at any time during the winter, it may need another bleeding.

Locate the bleeder valves on both sides of each radiator or convector (they'll be near the top). Some bleeder valves open with a screwdriver, others with a special key or an adjustable wrench (if you don't have the key). Hold a pan under the valve as you open it. There will be a hiss of air, followed by a surge of water. Be prepared to close the valve quickly as the water begins to flow. (You don't want a flood.)

Inspect the radiator shut-off valves—the devices that control the amount of hot water or steam that reaches the radiator. If you find a leak, use an adjustable wrench to tighten the large nut just below the valve handle. However, this may not work, and you might need a plumber to repack the valve. You will find it most economical to try to stop the leak temporarily (with waterproof tape or rubber patches) and have the plumber fix it permanently when he's at your home for another repair. Or wait until spring (when your heating system is off), and repair it yourself.

When the radiator is in the off position the radiator should be cold. When it's at the maximum heat setting you should have plenty of heat. Keep in mind that you can experiment with hot water radiator valves because they have a wide range of settings. Steam radiator valves have only two settings: on or off.

If you suspect that a radiator valve is

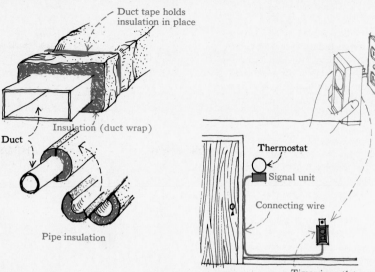

Duct tape holds insulation in place

Insulation (duct wrap)

Duct

Pipe insulation

Thermostat

Signal unit

Connecting wire

Timer in outlet

Some clock thermostats operate by use of a signal unit. They're simple to install, because you don't have to remove your present thermostat.

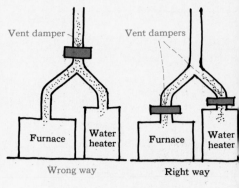

Vent damper

Vent dampers

Furnace | Water heater

Furnace | Water heater

Wrong way

Right way

CAUTION: It's dangerous to install one vent damper to control the heat loss from two heating appliances. Each furnace, boiler, or water heater must have its own damper, or poisonous exhaust fumes can come back into the house. Vent dampers are open while the appliance is operating, and closed when the appliance is off. Obviously, no two heating appliances will have the same on/off cycle.

not working, consider replacing it. If you want to avoid the cost of a plumber, wait until summer: remove the valve, and go shopping for a replacement. (Don't remove a shut-off valve while the heating system is in operation unless you know how to drain the radiator.) For your hot water system, look for a radiator shut-off valve that has a thermostatic control. On steam systems, look for a reliable manual control (any thermostat will be part of the air valve, not the radiator shut-off valve).

If you need more heat from a radiator, install a sheet of aluminum foil behind it to radiate more heat into the room. Or paint the radiator black. If you want *less* heat, paint the radiator with metallic (aluminum) paint. Aesthetics won't be a consideration if your radiators have covers, and most do.

If you can't get the heating control you need, call in one or more contractors experienced in hydronic heating. A contractor can add or subtract radiators to suit your needs.

Duct and pipe insulation. In

many homes, heating ducts or pipes go through attics, under floors, through garages, or through other non-insulated spaces. Heating ducts and pipes in these unheated spaces should be insulated. Although some of the duct or pipe heat loss is regained by the house, a significant amount is not.

Because of the high temperature differential between the air in the attic and the heating ducts or pipes, these are the

most important ones to insulate. Ducts and pipes in basements and crawl spaces should also be insulated, particularly if the floor above is heavily insulated. When insulating basement ducts, don't cover the registers (if you want them closed, use the dampers).

Before insulating ducts, tape all of the joints with duct tape to seal air leaks. Be sure to use *duct tape*—not cheap, but worth the extra expense. It's very sticky, and has a myriad of other uses too.

Insulate *only* with duct wrap insulation and pipe insulation, which have a vapor barrier on one side. (Install with the vapor barrier on the outside.) Substitutes may be less expensive, but they may not be safe to use.

Clock thermostats. Some

electric utilities are arguing against night thermostat setback because it causes an increased peak demand (for the utility) on winter mornings. However, lowering your thermostat at night is a *proven* way to reduce *your* heating bills, so try to get in the habit of doing it.

A clock thermostat can be installed to turn down your thermostat automatically, so you can't forget. It can also be programmed to turn on the heat *before* you wake up, so you don't have to wake up to a cold house.

Some clock thermostats allow you only one setback in each 24-hour period. If your home is usually empty during the day, buy the kind that gives you two or three setbacks, so you can turn your heat down in the daytime as

well as at night.

Before buying a clock thermostat, read the instructions carefully. Some are more complicated to install than others. Will you be able to install it yourself? Or will you need a handyman to rewire your existing thermostat?

Clock thermostats cost between $30 and $70, and will quickly pay for themselves in fuel savings in all but the warmest climates.

Vent dampers. If you buy a *new* furnace, boiler or hot water heater that is fueled by gas or oil, it should have a vent damper to reduce the heat lost up the chimney. The vent damper closes the stack (chimney) when the heating appliance is off, and opens the stack automatically when the oil or gas burner is firing. (A fireplace damper serves the same purpose, but it's operated by hand.)

Having a vent damper installed on your *existing* gas or oil furnace, boiler or water heater is also highly desirable, and will save you fuel dollars. *But proceed with caution.* Vent dampers (often called "flue dampers," erroneously) are relatively new devices, and there has been a great deal of controversy over the safety aspects of adding vent dampers to existing heating equipment.

Until recently, most building codes wouldn't allow you to add a vent damper. Currently, codes are being rewritten to include vent dampers, and in another two years most codes will probably

Free Information Center.
For products, planning, decorating and remodeling.

Many of the advertisers in the HomeBook are offering free full-color catalogs to HomeBook readers. Just turn to the back of the book and circle the catalogs you want on the postage-paid postcards. Drop your card in the mail, and we'll send back the catalogs you requested as soon as possible. Often as fast as three days of receiving your request. So that very quickly the information you need will be found right in your new mailbox.

More help from the HomeBook.

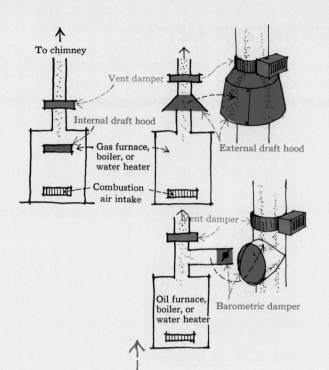

To chimney

Vent damper

Internal draft hood

Gas furnace, boiler, or water heater

Combustion air intake

External draft hood

Vent damper

Oil furnace, boiler, or water heater

Barometric damper

allow them. To some extent, whether or not you can install a vent damper (and how soon) will depend upon your local code.

Call your local building inspector. Are vent dampers allowed? Do you need a building permit? Does your building department inspect completed installations? Have they inspected many? Are one or two contractors doing most of the installations? What does he think of vent dampers?

Any vent damper you buy for an oil heating appliance should be UL listed. For gas appliances, an AGA certification is necessary. At least a dozen manufacturers now make vent dampers with a UL listing or an AGA certification.

Look for a vent damper that opens *quickly:* within five seconds or less after the burner goes on. If the vent damper takes too long to open, your furnace or boiler can be "fooled" into shutting itself off as a safety precaution. (It would have to be reset each time this happened.)

Your biggest problem in adding a vent damper will be to find a qualified installer. There aren't many. Try asking your local building inspector. Or write to the Automatic Damper Manufacturers Association, P.O. Box 478, Madison, Ohio 44057, and ask for their advice. ADMA is working with the U.S. Department of Energy and the American Gas Association to develop training programs to help assure the safe installation of vent dampers on existing equipment.

Barometric dampers. If you have oil heating equipment, you need a barometric damper to keep heat from going too quickly up the stack. If you don't already have a barometric damper, get one installed. This device has been around for a long time. It saves energy, and there's no safety controversy.

Hot water heaters. Locate the thermostat control on your water heater and turn it down slightly. See if you still have enough hot water. Keep edging the thermostat downward until you find the setting that gives you just enough hot water for normal use. Mark the setting with a grease pencil so you can find it easily.

On days when you are washing clothes, turn up the water heater thermostat. You can also do this a couple of hours before running your dishwasher. But, when you're finished, remember to return the thermostat to its "normal use" setting.

Put insulation on the outside of your water heater, even if you have a newer "insulated" model. Gas and oil water heaters are insulated around the sides (don't block air intakes). Electric water heaters get insulated on the top too. A $20 investment in water heater insulation will save you about $15 to $20 a year in fuel costs on a 40-50 gallon tank.

Hot water supply pipes, like hot water heating pipes, should be insulated where they run through unheated spaces. (Follow the same procedure.)

It's not normally economical to insulate the cold water supply pipes, but insulation can put a stop to dripping (if you have this problem).

Fireplaces. Only about ten percent of fireplace heat makes it into the room—the rest goes up the chimney. For this reason, fireplaces are not usually considered an economical means of heating, except perhaps in milder climates where they can provide all of the heating for your home on a room-by-room basis.

On the other hand, who can resist a roaring fire on a snowy evening? Consider yourself fortunate if you have a fireplace, and as an investment in your comfort and happiness.

Your first concern should be to keep heat from disappearing up the chimney when your fireplace is *not* being used. The chimney should be closed off when there is no fire in the fireplace, or your *central* heating will be wasted. A tightly-fitting damper installed at the bottom of the flue is what you need.

The damper consists of a cast-iron frame with a hinged lid. It is opened (or partially opened) to control the smoke and heat of the fire, and closed when the fireplace is not being used. Dampers are not always installed, but they are definitely recommended, especially in colder climates.

Use a flashlight to find out if you have a damper on your fireplace, and what condition the damper is in. The damper will be located at the top rear of the

The Heatilator EP Fireplace saves money as it saves heat

Puts more heat into your home, then keeps it there.

For more information circle 37 on the Reader's Service Card following the Index.

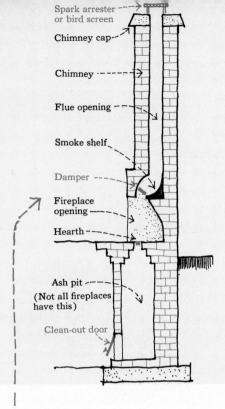

Spark arrester or bird screen
Chimney cap
Chimney
Flue opening
Smoke shelf
Damper
Fireplace opening
Hearth
Ash pit (Not all fireplaces have this)
Clean-out door

Chimney sweeps really do exist. If you can't locate one in your town, write: The Chimney Sweep Guild, c/o Kristia Associates, P.O. Box 1118, Portland, Maine 04104.

fireplace opening. It should fit tightly, operate easily, and have a handle or a ring that's easy to reach. Before the first heating season in your home, fix any damper that's not working properly or, if necessary, have a new one installed.

At a later date, you can install glass doors on your fireplace to further cut down on heat loss. Some of these doors are now made with insulating glass (two thicknesses of glass with an air space between).

To increase the amount of heat delivered to the room when a fire has been set, decorative metal plates can be installed on the back and sides of the fireplace opening. These metal heat reflectors can be purchased in many sizes and designs from manufacturers of fireplace accessories, but as a temporary measure you can install any metal sheeting (such as aluminum flashing, or even heavy-duty foil).

Most home fireplaces in the United States are seldom (if ever) cleaned and inspected. Particularly if you've moved into a very old home, you have reason to be concerned about the efficiency, safety, and state of repair of your existing fireplace and chimney. Do you know when it was last used? How often it was used? If there were any problems?

Before you operate your fireplace for the first time, hire a professional to clean and inspect your fireplace and chimney. You can also do it yourself if you know what to look for and don't mind the dirt. But for as little as $50 (for a one-fireplace, one-chimney home),

you can have a cleaning and inspection *and* a lesson in fireplace construction and future maintenance, if you ask questions. It's well worth the expense.

Ask your local hardware store or home center if they have a handyman available (or know of one) who's experienced with fireplaces and chimneys. Local fire marshalls or building officials may also be able to suggest someone. But your best source will probably be The Chimney Sweep Guild, which now has members in about 26 states.

How often you need to have your chimney swept will depend upon how often you use the fireplace and what kind of fuel you burn. Cleaning may be advisable after 150-200 fires have been set, particularly if you burn greenwood, or regularly throw trash into the fire.

Adding a fireplace or wood stove.

The simple addition of a fireplace or wood stove can transform a drab room into a showplace. Properly planned, this addition can also add to the energy efficiency of your home.

Prefabricated fireplaces and wood stoves are available in a myriad of designs, and many of them are designed to operate much more efficiently than regular fireplaces. Some of these units come with do-it-yourself instructions, others have to be installed by a contractor. To make the best use of your new fireplace or wood stove, locate it where you need the extra heat (such as a chilly corner of a large family room).

Before adding a fireplace or wood

stove, be sure to check with your local building department and your insurance company about safety requirements.

Air conditioning.

Like any piece of mechanical equipment, your air conditioning needs attention from time to time. A once-a-year checkup and cleaning by a qualified service technician will make it last longer and run better, as well as help keep operating costs lower.

If you live in a warm climate where air conditioning is practically a necessity, you'll want to have your equipment checked shortly after you move in. That way, you won't be surprised by a sudden air conditioning failure, or by inadequate cooling during your first big party. To keep the temperature down when you're entertaining a large group, your air conditioning will have to be operating at top efficiency.

The service technician will check the amount of refrigerant in the cooling coils. If your air conditioner does not have a full charge of refrigerant, it can't remove as much heat as it should. Motors should be oiled once a season (unless they are the sealed bearing type). The service technician should also clean the entire air conditioner.

As with warm air furnaces, clean filters are essential to the efficient operation of air conditioners. Dirty filters restrict air flow inside your air conditioner, increase temperatures, and reduce efficiency—and the result is a higher cost of operation. If you have central air conditioning, clean or re

Dramatically cut heating costs and enjoy 'comfort insurance' in a fuel shortage or blackout!

If you have a fireplace . . . or if you don't

Convert your fireplace from a potential heat waster into a highly efficient and effective heat producer. Install a beautiful Glass Door THERMOGRATE Fireplace Furnace heat exchanger Insert. (It's easy. No construction is needed.) It can produce up to 60,000 BTU per hour — even without the auxiliary blower — and up to 100,000 BTU per hour if you add a blower. That's enough to heat a house!

Tested and listed for safety by Underwriters Laboratories, THERMOGRATE Fireplace Furnaces feature welded construction for long life.

Send for Item No. 00

If you don't have a fireplace, you're still in luck! The all-new THERMOGRATE Free-Standing Fireplace/Stove is a 'third generation' breakthrough in wood-burning, capable of producing high heat outputs with high efficiencies. The full-view double bi-fold tempered glass doors give you a 'picture window' view of the fire. You enjoy all the aesthetic benefits of a fireplace and get both higher heat output and greater efficiency than from any other woodstove.

Send for Item No. 0000

An investment in a quality wood-burning appliance will pay greater dividends every year as fossil fuel costs soar.

THERMOGRATE products are built to perform efficiently and effectively for many years. Exclusive chromium nickel stainless steel heat exchanger tubes are guaranteed unconditionally for 5 years . . . and should last a lifetime! Long life and efficiency are important if you are to get the return on your investment that you're looking for. At Thermograte, we won't build less than the best . . . and we guarantee performance and your satisfaction as well.

**Or call TOLL FREE: 1-800-328-0882
In MN call COLLECT: 612-633-1376**

Here's how the System works:

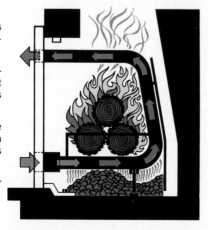

THERMOGRATE products utilize natural heat convection principles.

As air in the heat exchanger tubes is heated it expands, rises and rushes out into the room.

The flow of air through the tubes and into the room increases dramatically as the fire becomes hotter.

It really works . . . with or without a blower!

© 1978 THERMOGRATE ENTERPRISES, INC. ST. PAUL MN 55113. ALL RIGHTS RESERVED. U.S. PATS. 247,973 & 4,129,113. OTHER PATENTS PENDING.

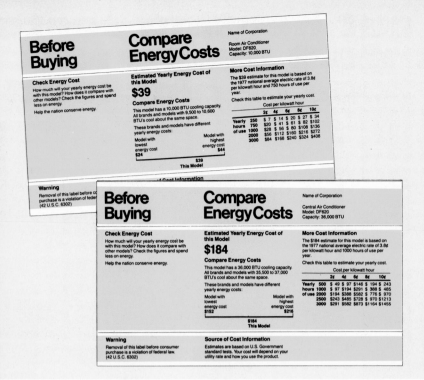

$$EER = \frac{\text{Capacity of air conditioner (Btuh)}}{\text{Power input (watts)}}$$

By looking at product literature or at the machine itself, you find that a room air conditioner you're considering has a capacity of 8,500 Btuh, and operates on 850 watts. This is a very efficient unit, with a high EER:

$$EER = \frac{8500 \text{ Btuh}}{850 \text{ watts}} = EER\ 10.0$$

You can use this same formula to get a rough idea of the efficiency of air conditioners you already own. They usually have labels that give the Btuh capacity and wattage. If your existing air conditioners have EER ratings of only 5 or 6, they could be wasting a lot of your money. Monitor your electric bills, and consider replacing these inefficient units.

place filters at least once a month. With room air conditioners, once or twice a season is usually sufficient.

If you have central air conditioning, you will have an air conditioning unit (or more than one), and ducts to distribute the cool air throughout the house (just like a warm air furnace). Most homes with central air conditioning have a "split-system" air conditioning unit to produce cool air. Part of the equipment (the evaporator coil and the fan) is located indoors, and part (the condenser unit) is located outdoors. "Single-package units" are sometimes used in centrally air conditioned houses too. In this system, all of the components are combined into a single indoor unit that has an air exhaust connection to the outdoors.

All central air conditioning systems should have thermostatic controls (like heating systems) to automatically turn the unit off or on as needed. If your system doesn't have a thermostat, have one installed. Consider buying a clock thermostat (they can be used on cooling systems, as well as for heating). But don't worry if your *room* air conditioners don't have thermostatic controls. You can always shut off room units when you don't need them (which you shouldn't do with central air conditioning, unless you'll be away a few days).

Set your air conditioning thermostat at 75°F., or even 78°F., and dress lightly so you'll be comfortable. If you have room air conditioners with high-medium-low settings, see if the low setting will give you enough cooling. Your electric bills will be reduced drastically.

Common sense will tell you to keep all doors and windows closed while your air conditioning is operating. But, when the outside temperature drops below 75°F., you *can* open the windows and let fresh breezes cool your home. Just make sure the thermostat on your central air conditioning system is set *higher* than 75°F. (so your system will stay off). And, of course, be sure to turn off your room air conditioners. (To keep track of the outside temperature, install an outdoor thermometer that you can glance at through a window. The thermometer should be installed in the shade, not in direct sunlight.)

Heat and moisture produced by your daily activities will make your air conditioner work harder, so give some attention to your living habits. Try to avoid using your appliances (oven, stove, clothes dryer, etc.) between 9:00 a.m. and 6:00 p.m. Keep unused lights turned off—light bulbs produce heat too. And, if your family is fond of hot steamy showers even in summertime, try to schedule them late at night or early in the morning.

If your home has high summer humidity, it may be more economical for you to buy a dehumidifier than to have your air conditioner remove the moisture. Exhaust fans in problem areas (kitchens, baths, basements) can also help reduce air conditioning costs. But use exhaust fans *only* when they are needed to remove moisture and odors. They exhaust cool air too.

Any portion of your air conditioner that is outdoors should be in a shady location, and have free air circulation around it. This reduces the heat load the unit must handle and helps it operate more efficiently. Check your central system and all room units to make sure they are shaded from the sun's rays, and that landscaping or other objects aren't preventing good air circulation.

Sometime in 1979, you will begin seeing cost-of-operation labels on air conditioners and other appliances, which will make your buying decisions easier. In the meantime, however, manufacturers are no longer permitted (by the government) to use EER (Energy Efficiency Ratio) ratings. EER ratings on air conditioners ranged from 4 to 11 (the higher the better). Until the new labels come out, the only way you can have any indication of the efficiency of an air conditioner is to calculate your own EERs.

Adding air conditioning. If you have forced warm air heating, you can almost always add central air conditioning to your existing system for under $2,000. The cost will be lower for newer homes (built in the last 15 or 20 years) with a heating system that was "prepared for air conditioning" by installing larger ductwork and providing 240-volt electrical service. Since each home is different, however, you will have

YOU'VE JUST SPENT A BUNDLE ON YOUR NEW <u>USED</u> HOME. HAVE YOU HAD ITS PULSE CHECKED YET?

90 Lakewood Avenue 34 yrs. old

$61,000   (SOLD)

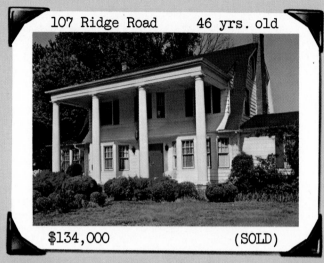

107 Ridge Road   46 yrs. old

$134,000   (SOLD)

52 Povershon Road   24 yrs. old

$85,000   (SOLD)

32 Patten Terrace   17 yrs. old

$55,000   (SOLD)

When most people move into a new <u>used</u> home, they have it checked for termites, structural defects, lack of insulation and any number of other things.

But they often forget to check one of the most important life-support systems in any home: the heating and cooling system. Which is unfortunate.

The prices of new homes today are so high, nobody wants to spend even more money repairing or replacing a heating/cooling system that breaks down.

So why take a chance? Simply call your Carrier air conditioning and heating dealer (he's in your Yellow Pages). He's trained to examine your heating and cooling system regardless of make or model, tell you what kind of shape it's in, and perform preventive maintenance if necessary.

Call him now. He's a good man to know. It'll only cost you a little. And it may save your family a bundle.

WE CAN'T CONTROL THE WEATHER. BUT WE CAN HELP YOU CONTROL ITS COST.

Number One
Air Conditioning
Maker

Carrier ®

Division of Carrier Corporation

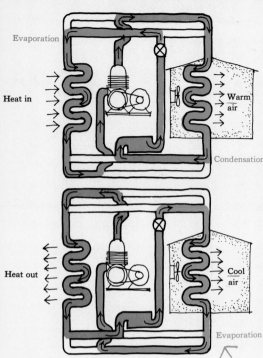

Evaporation

Heat in

Warm air

Condensation

Heat out

Cool air

Evaporation

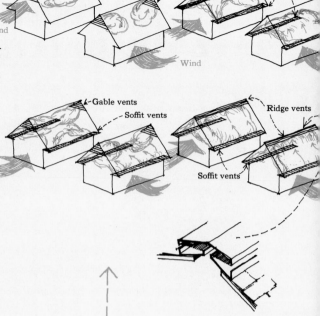

Gable vents

Soffit vents

Wind

Wind

Gable vents

Soffit vents

Ridge vents

Soffit vents

How the heat pump works in the heating cycle (top) and in the cooling cycle (bottom). Most heat pumps currently on the market are designed to economically extract heat from outside air as cold as 20°F., and bring it inside to heat your house. At about 20°F., the heat pump goes off automatically and back-up electrical resistance heating takes over. Heat pumps are the most economical to operate of all electrical heating systems. In the cooling cycle, the heat pump works just like an air conditioner. But the heat pump's cooling efficiency won't be quite as good as the cooling efficiency of the newer model air conditioning units that are sold separately. The heat pump provides *both* heating and cooling, and so design compromises are necessary to balance the system.

to call in an air conditioning contractor to tell you how easy (or difficult) it would be for you to add central cooling. He will also help you choose an appropriately-sized system.

If you don't have forced warm air heating, it could cost you as much as $4,000 or $5,000 to add central cooling, because the air conditioning system must be completely separate from the heating system. You will need a good air conditioning contractor that can make recommendations on the most economical and efficient way of providing cooling for your home.

Consider installing room air conditioners. Prices start at about $200 for a small unit, and you can concentrate cooling where you need it—in the bedrooms, or dining room, or in the living room where you entertain. You can buy the units one at a time, as your budget permits.

When buying any central or room air conditioner, buy the most efficient model you can find. With fuel costs increasing, you need to consider *both* the first cost for equipment, and the long-term operating costs. Although efficient air conditioners are more expensive, and often larger than inefficient ones, they are still the best buy.

Before adding air conditioning, have you considered other alternatives? Maybe opening windows, installing fans or dehumidifiers, or improving ventilation will cool your home just as well—at a lower operating cost. And have you thought about heat pumps?

Heat pumps. If your home is electrically heated and you've decided you *must* add air conditioning, the heat pump could be your wisest investment. Heat pumps work like reversible air conditioners, and provide efficient heating as well as efficient cooling. Like air conditioners, they are available in split systems.

If you have a warm air furnace that operates on electricity and you want to add central air conditioning, consider the heat pump alternative. A heat pump can replace the entire furnace. Or it can be used as an "add-on" unit to provide lower-cost heating as well as the air conditioning you want. Again, talk with your local contractor about the economics.

Keep in mind that heat pumps which supplement or replace oil or gas heat may have *higher* operating costs than your existing heating system. Buying a heat pump when you have oil or gas heat requires more careful consideration.

Ventilation. Use mechanical ventilation sparingly—electric fans can waste more energy than they save, if not used properly.

When your heating or cooling systems are operating, use exhaust fans when they're needed to eliminate moisture or odors, but don't leave them running. Your heating and air conditioning are also being exhausted by these fans.

In the spring and fall, when your

heating and cooling systems are off, open the windows! A cool breeze can rid your house of unwanted moisture better and faster than an electric fan.

If your home isn't air conditioned, electric fans *can* be used to cool your home both economically and efficiently. Use window units rather than floor models—they move more air, and they're out of your way.

Attic ventilation. Summer attic temperatures may be as high as 140°F. to 160°F. If this is your house, adding attic ventilation will make your whole home cooler.

Many homes have attic fans, but it's better to install a natural ventilation system that doesn't operate on electricity. Attic fans are particularly uneconomical in homes that are air conditioned.

Most of the engineers agree that the combination of soffit vents and a roof ridge vent gives the best air circulation in attics. The roof ridge/soffit ventilation has been around for about 30 years, and is being installed on more and more new homes every year. You can have a roof ridge system installed on your house too—it can be done in less than a day.

Not all homes have a continuous ridge on the roof—your home may have a series of gables and dormers. In this case, you should consider the other types of natural ventilation that don't use electricity, such as wind turbines and ventilating skylights.

It's your energy dollar.
Make it go further, with Alaskan Windows and Vent-A-System, by Alcoa.

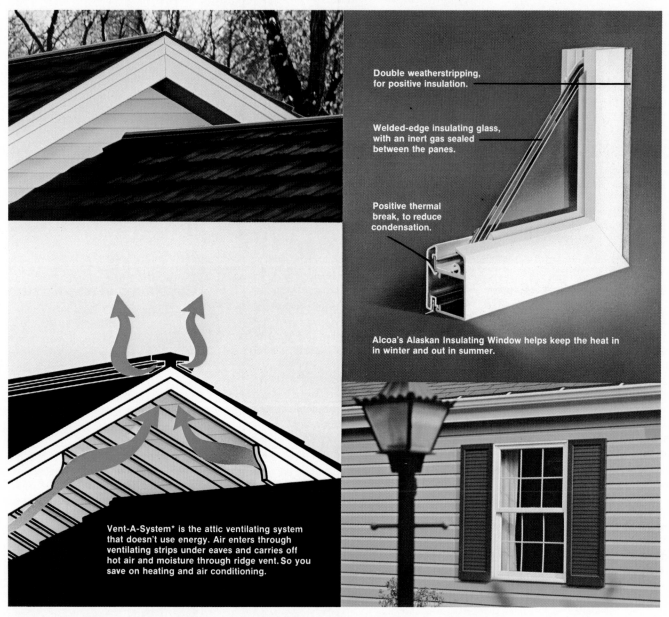

Double weatherstripping, for positive insulation.

Welded-edge insulating glass, with an inert gas sealed between the panes.

Positive thermal break, to reduce condensation.

Alcoa's Alaskan Insulating Window helps keep the heat in in winter and out in summer.

Vent-A-System* is the attic ventilating system that doesn't use energy. Air enters through ventilating strips under eaves and carries off hot air and moisture through ridge vent. So you save on heating and air conditioning.

Insulation is the key to conservation.

The Alcoa® Alaskan™ Window is the high-performance window that helps save energy year-round. In the winter it helps keep the heat where it belongs, inside your home. In the summer it helps keep the heat out and the cool in.

Alcoa's Vent-A-System* gives your attic insulation a helping hand. In the summer it helps prevent heat build-up. In the winter it helps keep your attic insulation dry, so it works more efficiently.

Two great ways to save energy. Vent-A-System and Alaskan Windows, by Alcoa.

Don't forget these other beautiful Alcoa Building Products.

Gutters and downspouts. Soffit and fascia. Columns and railings. Siding. Outer doors. Insulated siding. Country Cedar Shakes™. Every one from a company you know and trust, Alcoa.

*Registered trademark of HC Products Company.

We can't wait for tomorrow.

For more information circle 20 on the Reader's Service Card following the Index.

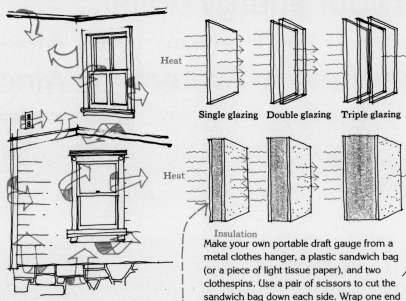

Single glazing   Double glazing   Triple glazing

Whether you are planning to do the work yourself or intend to hire contractors, send for these booklets to help you make better decisions on how to seal your home's thermal envelope.

In the Bank... or Up the Chimney?, Price: $1.70
Superintendent of Documents
U.S. Government Printing Office, Washington, D.C. 20402

Making the Most of Your Energy Dollars, Price: 70¢
Consumer Information Center, Pueblo, Colorado 81009

How to Save Money by Insulating Your Home
Price: 30¢
Mineral Insulation Manufacturers Association
382 Springfield Avenue, Summit, N.J. 07901

The small air leaks in the average home can add up to the equivalent of a one-square-foot hole in the wall.

Make your own portable draft gauge from a metal clothes hanger, a plastic sandwich bag (or a piece of light tissue paper), and two clothespins. Use a pair of scissors to cut the sandwich bag down each side. Wrap one end of the bag over the crossbar of the clothes hanger, using the clothespins to fasten the bag in place.

Sealing the thermal envelope.
The walls, ceilings and floors of your home are its thermal envelope, its protection against the outside elements. A tightly sealed thermal envelope slows down the escape of heat in winter and the entry of heat in summer, and it's essential to the energy efficiency of your home.

With a tight, well-insulated home, your heating and cooling systems won't have to work so hard to keep your home comfortable. Heating and cooling will stay inside where they belong, and the result will be lower fuel bills both summer and winter.

How your home loses heat in winter.
Your home loses heat in two ways: through air leaks and by the movement of heat through solid walls, windows, doors, floors and ceilings (conduction). Excessive heat loss of either type means higher heating bills.

Older homes are particularly drafty and subject to air leaks. But no matter what the age of your home, air leaks and drafts will almost always be the greatest source of heat loss. Concentrate your first efforts on locating and eliminating small leaks with caulking, weatherstripping, putty, glazing compounds, and filler materials like fiber glass sill sealer and oakum. Install fireplace dampers and exhaust fan covers to get rid of big "leaks."

Cutting down on conductive heat loss through walls, ceilings, floors, doors and windows is the second step. Do you need more attic insulation? Storm windows? Wall insulation? Storm doors? Draperies lined with insulating material? Tight window shades? Floor insulation?

How your home gains heat.
Your home gains heat from sources other than the heating system. Artificial and natural lighting, appliances, and the daily activities of your family all contribute to the amount of heat your home gains.

In winter, heat gain may result in lower fuel bills. Sunlight coming in through the window turns into heat. Heat is created as a by-product when using appliances (ovens, dishwashers, clothes dryers, etc.) and when your family takes steamy showers. All of this heat can be used to supplement your home's heating system.

In summer, heat gain is unwanted. It can raise air conditioning costs considerably. Awnings, draperies, window shades, venetian blinds, trees, and other sun screens should be used to shade windows from direct sunlight. Electric lights should be turned off when they're not needed. Heat-producing appliances should be used only in the coolest parts of the day (morning or evening).

A tightly sealed thermal envelope is just as important in summer as it is in winter. Tight and well-insulated walls, attics and floors will help reduce the summer heat from outdoor sources, much the same way they help prevent heat from escaping in winter.

Caulking and weatherstripping.
Sealing air leaks with caulking and weatherstripping is an easy do-it-yourself project, doesn't cost much, and you'll notice reduced fuel bills immediately. How much it costs will depend on the type and amount of materials you use. How much you save on your fuel bills will depend on how badly your home is leaking and the quality of your workmanship.

An inspection of your home will show where caulking and weatherstripping are needed. Begin the inspection inside your home, on a cold day, using a draft gauge to check for drafts in all suspected areas. If any breeze is coming in, the movement of the plastic will show you where. On the outside of your home, inspect visually for cracks and crevices that need repair.

Caulking.
Wherever two different materials or *unmovable* parts of the house meet, you can use caulking compound to seal air leaks.

Caulking compound is available in cartridges for use in caulking guns, and in preformed ropes for application by hand. The rope type isn't very durable, so buy the cartridge type even if it is a bit harder to apply. Your first attempts at using a caulking gun may be messy, but with a little practice you'll be able to draw a good bead of caulk. (See the diagrams on the next page.)

Better quality, more durable caulking compounds are more expensive, but a better investment. An oil-base caulk

For free help in a hurry, turn to the back of the book.

Many of the advertisers in the HomeBook are offering free full-color catalogs with detailed product information and decorating ideas.

Refer to the back of the book to find descriptions of the free catalogs, along with postpaid cards for ordering them.

You send the card, and we'll send you the catalogs fast. Often it'll be mailed within three days after we get your request.

More help from the HomeBook.

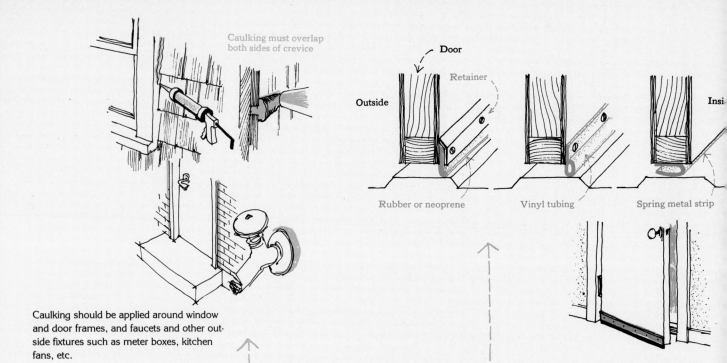

Caulking must overlap both sides of crevice

Door

Retainer

Outside

Rubber or neoprene

Vinyl tubing

Spring metal strip

Insi

Caulking should be applied around window and door frames, and faucets and other outside fixtures such as meter boxes, kitchen fans, etc.

may be cheap, but it won't last more than 2 or 3 years. Butyl rubber and acrylic latex caulks are only slightly more expensive, and have a service life of 5 to 10 years. Best of all (and most expensive) are the elastomeric caulks (including silicones, polysulfides, and polyurethanes) which last 15 or 20 years. Before buying, read the label to find out the contents and expected service life of the caulking material you're considering.

Consider, also, how the caulking material will be used. Not all caulks bond to all surfaces. Some caulks cannot be painted, but are available in a number of colors. Alternative materials like fiber glass sill sealer, oakum, mortar, putty, wood filler or glazing compounds may be a better choice for some jobs.

For best results, surfaces should be cleaned with solvent and a putty knife or large screwdriver before applying the caulking compound. On bare wood, caulk adheres better if the surface is primed with linseed oil or paint.

Indoors, caulking may be done anytime. Outdoors, caulking compound should be applied only when the temperature is above 40°F., since it becomes stiff and unworkable in cold weather. Keep the material at room temperature until just before use.

Weatherstripping doors.
In most homes, cold drafts from underneath doors are a common problem. Inspect your exterior doors (and doors leading to any unheated areas like

attics, basements and garages) for gaps at the bottom. These gaps should be weatherstripped immediately.

Nailing rubber or neoprene strips or vinyl tubing onto the bottom edge of the door (on the inside) is a quick and effective way to stop under-door drafts. If you find this unattractive, you can still use it as a temporary measure. Later, remove the door from its hinges and install a spring metal strip on the bottom edge to provide more permanent (and invisible) weatherstripping. You can also install a spring metal strip directly on the door sill, if you prefer.

Air leaks at the tops and sides of exterior doors will usually not be as troublesome as those at the bottom. But these leaks do waste fuel, so weatherstrip all sides of exterior doors as soon as you can.

A variety of weatherstripping materials will be available at your home center or hardware store including felt, sponge rubber, vinyl tubing and spring metal. Spring metal strips are the most durable and unobtrusive material (and the most expensive).

Storm doors
will have *some* impact on your fuel bills, but not as much as most other energy improvements you can make. In a recent analysis of energy-saving options, the National Association of Home Builders determined that storm doors pay for themselves in fuel savings only in the coldest climates where fuel costs are high.

Replacing an exterior door.
Warped doors that won't close tightly and that are beyond the help of weatherstripping should be replaced. If you need a replacement, look for a prime door with insulation value as well as beauty. Doors with a polyurethane core insulate better than solid wood doors.

Weatherstripping windows.
Your home probably has at least a few double-hung windows which are likely candidates for weatherstripping. (The double-hung window has two sashes which move up and down independently in the frame. In older homes, the top sash has sometimes been painted shut.) Horizontal sliding windows and sliding glass doors may need similar attention.

Begin by weatherstripping between the meeting rails of the two sashes—the most likely source of air infiltration. Use spring metal if you have wood windows, and fabric pile weatherstripping if you have metal windows. Other materials will work too, but aren't as durable. Make sure the window still operates easily after you've installed the weatherstripping.

The top, bottom and sides of a window may be drafty too. If so, install the weatherstripping in the window channels so it won't be seen when the window is closed. Materials like foam rubber and vinyl tubing may be used but, again, spring metal is more durable and permanent.

Check your casement, awning and hopper windows to make sure they

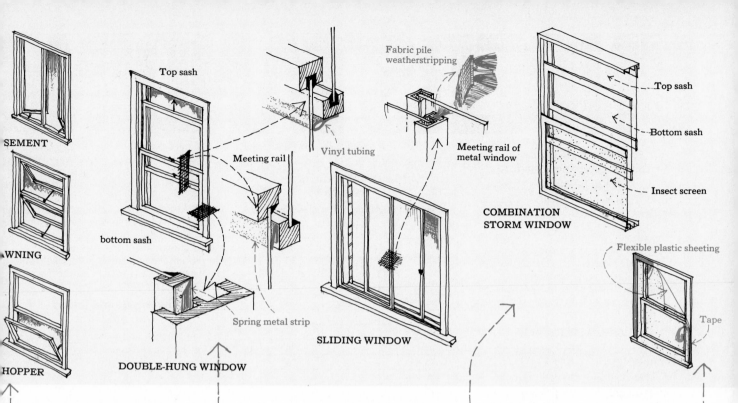

SEMENT

WNING

HOPPER

Top sash

bottom sash

DOUBLE-HUNG WINDOW

Meeting rail

Vinyl tubing

Spring metal strip

Fabric pile
weatherstripping

Meeting rail of
metal window

SLIDING WINDOW

COMBINATION
STORM WINDOW

Top sash

Bottom sash

Insect screen

Flexible plastic sheeting

Tape

---

provide a tight seal when closed. If they don't, glue rubber weatherstripping along the edges. However, if one of these windows is badly warped, it may need to be replaced—no amount of weatherstripping can save it.

While weatherstripping windows, check for loose window panes—they can also be the source of air leaks. Reset loose panes with glazing compound (more durable than putty).

Storm windows.

A winter necessity in most parts of the country, storm windows fit either on the inside or the outside of the prime windows. Storm windows are usually made of aluminum, although older homes sometimes have wooden ones and newer homes may have the plastic type.

Storm windows can reduce summer air conditioning bills as well as winter heating costs. Many homeowners who have air conditioning now leave on their storm windows year-round. If you live in a hot climate like Florida or Arizona, consider buying "summer storms" with tinted glass to help cut cooling costs.

You may hear two opposing theories on how storm windows should fit: *tightly* to avoid air leaks and *loosely* to allow ventilation and prevent the storm window from fogging. In a way both views are correct, but a tight-fitting storm is preferable because it will save more of your fuel dollars.

If your outside storm windows are fogged or iced in cold weather, this usually means inside *prime* windows

are leaking warm, moist air to the outside. Tightening the inside window with caulking and weatherstripping may eliminate the problem. Lowering the humidity level in your home (if it's too high) can also help: better (or more) exhaust fans and attic ventilation, or fewer steamy showers are possible remedies. Vent holes can be drilled into the storm window frame to provide ventilation and eliminate the visible moisture condensation, but at the same time this increases your energy loss through the window.

In very cold climates, fogged storm windows may indicate that you need triple-glazed windows. Each additional pane of glass you add reduces the likelihood of moisture condensation and, of course, cuts down on heat lost through windows.

Adding storm windows.

Homes in most parts of the country can benefit from double-glazed windows, but storm windows are not always the best way to provide double glazing. Buying a new storm window for installation on a leaky, rotted prime window is a waste of money.

If your prime windows are solid, storm windows are usually a good investment. The triple-track, self-storing unit that has both screens and storm windows built in is the most convenient type to have because it is installed permanently. You can switch from a glass panel to a screen panel easily by moving the panels up or down in their

tracks, and you don't have to be concerned about storage during off-seasons. Of course, the panels should also be removable for easy once-a-year cleaning with a garden hose. Most of these combination units are made of aluminum: look for enamel and anodized finishes which are more durable than the plain mill finish. Vinyl combination units are also available.

You can install *temporary* storm windows quickly and fairly inexpensively. Tape see-through plastic sheeting (flexible or rigid) onto the inside of your windows, extending the plastic sheeting beyond the window frame. (The tape won't show if it's behind draperies or curtains.) Plastic sheeting is available in home center stores as storm window kits, or you can buy it separately in craft stores.

If you choose this method of adding storm windows, consider it a temporary not-very-attractive solution. Materials have to be purchased every fall, and costs add up. Invest in permanent windows as soon as your budget allows.

Replacement windows.

If some of your prime windows are rotted, warped and beyond the help of weatherstripping, caulking and storm windows, you should consider replacing them. (The average window takes less than an hour to replace—not a difficult task.)

Usually only some windows will be in poor condition, not *all* the windows in your home. Since prime replacement windows cost at least $150–$200 per

UNDERSTANDING

From Owens-Corning, the company that's made it for 30 years.

In 30 years, we've grown to be America's leading insulation company by preaching that pink Fiberglas* insulation can save energy—*and money*.

Now the energy crunch and soaring fuel bills have made believers out of nearly everyone. In the last four years alone, over 11,000,000 homeowners have added insulation.

If your home is still an energy-waster, tear out this ad. It'll help you save *plenty*.

Types of insulation.

Blanket

Loose-Fill

Rigid

Foam

<u>Blanket</u>—soft, woolly, made from fibers of glass, rock or slag. Comes in slab-like "batts" or rolls. Probably in your attic right now.
<u>Loose-Fill</u>—sold by the bag, to be poured or "blown" into place. Made from glass, rock, slag, even macerated *paper*.
<u>Rigid</u>—panels of foam-plastic. Good under exterior siding or below concrete floor slabs.
<u>Foam</u>—chemicals that foam when pumped into wall cavities by professional contractors.

NOTE: All insulations are not alike. There's one way of being sure you get your money's worth. Insist on a brand with *this label:*

It means samples have been tested by *independent* experts—the NAHB (National Association of Home Builders) Research Foundation, Inc.—and found to deliver the thermal performance *claimed*.

Insulation is cheaper than oil.

Just as in figuring automobile gasoline mileage, the amount of money you save on your

Estimated Annual Fuel Savings**			
	Oil Heat & Electric Cooling	Gas Heat & Electric Cooling	All Electric
Albany, N.Y.	$364	$288	$679
Chicago, Ill.	336	222	422
Kansas City, Kan.	284	173	399
Columbia, S.C.	211	144	290
Tampa, Fla.	144	132	199
Los Angeles, Cal.	156	80	286

home heating and cooling bills with insulation depends on a great many different factors.

**The estimated dollar savings listed in the chart above are based on April, 1977, average energy costs in each of the cities shown, taking into account the local climate conditions.

Estimated savings are calculated for a typical three-bedroom ranch home of 1,370 square feet, going from no insulation in the attic to Owens-Corning's recommended minimum standards for that city.

These savings represent guidelines or estimates only. They do not reflect actual savings, which may vary depending on the type and condition of a home, heating and cooling system, unusual weather conditions, personal temperature preference, family life-styles, increase in energy rates and other unpredictable factors.

<u>Important</u>: keep all receipts for insulation you install, so you can take advantage of the tax credit recently approved by Congress.

What's an R-value?

Take a look at that brick wall below, and you can see why it's important to understand "R-values."

R stands for Resistance—to the flow of heat. The R-value of any material is simply a measure of how *good* an insulator the material is. The higher the R number, the better the insulator.

Pink Owens-Corning Fiberglas, for example, is a highly *efficient* insulator. A blanket just 6 inches thick has the same insulating R-value—R-19—as a wooden wall 15 inches thick or a brick wall 7 *feet* thick.

Check the Owens-Corning insulation map on the right-hand page, and then consult your local building supply dealer or insulation contractor about the R-values—*not inches*—recommended for insulation in the ceilings, the walls, and the floors of your home.

Why you should insulate your attic first.

Below is an *infrared* photo of a typical uninsulated house. Places where heat is escaping show up red. The windows. The door.

But look at the attic.

Proof of where much of the heat is being wasted. (In the summertime, the sun's heat seeps *in* here, to run up air-conditioning

bills.) This is why the attic is one of the most important places for you to tackle *first*.

Where else you should insulate.

When you've taken care of one of the worst energy-wasters, the attic, you can turn your attention to two more areas: Exterior walls. Crawl spaces.

Walls may be toughest. If they're enclosed on both sides, but hollow, the best thing is usually to have a professional contractor inject loose-fill insulation through small, drilled holes. With unfinished walls, of course, you can add blankets of insulation and then enclose them.

Floors over unheated areas should be insulated from below. It's usually easy to apply blanket-type insulation, fastening it up into position with wire mesh, wooden cross braces or other devices.

Doing it yourself vs. having it done.

If you're handy around the house, and can spare the time, you'll probably be able to manage the biggest part of the job on your own—maybe two thirds the cost of having a professional contractor do it.

Your *walls* could stump you, though. For them, a pro and his special blowing equipment might be the answer.

Forget inches: It's R-values that count.
6 inches of Fiberglas have the same R-value as 15 inches of wood or 7 feet of brick

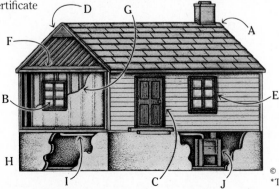
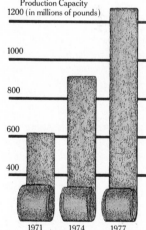

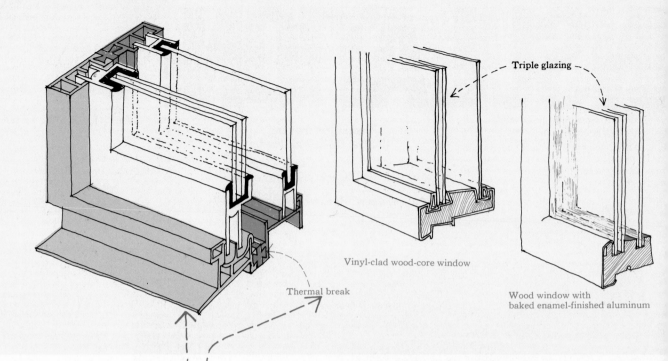

Triple glazing

Thermal break

Vinyl-clad wood-core window

Wood window with
baked enamel-finished aluminum

window (depending on the size), try to replace only the windows that really need replacement. This means shopping for windows that are similar in appearance to the rest of the windows in your home.

Prime replacement windows are available in aluminum, wood and vinyl, and in combinations of these materials. Aluminum ones should have a "thermal break" which reduces heat loss through the frame. In terms of *conductive* heat loss (U-value), one double-glazed window will not be much different from another, one triple-glazed window not much different from another—regardless of the material used in the frame. Don't be misled by claims that wood or vinyl are better insulators. You are interested in the performance of the *entire* window, not the insulation value of its parts.

Prime replacement windows *do* differ greatly in their ability to guard against air infiltration. Don't buy any window without weatherstripping on all movable parts. Look at the frame construction too—are there any places where air leaks could occur?

Consider buying triple-glazed windows that have detachable storm units, particularly if you live in a colder climate. Get prices on both double- and triple-glazed windows before you decide. Often the difference won't be that great.

You can sometimes save a little on installation costs by buying a "true" replacement window (available in alu-minum only) which is installed without removing the frame on your existing window. However, almost any window can be used as a replacement window.

Proper sizing and installation of prime replacement windows are the real keys to performance. These windows are custom-made and sized specifically to a particular window opening. Usually a contractor does the installation. Some home centers that sell replacement windows will give you instructions on measuring and installing the windows.

After installation, test for infiltration. Get a sheet of very thin plastic (a garment bag from the dry cleaners or a cheap drop cloth from the local paint store) large enough to cover the entire window. Use masking tape to attach the plastic, making sure to extend it over the window frame. Allow some slack in the plastic—don't pull it taut. If the plastic billows, this is a sign of air leaks and improper installation. Call back the contractor, or correct the installation yourself. Use your portable draft gauge to locate the specific leaks.

Insulating your home. How much insulation your home should have depends on your climate, your fuel costs, and your family's comfort. There is no one answer that will be right for all homes.

In general, the higher your fuel costs, the more insulation you need. Homes with electric resistance heating need more insulation than homes where heat is supplied by oil, gas, or a heat pump.

More is needed in homes with air conditioning. Homes in very warm or very cold climates need more insulation than homes in temperate climates.

Until the 1940s, we thought we were insulating against cold. Today, we know we are insulating against fuel costs as well. But even if economic factors were considered when your home was designed and built, your home will have the amount of insulation justified by fuel costs *at the time of construction*, not enough insulation to protect you from *today's* fuel prices.

Make an inspection of your existing insulation to find out how much you already have. To get an idea of how much insulation you should add to combat current heating and cooling costs, call your local gas or electric utility (or both). Ask what their minimum insulation recommendations or requirements are for *new* homes in your locale. Bring your insulation levels up to current standards (or higher, since fuel costs will continue to rise).

Insulation materials. Any material with an R-value greater than R-2 per inch is considered an insulating material. The higher the R, the better the material will resist heat loss and heat gain. Brick (about R-0.2 per inch) and wood (approximately R-1 per inch) are not considered insulation materials.

R-values are determined by laboratory testing (not in-use testing in actual homes) and should be used only as a *design* guideline. They will help you

Re-siding?
Perfect chance to add extra insulation. And nothing, no way, no how, is more efficient than Thermax.

If you're thinking of re-siding, you're lucky. Now's your chance to add extra insulation without tearing out any walls. And reduce your energy bills month after month for the life of your home.

Thermax Insulating Sheathing is a rigid foam board with foil facers on both sides. It goes up right over your old siding enclosing your house in a silvery envelope of insulation. Then your new siding goes right over the Thermax. And Thermax is more efficient than fiberboard, than polystyrene, even more efficient than the fiberglass you may have between your studs. In fact, nothing is more efficient than Thermax.

Talk to your dealer or your siding salesman today.

Comparative R values (at 75° mean temperature) of sheathing in available thickness.

Celotex ¾" Thermax Sheathing | Dow Styrofoam TG ¾" Extruded Polystyrene | ¾" Expanded Polystyrene | ½" Fiberboard Sheathing | ½" Plywood | ½" Gypsum | Thermo-Ply

SOURCE: ASHRAE 1977 Fundamental Handbook and published product literature. Thermo-Ply—Reg. trademark of Simplex, Adrian, MI. Styrofoam—Reg. trademark of Dow Chemical Corp.

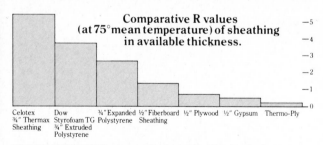

New tax benefit for energy savers!
You are entitled to a credit of 15% of the cost of insulating your home (up to a maximum credit of $300) on your Federal Income Tax Return. A credit is better than a deduction— the total amount is simply subtracted from the tax you owe.

Celotex ®
BUILDING PRODUCTS
The Celotex Corporation, Tampa, Florida 33622

a ᴊɪᴍ Ⓦalter company

U.S. Farmers Home Administration's minimum insulation standards for new homes

Degree Days	Ceilings	Frame Walls	Floors over Open Spaces
7001 or more	R–38	R–19	R–19
6001–7000			
2501–6000	R–33		
1001–2500	R–25	R–14	R–14
1000 or less	R–19	R–13	R–13

Minimum insulation standards for new homes reflect the thinking of experts on how much insulation you really need at today's fuel prices. In 1978, Farmers Home Administration (a U.S. government agency which gives mortgages to rural homeowners) adopted the highest insulation standards in the nation because too many of their mortgages were being defaulted by homeowners who couldn't afford the utility bills. According to Farmers Home, the new insulation standards will result in *lower* monthly payments for mortgage + interest + taxes + utility bills than previous standards. Degree days (a measure of how cold the climate is) give an indication of how much insulation is needed. To find out the degree days for your town, call your local weather bureau or utility. (Some samples. Phoenix: 1800 degree days. Atlanta and San Francisco: 3000. Baltimore: 4600. Boston: 5600. Detroit and Denver: 6200. Minneapolis: 8400.)

Do you need more attic insulation? If in doubt, wait for the first winter snow. Look at your home and the other houses in your neighborhood to see how quickly snow melts off the roofs. (Keep in mind that snow melts faster on metal roofs, and that other factors such as trees can influence the results.) If the snow on your roof is melted first, that's an indication you're losing heating dollars through your attic. Consider installing more insulation.

determine how much insulation of a particular type you need to get the performance you want.

In most situations the R-value per inch is not important. If one insulation material has a lower R-value per inch than another, you can buy additional material to achieve the total R-value you want. To add R-19 to your attic, for example, compare the prices of different materials on the basis of *the cost per square foot of R-19*. Although you may need more of one material or less of another, you'll find that the cost will usually be similar for equal R-values.

The most popular types of insulation are batts and blankets, which are delivered in preformed rolls of R-11, R-13, R-19, etc., so there can be no mistake about what you're buying. Batts and blankets can be used in more parts of your home than any other insulation. They are consistent in quality, and are relatively easy to install. There are, of course, other materials you can use, and in some cases other materials may be either preferable or necessary.

Attic insulation.
Check your unfinished attic floor to see how much insulation you already have. If you have less than two inches, installing more insulation is a necessity; less than four inches, strongly recommended; less than six inches, desirable. If you do re-insulate, add at least R-19 (more in colder climates).

If you don't have any insulation at all, install a vapor barrier first. You can use polyethylene sheeting if you like, but an easier way is to buy mineral wool batts that have a vapor barrier attached to one side. The batts should be installed with the vapor barrier *downward* toward the warm house. Follow the directions on the package.

If you already have some insulation, buy *unfaced* mineral fiber batts (no vapor barrier), loose-fill mineral fiber, or loose-fill cellulose fiber.

Insulating an unfinished attic floor is relatively easy. You can do the work yourself (order copies of the booklets listed on p. 90), or hire a contractor if you prefer. But if you have a finished or partially finished attic, adding insulation may be more complicated. Get estimates from one or more professional insulation contractors whenever you are in doubt about how to insulate properly.

Wall insulation.
There are three ways to add insulation to your exterior walls: on the inside, on the outside, and in the wall cavity itself. You can install decorative cork on the inside to help insulate (not particularly effective). You can buy new siding and install insulation board underneath (practical only if you also want new siding). Or you can add insulation material to the wall cavity (if the cavity is completely uninsulated).

The key to knowing what to do is finding out what you already have. An inspection should always be made before buying wall insulation. This is usually done by removing the plate from an electrical outlet and poking around with a screwdriver and flashlight (Warning: pull the fuse first). Sometimes, however, it will be necessary to remove a baseboard or part of the wall to make an accurate evaluation.

The age of your home will give you a general idea of how much insulation you already have in exterior walls. Most homes built before 1945 will have uninsulated walls. Most homes built between 1945 and 1965 will have partial wall insulation (1½"–2½"), and most homes built after 1965 will have full 3½" wall cavity insulation. But there are exceptions, and you may not know if previous owners added more wall insulation after your home was built.

If you suspect your exterior walls are completely uninsulated, call a professional insulation contractor. He will help you make an inspection and then give you an estimate on re-insulating the wall cavities (if they are empty). Most experts now advise against re-insulating wall cavities that are already partially insulated (you have to spend too much money to get too little thermal improvement), so don't buy unless the cavities are empty.

If your home has partial or full wall cavity insulation, experts agree that your best choice will usually be adding insulation board to the outside of the wall underneath new siding. But this choice will be appealing only if you need *both* insulation and siding. Because of the added cost of the siding, this choice is never economical on the basis of fuel savings alone.

Of course you're going to insulate.

But before you insulate, find out what the Sam Hill you're doing.

This free booklet could save you hundreds of dollars when you insulate your house. And thousands of dollars in the years ahead.

With a project this important, you don't want just any Tom, Dick or Harry passing out free advice. But maybe you'd listen to a nationwide association of insulation professionals with a quarter of a million customers in every climate, any one of whom will tell you about us. This nationwide network is called The Homefoamers®, and we have a representative who lives, works, shops, pays his taxes, and sends his kids to school right in your own area.

The Homefoamers will send you a free 8 page book about insulating. It'll answer just about every question you can think up about this suddenly hot subject. It compares the various types of insulation, tells you where they work best, and even tells you which parts of the job you could do yourself. And admittedly contains a strong plug for foam insulation installed by a licensed, insured, local Homefoamer.

Call the toll-free number to get your book, or a free no-hassle estimate if you like.

almost all about home insulating

Call toll free
800-553-5601
(Iowa residents call 800-582-2309)

The Homefoamers®
America's largest network of foam insulation specialists

Look for your nearest Homefoamer® Dealer in the Yellow Pages; he is listed under the classification:

INSULATION CONTRACTORS — COLD AND HEAT.

©Scientific Applications, Inc. 1979

Mineral fiber

What it is, how it is made

Types of mineral fiber include slag wool and rock wool (usually gray or black), fiber glass (usually blond, brown, or pink), and white wool (white and cotton-like). Mineral fiber is made by subjecting molten glass, furnace slag, or natural rock to a strong blast of steam or air to draw the material into long, thin threads. The threads solidifying into a woollike mass that traps many pockets of air and thus provides its insulating value. Mineral fiber can also be formed by spinning or by a combination of spinning and blowing.

In mineral wool batts and blankets, a heat-resistant binder is used to bond the fibers together. Batts and blankets are available plain (no facing) and with vapor barriers (kraft paper or aluminum foil facing). Vapor barriers must not be left exposed (for safety reasons).

R-Values

Range: Between R-2.1 and R-3.8 per inch.
Mineral fiber R-values vary according to the type of product, how it's being used, and in what thickness. White wool has the highest R-value, followed by rock or slag wool, then fiber glass. Batts and blankets usually have higher R-values than loose fill products (except white wool). The thicker the material, the lower the R-value per inch. Blown mineral fiber will have a higher R-value when it is blown into a closed space (like a wall cavity), and a lower R-value when blown into an open space (like an attic floor).

Mineral fiber has a lower R-value if it becomes wet. To protect it from moisture, a vapor barrier is often installed between the insulation and the heated part of the house.

Cellulose fiber

What it is, how it is made

Usually grayish in color, cellulosic insulation is made by shredding and milling waste paper (like newsprint) into an extremely fine, fluffy material. Other milled paper or wood pulp may also be used. The product must then be chemically treated to become fire retardant and vermin resistant while not becoming corrosive to metals in your home. Preferable fire retardant chemicals are boric acid or borates (ammonium or sulfate compounds can corrode metal in plumbing pipes or electrical wiring).

Under a new law passed by the U.S. Congress in 1978, all cellulose insulation products on the market must meet a minimum (mandatory) standard for flame resistance and corrosiveness. Buy only a product that has the following label (required by the new law): "Attention: This material meets the applicable minimum Federal flammability standard. This standard is based upon laboratory tests only, which do not represent actual conditions which may occur in the home."

R-Values

Range: Between R-2.8 and R-3.8 per inch.
Cellulosic fiber R-values also vary according to the type of product, how it's being used, and in what thickness. Cellulose products made from newsprint generally have higher R-values than products made from other types of paper or from wood pulp. The thicker the material, the lower the R-value per inch. Blown cellulose fiber will have a higher R-value when it is blown into an open space (like an attic floor), and a lower R-value when blown into a closed space (like a wall cavity).

Cellulose has a lower R-value if it becomes wet. To protect it from moisture, a vapor barrier is often installed between the insulation and the heated part of the house.

Types available

Types available	Rock or slag wool: Batts and blankets	Rock: Loose fill (blown)	Rock: Loose fill (poured)	Fiber glass: Batts and blankets	Fiber glass: Loose fill (blown)	White wool: Loose fill (blown)	Cellulose fiber: Loose fill (blown)	Cellulose fiber: Loose fill (poured)
Installed by contractor	●	●		●	●	●	●	
Do-it-yourself	●		●	●				●
Use in attics	●	●	●	●	●	●	●	●
Use in crawl space	●			●				
Re-insulate wall cavities		●			●	●	●	
Install on outside walls under new siding								
Add to basement or garage walls	●			●				
Use for perimeter insulation	●			●				
Use to insulate under floors								

Urea formaldehyde

A foamy white material that looks like shaving cream, urea formaldehyde is generated on-site with a foaming gun by the contractor (while it is being installed) from three ingredients: a urea-formaldehyde based resin, a foaming agent that includes an acid catalyst or hardening agent, and air. Urea-formaldehyde ingredients may be supplied to the contractor fully diluted, partially diluted, or in a dry-mix form. UF foam has a shelf-life: 3 months for diluted solutions, one year for dry-mix products. The contractor usually buys his material from a national manufacturer who has licensed and trained him to apply UF foam: ask him for his identification card that shows he is authorized, and make sure to get a manufacturer's warranty when you buy.

A faint paint-like odor is normal for a short time after installation (1 week to 3 months), but shouldn't cause discomfort. Many homeowners don't notice any odor at all. Complaints about odor problems are few: the U.S. Consumer Product Safety Commission had documented only 36 cases nationwide as of March 1978. Problems that do occur are usually due to faulty installation. Odor problems can result from either an improper foam mixture or from using materials that have passed their shelf life.

Range: Between R-2.8 and R-4.3 per inch.
The thicker the material, the lower the R-value per inch. The National Bureau of Standards uses R-4.0 or R-4.1 per inch as its average for urea formaldehyde. R-values stated in manufacturers' product literature will not be higher than 4.2 or 4.3 (if the values are based on laboratory testing and reported according to standard industry methods).

Shrinkage occurs as the product is curing, and this affects the R-value. (Manufacturers report shrinkage rates of between 1% and 6% in product literature. Any shrinkage greater than 6% should be considered a faulty installation.) Based on research from the National Bureau of Standards, the U.S. Department of Housing and Urban Development developed a chart for de-rating urea-formaldehyde R-values according to the percentage of shrinkage. Using this chart, an R-4.0 products with 5% shrinkage would be de-rated to R-2.8 per inch, and with 3% shrinkage to R-3.4 per inch. Manufacturers disagree with HUD's de-rating method because the numbers are theoretical (a valid argument), but the HUD method is the only one currently available.

Isocyanurate & Urethane

Isocyanurate (also called polyisocyanurate, modified polyurethane, or trimer foam) and urethane (also called polyurethane) are complex plastic polymers formed by the reaction of liquid components. For use in homes, these two products are formed into rigid boards that are applied like polystyrene board. Like polystyrene, these materials are plastics and must never be left exposed. Follow package or label instructions to insure safe installation.

Isocyanurates have a greater degree of heat stability and lower flammability characteristics than conventional urethanes. The product most readily available to you is an isocyanurate that is yellow in color, reinforced with fiber glass, and has aluminum foil laminated to both sides. Urethanes are more often used in commercial and industrial buildings.

Range: Between R-5.75 and R-10 per inch
Isocyanurates and urethanes are usually made with a special blowing agent that increases their R-value. Over a period of time, the R-value on these products is reduced as air replaces the blowing agent. Aluminum foil and other facings laminated to the products help slow down the drop in R-value.

When manufactured, isocyanurates and urethanes may have R-values as high as R-10. Many product brochures will give two R-values: initial and aged. "Aged" usually means "aged 30 days" which doesn't reflect the performance of the product over a long period of time. The best working R-value to use for isocyanurate is R-7 per inch, for urethane R-6.25 per inch (no matter what the brochures say).

Polystyrene

There are two types of polystyrene insulation board: extruded and expanded. The extruded type is made by forcing the polystyrene material through a shaped opening to form a continuous board. The expanded type is made by "exploding" small beads of polystyrene so that they trap air, and then molding and bonding the beads together. This second type is often called "bead board."

Polystyrene is usually available in densities from 1 lb. to 2 lb. for building use. The higher the density, the stronger and more durable the material. For below-grade (underground) application where the board is exposed to moisture, use only the high-density boards: the lower-density products may break apart in time. Lower-density polystyrenes are less expensive, however, and may be used to advantage where breakage and moisture are not of concern.

Polystyrene is available plain, or with facing material (kraft paper or aluminum foil) on one or both sides. (The facing is sometimes a vapor barrier, sometimes not.) Thicknesses of up to one inch are usually available in home centers and through contractors, while thicker polystyrene may have to be special ordered.

Polystyrene is a plastic material and must never be left exposed. Follow the instructions on the package or label to insure a safe installation.

Range: Between R-3.5 and R-5.0 per inch.
The higher the density, the higher the R-value per inch. No matter how thick the polystyrene, the per-inch R-value will be the same (for the same product).

Polystyrenes formed with air as the blowing agent have R-values between 3.5 and 4.3 per inch. Extruded polystyrene formed with a special blowing agent (instead of air) has the highest R-value per inch (R-5).

Since polystyrenes formed with special blowing agents change in time, they have two R-values: initial and aged. The R-5 value is an aged R-value (based on testing 5-year-old samples). Product literature does not usually state the initial R-value (which is higher). Polystyrenes that use air as their blowing agent do not change in R-value over time.

Urea-formaldehyde: Foamed-in-place	Isocyanurate	Urethane	Polystyrene board: Bead board, 1-lb. density, about R-3.5 per inch	Bead board, 1½-lb. density, about R-4 per inch	Bead board, 2-lb. density, about R-4.3 per inch	Extruded polystyrene, 2-lb. density, R-5 per inch (blue tongue-and-groove sheets)
●	●	●	●	●	●	●
	●	●	●	●	●	●
●						
			●	●	●	●
	●	●	●	●	●	●
	●	●			●	●
	●	●				

101

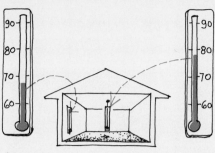

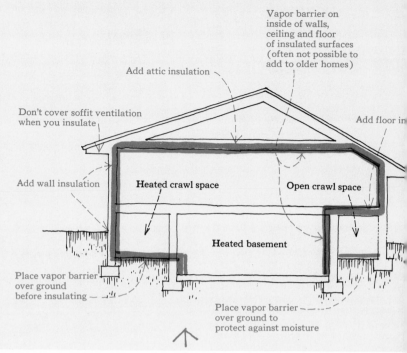

Add attic insulation

Vapor barrier on inside of walls, ceiling and floor of insulated surfaces (often not possible to add to older homes)

Don't cover soffit ventilation when you insulate

Add floor in

Add wall insulation

Heated crawl space

Open crawl space

Heated basement

Place vapor barrier over ground before insulating

Place vapor barrier over ground to protect against moisture

Do you need more wall insulation? Saving fuel dollars is one good reason to re-insulate your walls, but creature comfort is an even more important one. When walls are uninsulated, parts of the house are often too cold. Do you feel chilly when you're sitting near an outside wall? Here's a simple "comfort test" you can make on a cold day (when your heating system is operating). Place a thermometer firmly against the inside surface of an exterior wall (on a picture hook), and another thermometer in the middle of the room. Record the two readings (after allowing sufficient time for the temperatures to register). If the difference between the two readings is more than 5°F., your home could probably benefit from additional wall insulation. The example illustrated above shows an exterior wall temperature of 67°F. and a center-of-the-room temperature of 78°F.

If you are planning to re-side your home and also have uninsulated wall cavities, wait until you can afford to do all of the work at once. You will save a bit on wall cavity insulation because the contractor won't have to make the cosmetic repairs that return your home to its original appearance. Complete the work by installing insulation board under the new siding. (You will probably have to hire two different contractors and coordinate their efforts.)

Floor insulation. If you suffer from cold feet, more floor insulation can make your home comfortable. Additional floor insulation will also help reduce your fuel bills.

Any floor located over an *unheated* space of your home should be insulated. Since new construcion standards used to have minimal requirements (or no requirements) on floor insulation, floors in most homes are under-insulated.

Inspect your floor insulation by checking the *ceilings* of your unheated garage, unheated basement, and unheated crawl spaces. If you don't find any mineral wool batts between the ceiling rafters, install batts that have a vapor barrier on one side. The vapor barrier should face *upward* (so you can't see it) toward the warm room above. If you find thin batts that don't fill the entire rafter space, add *unfaced* batt material.

Whether you should buy R-11, R-13 or R-19 batts will depend on your cli-

mate and how much space you have between rafters. If you plan to do the installation yourself, take complete measurements before you buy materials. Measure the depth (to determine what R-value and thickness to buy), the width between rafters (to determine whether you need batts 15 or 23 inches wide), and the total length (to determine how much material to buy).

Crawl space insulation.
Open, unheated crawl spaces should have insulated ceilings to keep floors warm in the living area above.

Insulate the *walls* of closed, heated crawl spaces with *unfaced* mineral wool batts or blankets (R-11, R-13, or R-19). Before installing the insulation, cover the entire floor area with polyethylene plastic sheeting to protect the crawl space (and the insulation) from ground moisture. Cut batts 6 inches longer than the height of the wall and let them overlap the plastic sheeting.

Basement insulation. Ceilings of unheated basements should be insulated to keep floors warm in the living area above.

If you are converting your basement into a recreation room, insulate the walls first. The easiest and most economical method is to install vertical wood framing (wood studs) along the walls and then place mineral fiber batts between the studs. (A "stud" is simply a beam that runs vertically. Horizontal beams are called "joists.") Since the

wood framing doesn't have to provide structural support, you can use a minimum amount of wood: buy 2x3 lumber to make your studs, and place the studs 24 inches on center (which will give you a 23-inch space between them). Attach the studs to the floor and ceiling, positioning them one inch away from the wall (which will create cavities about 3½ inches deep). Buy R-11 or R-13 mineral wool batts (23 inches wide) that have a vapor barrier on one side. Install the batts between the studs, with the vapor barrier facing into the room. Warning: The vapor barrier is flammable and should not be left exposed. Any material that has a flame spread rating of *200 or less* can be used to finish the wall: plywood thicker than ½" can be used or ½" gypsum wallboard. If in doubt about which materials qualify, ask your local building inspector.

Insulation board can also be used to insulate basement walls, but it's usually more expensive than batts. To provide a nailing surface for the insulation board, wood strips are attached to the concrete wall with masonry nails or screws. Use a 2-inch thickness of extruded polystyrene (R-10) or a 1½- to 2-inch thickness of polyisocyanurate board (R-10.5 to R-14). (Boards thicker than 2 inches may be difficult to attach to the wall.) Warning: These board products are flammable and must never be left exposed. Follow the above instructions for vapor barriers.

Insulating basement floors will not have much effect on your fuel bills. On

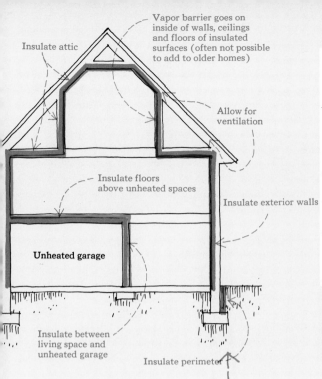

Insulate attic

Vapor barrier goes on inside of walls, ceilings and floors of insulated surfaces (often not possible to add to older homes)

Allow for ventilation

Insulate floors above unheated spaces

Insulate exterior walls

Unheated garage

Insulate between living space and unheated garage

Insulate perimeter

	How many **days** *it will last*	How many **hours** *it will last*	*How much it costs for electricity*
When the bulb burns 5 hours a day with frequent off and on switching	800	4,000	Less than 1¢/day $6.40/life of bulb
When the bulb burns 12 hours a day in cycles of 3 hours or more	500	6,000	Less than 2¢/day $9.60/life of bulb
When the bulb burns continuously	417	10,000	4¢/day $16.00/life of bulb

How long will a fluorescent bulb last, and what is the cost of operation? (Example: 40-watt fluorescent bulb with a rated life of 6,000 hours, at an electricity cost of 4¢/kilowatthour.)

the other hand, basement floors are often too cold for comfort. The best solution is to finish your remodeling by installing carpet with a thick padding underneath.

Perimeter insulation.
There are two ways to insulate around the outside perimeter of your house at the ground level. The easiest method is to create a *soil bank* up against the masonry foundation of your home. (But keep the soil level at least 3 or 4 inches below where the siding begins to discourage moisture problems and termites.) The other way is to dig around your foundation, install moisture-resistant plastic board insulation underground, and then replace the soil.

Both methods involve hard work and are usually not worth the effort. They should be used only if you can't find a way to insulate the *inside* perimeter walls. Consider *outside* perimeter insulation if you have a finished basement that's too cold, or if the first floor of your home is built on ground level without a basement or crawl space.

Lighting.
It costs 4¢ to burn a 100-watt light bulb for 10 hours (at the national average electric rate of 4¢ per kilowatt-hour). Inexpensive? Not really. If this 100-watt bulb burns continuously 24 hours a day, 7 days a week, it will add $35 a year to your electric bill. Since it's not unusual for a family to use 4 or 5 kilowatt-hours of lighting a day (at an annual cost of $60 or $70), you will save

money by turning off unnecessary lights.

Don't forget to turn off fluorescents. While it's true that fluorescent tubes will not last as many *hours* when you switch them on and off frequently, they will last more *days*. No energy is required to turn the light off, and the initial charge required to turn a fluorescent back on does not use a significant amount of energy unless the switch is flipped back and forth in rapid succession. You will use less electricity and replace tubes less often if you use fluorescents only when you need them, saving money both on utility bills and on replacement bulbs.

Plan your lighting so that you get as much light as you need, where you want it, and at the lowest energy cost. Careful choice and placement of lighting fixtures and bulbs will make your home more attractive—as well as save money on utility bills.

Overall, uniform lighting is drab and dull. Uneven, contrasty lighting is uncomfortable and can cause eye strain. Both waste energy: the first because you need more wattage to provide an acceptable level of illumination, and the second because you will be tempted to turn on or add more lights to relieve discomfort. Most rooms need a balance of directional illumination ("key" lighting to focus attention on specific areas of the room or to provide extra light for work areas like kitchen counters or a study desk) and general illumination ("fill" light to prevent excessive shad-

ows and contrast between light and dark areas). A "normal" room should have fill light that is about half the brightness of key lights. If you want to create special effects, vary the formula.

Daylight is your daytime fill light. Artificial fill lighting used at night is simply an attempt to simulate daytime conditions. You can reduce your electric bills considerably by using daylight for general illumination. If you need more light for specific activities like reading or washing dishes, turn on appropriate key lights (one at a time) as required.

Strategic placement of lamps and lighting fixtures will often allow you to use two lights instead of three to produce equally attractive and functional lighting. Move lamps around the room to see what results you can achieve. If you have permanent light fixtures that are poorly placed, consider repositioning them or perhaps not using them at all. Two tips on light distribution: Perimeter lighting will usually provide more brightness for the same wattage than central lighting; light-colored walls and bright surfaces will reflect more light into the room than dark surfaces.

When buying replacement light bulbs, read and compare information printed on the packages. *Lumens* (which measure the amount of light delivered) are as important as *wattage* (which measures the amount of electricity used).

A 100-watt bulb that delivers 1710 lumens will give you more light than one that delivers 1585 lumens—without

103

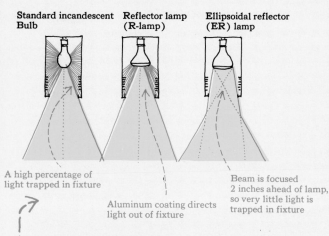

Standard incandescent Bulb   **Reflector lamp (R-lamp)**   **Ellipsoidal reflector (ER) lamp**

A high percentage of light trapped in fixture

Aluminum coating directs light out of fixture

Beam is focused 2 inches ahead of lamp, so very little light is trapped in fixture

Here's why reflector lamps deliver more light than standard incandescents in directional fixtures.

Efficiency of various light sources. Lumens per watt measure the efficiency of light bulbs (like miles per gallon indicate the efficiency of cars). The higher the lumens per watt, the better.

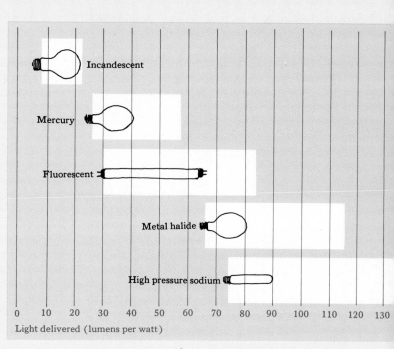

Incandescent

Mercury

Fluorescent

Metal halide

High pressure sodium

0   10   20   30   40   50   60   70   80   90   100   110   120   130

Light delivered (lumens per watt)

using additional electricity. You'll save both on utility bills and bulbs by using one large bulb in place of two smaller ones: a 100-watt bulb has the same lumen output as two 60-watt bulbs. Long-life bulbs, tinted bulbs and frosted bulbs deliver less light than clear bulbs. Reflector lamps are often a good investment for recessed or directional fixtures: a 50-watt reflector bulb will provide better lighting and use less energy than a 100-watt standard incandescent bulb.

Compared to incandescent bulbs, fluorescent lamps deliver more lumens of light for the same wattage. Although fluorescents are most often used in kitchens, baths and family rooms, they can provide economical and attractive lighting for other rooms too.

To create a pleasant atmosphere without the color distortion that's associated with fluorescents, use *deluxe* fluorescent bulbs. *Deluxe cool white* (best color rendition) and *deluxe warm white* (not far behind) are preferable to *warm white* (acceptable color) and *cool white* (sickly green). But keep in mind that deluxe fluorescents are not as energy-efficient as regular fluorescents because they don't give you as much light for the same wattage.

Fluorescent tubes may be long and straight, U-shaped, or circular. Although these tubes require special fixtures, screw-in adapters can be used to convert incandescent light sockets to fluorescent without rewiring. Specially designed adapters are made for both ceiling fixtures and table lamps, with

initial costs beginning at about $15 for both the adapter and the fluorescent tube. You will be reimbursed for this expense quickly through lower electric bills and bulb replacement costs.

Outdoor security and safety lights that burn for long hours deserve special attention. Your most appropriate choice for outdoor flood and spot lighting will usually be parabolic aluminized reflector (PAR) lamps. PAR lamps are incandescent reflector lamps with heavy, durable glass lenses that focus light where it's needed. They are more expensive than regular incandescents, but have longer lifetimes and lower operating costs. Available in 75, 150, and 250 watts, PAR lamps use less wattage to deliver more light.

More efficient for outdoor lighting (and more expensive initially) are the High Intensity Discharge (HID) lamps. HIDs may be mercury lamps, metal halide lamps, or high pressure sodium lamps. Of the three, mercury lamps are the most commonly used for outdoor lighting. They have the lowest installation cost and a very long life. Available in 40, 50, 75, 100, and 250 watts, they produce twice as much light as an incandescent bulb of the same wattage. Clear mercury lamps are unattractive because they accentuate blue, but color-corrected deluxe cool white or deluxe warm white mercury lamps are better (don't expect perfection). Mercury HIDs are not mass produced, and are therefore expensive. Compare bulb cost, installation cost, bulb life, and cost

of operation with PAR lamps before you buy. How long will a fluorescent bulb last, and what is the cost of operation? (Example: 40-watt fluorescent bulb with a rated life of 6,000 hours, at an electricity cost of 4¢/kilowatt-hour.)

Appliances. Go after the big energy users first. Most studies have shown that the energy used by small appliances (can openers, toasters, pencil sharpeners, mixers, etc.) is relatively insignificant. On the other hand, major appliances (ovens, water heaters, refrigerators, clothes washers, etc.) can use large amounts of energy.

According to the U.S. Department of Energy, water heating represents about 20% of the energy used in homes. If you have gas heat and an electric water heater, your *water* heating may be costing you more than your *space* heating. Insulating your hot water tank and turning down the thermostat on the water heater help reduce costs. But you can also make a substantial impact on your fuel bills by paying attention to how you use hot water for dishwashing, washing clothes, and showers and baths. Wait until you collect a full load of dirty dishes and laundry before using your dish washer and clothes washer. Take shorter showers and don't fill the tub completely when taking a bath. A water-conserving shower head is a good investment: its basic purpose is to conserve *hot* water, not to alleviate water shortages.

Control the amount of hot water you

Electric appliance	Average kWh... Used annually
Electric furnace (based on 1,500-sq.ft. fully-insulated home located in a 3,500-degree-day climate)	13,200
Electric heat pump (heat only, same home)	6,600
Central air conditioning (3 tons)	4,500
Quick-recovery electric water heater	4,200
Clothes washer (including hot water)	1,900
Refrigerator/Freezer (14-cu.ft. frost-free)	1,800
Freezer (15-cu.ft. frost-free)	1,800
Dishwasher (including hot water)	1,560
Room air conditioner (1 ton)	1,500
Refrigerator/Freezer (14-cu.ft. manual defrost)	1,200
Freezer (15-cu.ft. manual defrost)	1,200
Electric cooking range	1,200
Electric clothes dryer	1,000
Color television (tube type)	660
Color television (solid state)	440
Dehumidifier	400
Black & white television (tube type)	350
Microwave oven	300
Electric roasting pan	200
Electric frying pan	190
Electric blanket	150
Hand iron	150
Black & white television (solid state)	120
Radio-phonograph	110
Coffeemaker	110
Vacuum cleaner	50
Electric toaster	40
Electric clock	18
Electric mixer	10
Electric toothbrush	0.5

Annual electric energy use and cost. Electricity is measured and you are billed by the kilowatthour (kWh). A kWh is equivalent to the electricity used by ten 100-watt light bulbs burning for one hour. To get an idea of operating costs for the appliances listed below, contact your electric utility for your cost per kWh. Then multiply the estimated annual kWh by the electric rate. For example: at 4¢ per kilowatthour (the national average) it would cost you $66 a year ($.04 x 1,900 kWh) to operate your electric clothes washer. Actual use of appliances varies from family to family, so use this chart only for rough estimating. The "average use" figures were developed by the Tennessee Valley Authority specifically for electrical appliances. As a general rule, your operating costs will be lower when you have gas or oil appliances.

use in your automatic washer by using lower wash and rinse temperatures. Except for heavily soiled articles, a hot wash is seldom necessary. Cold-water rinses should be used exclusively.

Balancing satisfactory cleaning, sanitation and hot water/energy use, the optimum for most articles will be a wash temperature between 75°F. and 95°F. (usually the warm-wash setting), a cup of chlorine bleach for bacteria removal (not brightness), a cold-water rinse, and drying in a clothes dryer or on an outside clothesline. If your current detergent doesn't work, switch to a cold-water detergent (which will dissolve easily at these temperatures).

There are times when you will need other wash settings. For sanitary reasons, use only the hot-wash setting if you dry clothes on indoor lines. When you have illness in the family, or if you have infants, wash with hot water (plus chlorine bleach) to help guard against infection. In addition, garment-care labels may have special instructions (such as "do not bleach" or "wash in cold water only").

For economy and convenience, any *new* automatic washer you buy should have a water-temperature control with three wash/rinse settings: hot/cold, warm/cold, and cold/cold. Also look for a "variable fill" control that allows you to use less water for smaller loads.

The hottest water you ever need is for your dishwasher. But it's wasteful to operate your hot water heater full-time at a high-temperature setting just to supply hot water for relatively infrequent dishwashing. One energy-saving solution is to keep your water heater at a lower setting until an hour or two before using your dishwasher.

An easier solution is to own a dishwasher that saves hot water automatically without sacrificing sanitation. Some dishwashers have a booster heating element that heats wash and/or rinse water to between 145°F. and 180°F. Some have a high-temperature drying cycle. *When the final rinse or drying cycle reaches 180°F.,* dishes washed in an electric dishwasher have an average bacteria count of less than one (compared to an average bacteria count of 390 per dish after washing by hand). Obviously, if your dishwasher helps provide the extra-high temperatures needed for sterilization, you can turn your water heater down.

When buying a new dishwasher look also for a model that offers a short wash cycle (for lightly soiled dishes), a regular wash, and a scrubbing cycle (for pots and pans). A "rinse and hold" feature will allow you to rinse off gross dirt so that you can wait until you have a full load before running the dishwasher.

Because water heaters run continuously, they have the shortest life (10-15 years) of any major appliance. If your water heater is worn out and ready for replacement, shop for the smallest size that will serve your family's hot water needs. (A bigger-capacity unit costs more to operate.) Usually a 40-gallon gas water heater or a 52-gallon electric unit will be sufficient for a family of four. Fuel type affects operating costs too: electric water heaters almost always cost more to run that gas or oil.

The location of your appliances can also affect energy use. A water heater in close proximity to your dishwasher can be kept at a lower temperature setting. In the kitchen, heat-producing appliances (ovens, cooking ranges, dishwashers, toasters, etc.) should never be placed next to your refrigerator.

Whenever possible, use a small appliance rather than a large one. You can often use a toaster-oven in place of your regular oven—at a lower operating cost. Microwave ovens can cook many foods (but not all) less expensively.

If you are buying new home entertainment appliances (a television, stereo, or radio), keep in mind that solid-state equipment costs much less to operate than the tube type. The difference will be significant if you use the equipment often, insignificant if you don't. But don't buy an "instant-on" television that uses a continual supply of electricity: if you already have one, unplug it when it's not in use.

If you haven't already "fine-tuned" your heating and cooling appliances by improving their efficiency and by sealing your home's thermal envelope, go back to the beginning of your Whole House Energy Inspection. Climate-control appliances use about *70%* of the energy in residences, and that's where you'll make the biggest dent in your fuel bills. □

105

Tapping energy from the sun

You can adapt solar energy to your present home without spending a fortune

News of solar-heated homes appears in newspapers at least once a month, often once a week. Despite the glamour and the success stories, confusion persists, even among professionals. If uncertainty is rampant among experienced contractors, how are you expected to make a rational decision about buying solar equipment?

Yet, a rational decision is what this report intends to help you make. Will solar devices save you money right now? Can solar equipment work well enough on an existing house? How much will it all cost? Legitimate questions, every one, and you have a right to know.

Understand, first, that no matter how your house is built or where it's located, you can benefit from the sun's warmth, winter and summer. You can (1) draw solar rays to heat a swimming pool or whirlpool bath; (2) draw hot tap water pushed to scalding temperatures by the sun, and (3) heat all of the house part of the time with solar energy.

Swimming pools. Solar equipment can be added with relative ease to an existing pool or spa, or to one you plan to build. Solar collector panels produced for these uses are less complicated and less expensive than those for house heat. Panels are made of metal—aluminum or copper—and some are plastic. Pool water is pumped through piping attached to the panels, heated and sent back. The panels are not glazed, making them light and easy to install. (An exception: in a locale where strong, gusty winds blow constantly or often enough to shake loose installed panels, glazing is recommended. The weight of the glazing secures the panels.)

Ideally, collector panels are installed facing true south and at an angle that places the panel surface in the direct path of sun rays. If those guidelines are rigidly followed, where you install a panel is limited. Panels must be sloped just so, and face due south. Fortunately, pools and spas do not call for the same quantity of heat as a house. As a result, solar panel installation is quite flexible. For example:

• Pool panels can face south, southeast or southwest. They can even face east or west. Within United States latitudes, the only direction they can't face is north.

• Pool panels are effective at any angle between 5° and 90°. This means the collector panels can be attached to a roof with as low as a 1-in-12 pitch (one inch of rise for every 12 inches on the horizontal). A 1-in-12 pitch is set at an angle of about 7.5°.

Panels could be positioned on a flat roof and pitched to 5° on a wedged platform. Since 90° is vertical, the panels could be attached to the side of a building or fencing facing south. If so, some caution is needed to prevent people from touching an operating metal panel. Metal will grow hot enough in bright sun to burn bare skin.

So long as the surface has a clear shot at the sun, panels can be placed on the ground. Nor is distance from the pool or spa a critical determination.

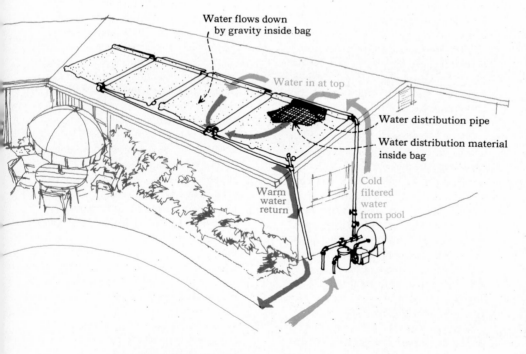

Water flows down by gravity inside bag

Water in at top

Water distribution pipe

Water distribution material inside bag

Warm water return

Cold filtered water from pool

In some locales, fuel-fired pool heaters are outlawed by code. If fuel shortages continue, the ban may spread. Solar heaters—plastic (as above) or metal—can meet 100% of pool heating needs. Circulating pump, already a part of the filter equipment, routes pool water through inexpensive collectors, back to pool.

Piping between panels and pool can always be insulated.

A rough rule of thumb says a pool can be heated with collector panels adding up to one-half the area of the pool. The most common in-ground pool size is 18 ft. by 36 ft., or 648 sq. ft. of area. Using the rule, 324 sq. ft. of panel surface area will heat the pool. Each panel maker will have exact specifications to tell how many panels are required. You simply bring along the pool dimensions.

Will you still need a fuel-fired pool heater? Yes, if you want an evenly heated pool, especially during nighttime swimming, early-morning dips or on sunless days. Of course, you could limit your swimming from noon to dusk on sunny days, in which case a solar system could probably handle all the heating.

A solar-heated pool does save money from the moment it's operative. How

much depends on how you use it. One Floridian used a fuel-fired heater twice during the cold 1977/78 winter. At all other times, the solar collector panels provided just enough heat. (A side note: in summer, this owner pumps water through the collectors at night; swims during the day in water made a few degrees cooler!)

Installed cost for the system bears directly on pool size. The range begins around $1,500 and climbs to about $4,000. There are exceptions on both ends of the scale, and a 30% to 50% saving for do-it-yourselfers. Just keep in mind you need better-than-average handyman skills to install a system.

Domestic hot water. In 1978, about 100,000 families ordered solar collectors installed on their homes to heat tap water. The technology for this job is established. Everyday, more contractors are learning the techniques. They

are also learning that the tasks are not substantially different from putting in a new fuel-fired hot-water heater. Of course, there's one difference that stands out—the collector panels.

Yet, even the panels are familiar. It is a stationary mechanism with an inlet and outlet pipe, and an air vent—all "old hat" to heating or plumbing contractors. Piping must be connected to both ends and run through the house to a storage tank. A pump is connected to circulate water or other fluid through the panels, and a piping tie is made to the existing hot water tank. This is the kind of work a contractor does every working day.

What is different is the way he must install the panels. They must face due south, or up to 20° east or west of South. If one roof on your house faces that direction, and you have no objection to the aesthetics of the panel on that

First of two collector panels (immediately below) has been attached to an existing south-facing roof. This sun heat-trap is part of a total package typically produced by leading companies now. Display (bottom photo) shows parts of a similar system—collectors, storage tank, controls.

Finished installation (below) of two solar collector panels beneath the wide dormer blends with the contemporary look of the home, and even resembles skylights on the roof above entry.

roof, you're in luck. That's where the panels will go with a minimum of fuss.

Will the lack of a south-facing roof be a problem? Somewhat, but hardly insurmountable. The options:

1. Build a frame on the roof to hold the panels in a south-facing position. Since hot-water demands rarely call for more than two panels, this is an easier job than it may sound initially.

2. Install the collectors on an outbuilding. Connect to the house storage tanks with insulated piping on the supply side.

3. Install the panels at the proper angle on the ground, and, again, connect to storage with insulated piping.

While each producer of solar collectors has computed the relationship between collector-panel area and hot-water needs, there is a rough guide. Figure about one square foot of collec-

tor surface for every two gallons of hot water required. Average needs for a home range between 20 and 35 gallons of hot water per day per person. Thus, a family of four might use 120 gallons a day. About 60 square feet of collectors will supply those needs. Many panels are produced in 4' x 8' modules. Thus, two panels (64 sq. ft.) would be sufficient.

Although solar collectors provide hot water summer and winter, the total rarely adds up to 100% of needs. The exceptions occur in areas of bountiful sun, such as southern California and south Florida. Elsewhere, icy winters and strings of sunless days cut down on collector efficiency. Yet, even in regions plagued with more clouds than sun, a system can heat 60% of the requirements. Collectors send down some heat on hazy, and even cloudy days.

To determine potential savings of a solar-assisted hot water system, com-

pute your yearly hot water use and the fuel needed to heat it (the utility or fuel oil supplier can help you compute this). Your savings will fall somewhere between 60% and 90% of that cost.

Prices for installing a solar domestic hot water system to an existing house now range betwen $1,800 and $3,800. The range is less for a house under construction, since less labor is involved. Doing the job yourself is risky unless plumbing or heating is your business.

Space heating. This is the glamorous member of the solar family, principally because it promises the greatest savings. Space heating in the average American home accounts for 57% of all energy used. It is therefore the largest single consumer of energy, and accounts for the major portion of home energy costs. A 50% reduction through solar economies will show up signifi-

When no side of your house roof faces south, or you simply don't want to see panels on it, have them installed on an outbuilding. Below, panels are fixed to a garden shed. Sun-heated fluid in panels will flow to the house through insulated pipes to storage tank in the basement.

Government help at hand

The U.S. Government is one of the best sources of information on all things solar. Whether you want more information, the names of companies or organizations in the business, the names of architects familiar with solar design, the names of specialists in the field, or sources for further study, there is a government number to call and an address to write to.

This single compendium of solar data was the inspiration of and is funded by the Department of Energy through the Department of Housing and Urban Development.

From any point in the country, except Pennsylvania, call, toll-free, (800) 523-2929. Residents of Pennsylvania can call, toll-free, (800) 462-4983. Or write the National Solar Heating and Cooling Information Bureau, Box 1607, Rockville, MD 20850.

cantly in fuel bills.

Of course, solar-assisted space heating also demands the largest investment. A wide spread exists among installed costs. The figure could be as low as $7,000 or as high as $20,000. How much you spend depends on:

• *The number of collector panels.* Panel prices are currently running between $15 and $20 per sq. ft. The size of your house is less important than the Btu (British thermal unit) energy loss per day in determining how many panels are needed.

That is why homes fitted with a solar space heating system are also packed with insulation, caulked carefully to prevent air leaks and protected by such items as double glazing. When the Btu loss is driven down, so is the need for panels.

• *Your own judgment.* Suppose you learn from the contractor that 11 panels will provide 70% of the heat required by your house. Compute the savings, and match them with the cost of the system. Then, you find out that six panels will provide 40% of heating needs. Compare. You may discover the second choice is less costly over the long run. Find out all the facts. Then make up your own mind.

• *The type of system.* Clearly, more than two panels are needed for space heating. A south-facing roof is required. Assume your roof meets the test. Installation of either an air-heating or fluid-heating collector system is costly. Not only are there many panels, much piping (or ductwork), controls and pumps to install, but some means to store collected heat must be provided (water, rocks or eutectic salts).

A solar "furnace" is a self-contained heat producer generally installed on the ground apart from the house. It is usually an air-heating type that delivers warm air to the house through insulated ducts. Rocks provide the means for thermal storage. This unit easily overcomes the lack of a south-facing roof, since it can be installed on the property wherever there is an unobstructed view to the southern sky. It is also easier to install, since only minor work on the house is required. As a result, it is considerably less costly than a roof-mounted system. Solar furnaces with fluid-heating systems are also available. Both air- and fluid-heating units can be tapped to help heat domestic hot water, as well as the house.

Whatever system you choose, you want one that works today, tomorrow and years from now. Your best bet is to deal with a contractor you know and trust. Ask for and examine a warranty. Make certain the contractor will provide service when it's needed.

The triangular structure (below), labeled a solar furnace by makers, uses sun energy to heat air, which then heats rocks inside the unit. Stored heat in the rocks is drawn to the house through insulated ducts when needed. Domestic hot water can be heated, as well, with system.

This sun "furnace" suits remodeling better than many other systems, since it's positioned anywhere on the property a measured distance from the house. Of course, unit must be turned so collectors face the south. Installation below is placed on the rear lot line of the house.

Solar energy in your future

Cooling a house with solar energy is a technology not quite perfected at present. But it's coming. So far, one company produces a complete system for solar cooling and has installed it on an experimental house in Evansville, Ind., and several designers have developed non-mechanical means of keeping a house cool.

Estimates by solar experts call for operable solar cooling by 1985. Some say the day will arrive sooner. One fact is certain. A great many people, including scientists working for the government, are exploring paths to solar cooling. It may happen sooner than we think.

Beyond that development lies one even more exciting—the direct transformation of solar energy to electricity. It's happening now in space. The hundreds of space vehicles circling the earth and on their way to various planets are supplied with electricity via solar cells, small wafers of silicon that convert sun heat to electric energy.

These tiny chips can manage the same feat on earth. But two problems crop up:

1. Because of atmospheric interference, solar cell efficiency drops to less than 8%.

2. They are dear. The electricity a silicon cell generates costs about $20 a watt.

However, experimentation is pushing forward at a rapid pace. Other materials—such as cadmium sulphide—are getting tested. Already, progress has been made in pushing up cell efficiency and lowering the cost. Some scientists see a breakthrough within seven or eight years. When it does, these scientists claim, individual homes will be the first to benefit.

Walls and windows

Whether you have just moved into a new-new house or a new-old house, chances are that redoing the interior walls is somewhere near the top of your priority list. The walls in an older home are often an eyesore and badly in need of repair. And in a new home, the walls were probably finished to a builder's specifications and taste—which may be vastly different from your own.

Walls and ceiling influence about 80 percent of a room's scale and appearance. A change here can have a remarkable effect on the background mood and identity of the room. When you want to expand the feeling of spaciousness or make a room seem cozier, it's how you handle the walls that does the trick.

The possibilities are dizzying. Fortunately, your wall and window decisions will be eased and shaped by the character and condition of your home and its furnishings, plus your own personal taste, objectives and budget.

Practical matters

Before you start collecting paint or paper samples galore, consider the practical side of the problem:

Do you plan to knock out any walls? With never enough living space, fixed interior walls seem inflexible and space consuming. Just be sure you can tell the difference between a "bearing" and a "nonbearing" wall before starting any demolition work. *What is structurally feasible?* If the walls are in poor condition, for example, it will probably be less expensive to hang a wallcovering rather than paint. *Should the wall finish be changed?* If the surface materials are impractical or unsuited to the purpose and activity of the room, change them. *What is available in the marketplace?* There are many more choices available than paint, paper and paneling today. Consider them before making up your mind. *Are you thinking of doing-it-yourself or do you plan to enlist the aid of an expert?* The answer to this question should influence the range and complexity of your plans. *Finally, how big is your budget?* If it's on the slim side, you can buy good quality paint for the same cost as cheap paneling.

After moving into a new house, it often takes a while to become "acclimated"—to get the feel of the proportions of the space, to sense its potential and visualize its possibilities. Read magazines and books, collect ideas, make sketches and talk to professionals. This will help accelerate the process. Soon you'll know whether a ceiling needs lowering visually, which room needs a strong dose of color, or how best to approach the windows in the living room.

Walls: in the background or forefront?

With soft and subtle color schemes, walls will seem to recede in space, forming an elegant backdrop for beautiful furnishings, art objects and people. On the other hand, you might prefer the more dramatic approach of intense color, pattern and gleam in a room. Such an exciting background turns the walls into the principal decoration and makes even ordinary furniture seem interesting.

Genuine barnwood siding is hard to come by, but this rustic paneling below makes the look both affordable and easily available.

The trend in paneling is to "go light" with textures of unbleached, unstained, or pickled wood or butcherblock surfaces. The result, above, is a room that is open and airy—and paneled.

Walls: plain or patterned?

There are two ways to use pattern in decorating: use a little or use a lot. Pattern can be delightful in the right room, pulling it together into a cohesive whole. Pattern-on-pattern schemes work best in small rooms because they share the same kind of intimate quality as the design. However, they are less flexible than solid color walls, and it's difficult to display paintings and pictures on busy walls.

The size and lavish use of pattern should also be influenced by the room at hand and *how much time is spent there.* Ignore the old cliché about the size of the room dictating the scale of the pattern. Vivid, overscaled designs are seldom pleasant to relax with in rooms of *any* size.

Generally speaking, the main "living room" in a house (which may or may not be The Living Room) should have solid color walls in one of the new soft neutral tones. Save the design theatrics for foyers, hallways, bathrooms and other rooms (large or small) in which you don't spend hours on end.

When selecting *floral patterns,* stay close to the delicacy or scale of the design in its natural form; oversized blossoms the size of bowling balls can seem grotesque on the wall. And if you like the look of print-on-print, several patterns can be successfully combined as long as there is enough distinction in color and scale among them to establish the difference at first glance.

Wood paneling

Paneling can be the ideal wallcovering solution to disguise minor disasters: rough walls, chipped paint or plaster, sagging coats of wallpaper, water damage, pipes or other obstructions.

It might also be chosen strictly on aesthetic merits. The visual impact of a beautifully paneled wall can't be matched by any other wallcovering.

Board paneling and *sheet paneling* (plywood and hardboard) are both considered wood paneling, but quite a difference exists between the two.

Solid board paneling is lumber milled from trees, with all the natural texture, warmth, fragrance, color and grain subtleties of wood. The narrow boards are easy to apply on walls broken up with doors and windows.

Sheet paneling, 4' X 8' panels, is faster to install over large, unbroken surfaces. *Plywood panels,* created from thin veneers of wood sandwiched together, have been heavily promoted for several good reasons.

First, if you want an exotic wood, it's available at fairly reasonable cost—barn wood to pecan to wormwood. Second, plywood is less likely to warp than real wood. And finally, installation can be successfully handled by a reasonbly skilled amateur to yield professional-looking results.

Hardboard paneling, also a sheet panel, is the basis for pegboard and other familiar products. It's a composition board formed under heat and pressure and noted for its strength. Hardboard panels are often finished to look like wood and grooved to look like board paneling. Only the top grades pass muster, however, as in the boy's bedroom (next page) with the partially pegged wall.

Paneling tips

• The trend in decorating with paneling is to use it on fewer walls for more drama and texture. The other walls should be coordinated in complementary paint, fabric, paper, brick, mirror or other wallcoverings.
• Board paneling has better acoustic and thermal insulation qualities than plywood.
• When buying genuine board paneling, take the time to personally select each piece.
• Paneling boards and sheets look better if they run the full height of the wall.

The dining room below from the restored Corbitt-Sharp house in Odessa, Delaware shows how formal paneling can be—and how beautifully it complements patterned walls in the same room.

The mood is serene when paneling provides a natural setting for a lovely outdoor view, as in this bedroom at right.

Dan Forer

Avoid piecing by ordering 9′ and 10′ lengths if necessary.

• Plywood paneling should not be used in damp basements or bathrooms; the moisture may cause it to delaminate.

• Some 4′ X 8′ panels on the market are only 5/32″ thick. Be forewarned. The heavier the paneling, the longer the life.

• Consider using exterior grade plywood on inside walls for a rustic effect.

• If you want to see the best quality, call or write the major plywood manufacturers and ask for literature on their architectural grade plywoods.

• Consider horizontal or diagonal installation on board paneling for an interesting variation on the usual vertically paneled walls. Other possibiities are a herringbone pattern or board-and-batten installation.

• A paneled room without good window light can seem terribly dark and dreary. Two illuminating solutions: One, add *track lighting* to highlight paneling, floor and furniture, thus brightening the room. Or two, buy *floor-based flood-lights* (or can lights) with swivels to "wash" the walls with pools of light.

• A more daring solution for a too-dark paneled room is to glaze it or stain it in a lighter color. Experiment on a scrap piece of paneling first or test it in an unobtrusive spot such as in a closet or behind a door.

However pattern is used, *avoid timid nondescript designs.* They are not interesting enough to add impact to a room nor plain enough to be good backgrounds. Unless pattern *does* something for a room it shouldn't be there.

Walls: strive for harmony

As you move from room to room in a house, you should not be bowled over by startling contrasts in wall surfaces, colors and patterns. That doesn't mean you have to live in monochromatic monotony however. It does suggest that you consider the *visual progression* of the rooms in your home. For example, an easy way to treat adjoining rooms is to use a patterned wall with coordinated woodwork in one, and the same woodwork with solid walls to match in another.

Paint

Paint takes the cake as the least expensive wallcovering and it's usually the fastest to apply as well. With the exception of a few sophisticated glazing, lacquering or **trompe l'oeil** techniques, an amateur painter can do a very professional job with just a little experience and a little more persistence. If existing walls are in good shape without too many large cracks, paint will be an excellent choice.

Color tips

• If your room is small, a light color paint can only make it look a *little* larger. So paint your walls the color you want in spite of the so-called "rules." A small room in rich deep-toned colors can be charming and intimate.

• One exception would be a very dark room with little or no natural light. Claustrophobia could set in unless a light, airy look was created.

• Strong colors should be painted in oil-base gloss enamel to reflect more light.

• Paint or paper all walls in a room in the *same* paint or paper unless there is a valid architectural reason for doing them differently. The cures for "diagnostic decor" ("horizontal stripes widen a room") are often worse than the problem.

• Get a *big sample* of each paint color being considered—at least 5″ x 7″ or 8″ x 10″. Even the experts can't tell a thing from looking at thumbnail-sized chips of color.

• Live with your color samples for at least a day. Look at them throughout the day and in all the lights of the room.

This boy's bedroom with a partially pegged wall of top-grade hardboard paneling shows how practical and handsome it can be.

The magic of color to change the mood of a room is well illustrated in this living room painted in the softest shades of aqua. The subtle variations in tone highlight the architectural detailing as well.

Photo: Elyse Lewin
Designer: Barbara Lockhart,

Let's see paint or paper do this.

OL' SAVANNAH® Chandlers Pine.

Georgia-Pacific paneling is so much more elegant than paint or paper.
And its beauty lasts. You can install it yourself in a day and enjoy it for years.
And compared to painting or papering, Georgia-Pacific paneling is a good investment.
Because paneling provides years of good looks with a minimum of maintenance.
Look for G-P paneling wherever you see our familiar blue and white sign.

Georgia-Pacific
REGISTERED DEALER
**Home of quality
building products
and service**

Georgia-Pacific paneling.

Georgia-Pacific Corporation, Portland, Oregon 97204
For more information circle 10 on the Reader's Service Card following the Index.

Creating illusions with paint

Ugly features in a room—such as radiators, air conditioners or heating ducts—can be "painted out" by painting them the same color as the wall or ceiling.

Low ceilings can be lifted by elongating the vertical elements in walls, such as painting the doors in a hallway a contrasting color. Ceiling should be light color.

A too-high ceiling can be lowered by painting it a darker color and extending the color part way down the walls to a picture molding.

Painted woodwork

If woodwork or moldings are not particularly attractive, paint them out in the same color as the walls. However, if the woodwork is indeed handsome, paint it in a contrasting accent color. Unless the walls are white as well, nothing looks fresher than darker walls with white trim.

Chair rails on walls are most effective when the color above and below the rail is contrasted. Otherwise, chair rails restrict the wall treatment and waste a lot of wall space. Chair backs can be kept from marking the wall by placing a strip of quarter-round molding around the bottom of the baseboard.

Surface	LATEX FLAT	LATEX SEMI-GLOSS	OIL-BASE FLAT	OIL-BASE SEMI-GLOSS	OIL-BASE GL. ENAMEL	EPOXY PAINT	VARNISH	SHELLAC	POLYURETHANE
Dry walls, ceilings (primed)	●	●	●	●	●			●	
Plaster walls, ceilings (prime-sealed)		●	●	●	●				
Wood paneling			●	●	●		●	●	●
Kitchen and bathroom walls				●	●				
Tile walls, glass, "formica"						●			
Wood trim	●	●	●	●	●		●	●	●
Window sills		●			●				●
Acoustical ceiling	●								
Wood cabinets, shelves				●	●		●	●	●

Paint can also create a feeling of excitement and turn eyesores into art objects. Here a heating duct becomes a sculptural element in this restored kitchen/dining area at left.

Below, an ornate stairway becomes a standout when the wall behind is painted a bright contrasting color. It's a dramatic touch that works best in areas where little time is spent.

Phillip MacMillan James

You've just made the smartest move of your life.

Now make another one.

Weldwood Paneling

The next best thing to buying your home is making it look like your home.

That's why now is a nice time to think about Weldwood® Paneling.

Weldwood offers you what paint or paper simply can't: the rich, warm look of wood. In a wide variety of classic real wood veneers or handsome reproductions for any room of your home.

And because Weldwood will be around for years after you've settled in, it's an investment that isn't expensive. Especially if you do it yourself.

Now, we know you've got a lot of important things to do in your new home. But while you're in the mood to make smart decisions, why not send in the order card in the back of this book. You'll receive our free full-color brochure, "All About Wall Paneling."

For the number of your nearest Headquarters/Champion Building Products® Dealer, call us toll-free **800-243-6000** (Conn. **1-800-882-6500**).

Weldwood®
PANELING

Wallcoverings

Wallpaper is the least expensive way to add drama to a room devoid of any architectural interest. Areas which would look empty if merely painted seem furnished when papered. An all-over pattern can also distract from a multitude of sins—jogs in the wall, window cutouts, rough wall surfaces—and its camouflage capability is exceeded only by its versatility. Wallpaper can be used in any room in the home.

For those who don't care for its "papery" look, there are many textures and vinyls available that look and feel like fabrics and other natural materials. *A cautionary note here:* Avoid wallpapers that try too hard to look like something they're not, such as a brick wall. Imitation may be a sincere form of flattery, but it's not always successful.

Buy the best quality paper you can afford. Look for patterns that are well-drawn, well-colored and nicely scaled. Pick a design you won't outgrow for a long time. Good wallpaper tends to last longer and may actually be less expensive over time than cheaper, thinner papers which are more difficult to hang.

Installation

If you're wallpapering for the first time, start small. Do a closet or a laundry room where a few mistakes won't be noticed. Every little error shows up in wallpaper and pattern matching must be perfect. Practice helps.

Old wallpaper should always be removed before applying new layers. However, if your walls are in poor condition and the paper is literally holding the plaster in place, don't touch it! Old paper should also remain when it's so smooth and in such good condition that it can serve as a liner.

Wallpaper should not be applied over wood paneling for two reasons: one, it will "settle" and the grooves will be apparent from the surface; and two, the expansion and contraction of the wood will cause the paper to rip. Also avoid applying paper between decorative wood moldings. What it does is to "chop up" the flow of the design and, therefore, looks a bit amateurish.

The *number of repeats* that will appear in a panel should affect the pattern chosen. Look at a full length of paper tacked to the wall before committing yourself. Seeing the design in multiple repeats could change the look of it completely.

Special effects

• Wallpapered walls that meet painted ceilings look more finished when joined by a *cornice molding.*

• *Papered ceilings* should be attempted only with a nondirectional design wallpaper. Run it so that the direction favors you as you walk into the room.

• A *wallpaper border* is a custom touch in a room that has no picture molding or cornice molding. This romantic attic bedroom uses three coordinating papers from Inaltera's "April in Paris" collection to create architectural features where none existed before. The border print framing the window is a lovely way to enhance a view.

• Textured wallcoverings—such as grasscloth, silk paper or vinyl—can be *painted over* if they have begun to fade or discolor. The handsome texture remains and only the color changes.

Paint or paper?

From a cost standpoint, it's hard to beat the value of paint. However, if aesthetics count (as they surely do), wallpaper offers choices in patterns, textures and multicolors that paint cannot match.

Wallpaper may also be a better choice if the wall is already prepared, or if a good deal of scraping and work is required to ready the wall for paint, or if more than two coats of paint will be required.

Michael Fitzwater

A combination of three related wallpaper designs seems to create architectural features where none existed before, as in this attic bedroom at left. The border print framing the window is a lovely way to enhance a view. Above: a plain white-walled bedroom acquires real personality, above, with the application of a handsome patterned paper and matching fabric quilted for the bedspread.

BEAT BLAH WALLS.

Grasscloth Greenfield™ *Burluxe Nutmeg™* *Someplace Avalon™* *Chaparral Arroyo™* *Sketchbook Villager™*

Woodglo Concord™ *Pattern Ply Rose Bosket™* *Adirondack Mohegan™* *Remembrance Eagle Rock™* *Vacationeer Horseshoe™*

 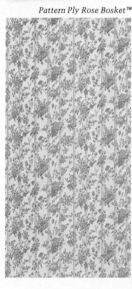   

CHECK OUT THESE CHRYSTIE JENNER IDEAS
AT YOUR WEYERHAEUSER PANELING CENTER.

Getting bored with those old, tired walls but can't face the mess and hassle of paint or wallpaper?

Then take a tip from Chrystie Jenner.

Decorate any room in your home the easy way with Weyerhaeuser Designer Wall Paneling.

It comes in more beautiful styles and patterns than you can shake a hammer at. Goes up in a jiffy. Is easy to clean and so tough it's practically childproof. And doesn't cost a fortune.

So come on down and visit your local Weyerhaeuser Paneling Center. You'll find all sorts of exciting decorating ideas.

And plenty of ways to beat the blahs.

 Weyerhaeuser

Mirrors

Mirrors create the most effective illusions of all the decorating tricks at hand. Short of knocking out walls, mirror is the best device for doubling space while adding brightness and sparkle to a room.

Professional tips

1. When thinking where to put a wall of mirror, consider what it will reflect: a pretty window? Or a messy kitchen?

2. Mirrors placed adjacent to a row of windows will give the illusion of more windows.

3. Avoid placing mirrors where anyone will look straight into them while seated in the room. It's distracting and unnerving.

4. Mirror is breakable, expensive to buy and to have installed. It can also be hazardous if not placed correctly. Put it far away enough from the main entrace to the room so that no one accidentally runs into it.

5. Mirrors show smudges (although they're easily cleaned). Avoid placing on a wall that is touched frequently.

6. A large mirror will seem to increase the amount of furniture—great if the room is sparsely furnished. An already crowded room will look more so.

7. Don't lavish mirror on a room in which you're hoping to create a feeling of quiet solitude.

8. Mirror tiles are not as effective as large expanses of mirror with few seams.

9. A floor-to-ceiling mirror should start at the floor and end at the ceiling— no baseboard, no cornice molding.

10. One center panel and two side half-panels are better than a wall of two equal-size panels.

11. When mirroring a high wall, the upper panel should cover the top ⅓, the lower panel should cover the bottom ⅔ of the wall.

12. Although acrylic mirror is half the weight and less costly than ¼" plate glass, it also produces a somewhat distorted, wavy image. Plate glass is the best choice for large installations and will insure that your mirrored wall doesn't resemble a funhouse.

How to use mirror

Mirror a dark wall to catch the sun, add life to a dead-end hallway.

Put a *half-circle table* against a mirror and you'll think you have a round table.

Mirror the long wall of a narrow room to make it look wider. Mirror a short wall to make it look deeper.

Mirror the *space between two win-* *dows* that are next to each other.

Mirror a solid column and it will seem to disappear.

Mirror the ceiling, the dining table, behind bookshelves for added dimension in unexpected places.

Mirror sliding closet doors to make a mirrored wall.

A slightly angled mirrored wall will seem to add another plane to the room. Mark ceiling line 10"-12" away from wall as starting point for mirror panels.

Mirror window shutters and/or reveals to bounce more light into a room.

Sheets & towels

The bedroom and bath are changing rapidly in both form and function. Bedrooms are becoming sitting rooms as well, baths are private retreats and mini-gyms. And is there anyone who still sleeps on plain white sheets? Very few, it would seem, unless those sheets are beruffled and beribboned as well. These changes are certainly reflective of the design revolution in sheets and towels over the last decade.

The bed has emerged from under the covers. With colorful designer sheets on hand, why hide them under a heavy spread? The boxspring may also be

The same wallpaper pattern used in adjoining rooms creates a pleasant feeling of harmony, left.

A new angle on the old "mirror trick" is pictured below. The wall of mirror on the left side not only makes this bedroom seem larger, but it also reflects all the window light to add to the feeling of spaciousness.

Dan Forer

A wallcovering sampler

Michael Fitzwater

Machine-printed wallpaper
Most wallpapers are machine printed. They are durable, fairly easy to handle and rolls match easily.

Burlap
Noted for its texture and durability, available with and without a paper backing. Backing eases handling and hanging. A vinyl-coated water-resistant burlap is also made.

Carpet
Extending the carpet partway or all the way up the walls gives a soft, warm look to an interior, with great acoustical control.

Ceramic tile
Wall tiles come in plain, textured, patterned, glazed, unglazed, mosaic, machine and hand-painted styles. Tiles are water-resistant, stain-resistant, long lasting, hard wearing and easy to clean.

Mirror
The most effective way to cosmetically enlarge a room is to mirror a wall or two. Wall-size mirrors should be ¼″ plate glass, and professional installation is recommended.

Felt
Paper-backed felt is made just for hanging. Adds warmth, plus some acoustic and insulating qualities. Vacuum to keep clean.

Grasscloth
Ranges from textured linen-like open weaves to coarse straw looks laminated to paper backing. Colors will fade in strong sunlight. Difficult to clean, costly and beautiful.

Hand-printed wallpaper
One roll is produced at a time with silkscreen, wood block or stencil printing. The image is sharper than machine prints, and hand-printed papers are priced accordingly.

Paneling
Available in large sheets (4′ X 8′) or installed as individual boards. Wood paneling has a warmth and grain that cannot be duplicated by other wallcoverings.

Fabrics
Chintz, cottons, linens, moiré, silks, crewels and velvets can be installed with a staple gun or cellulose wallpaper paste. Fabrics can also be laminated to a paper backing for wallpaper-like hanging.

Foil
Metal foils are laminated to a paper or cloth backing. Designs can be plain, random, hand-printed, flocked or three-dimensional.

Vinyl wallcoverings
Made with a paper or cloth backing and a printed or textured surface. Waterproof, stain-resistant, durable. Ideal for kitchens, baths, children's rooms, hallways.

Flocked
Hand prints with velvety pile on surface. Tricky to handle and hang.

Cork
Solid cork is available in pieces, tiles and rolls. It's a good sound absorber, but is also susceptible to staining and fading. Cork looks best in natural colors.

skirted or upholstered to show off a comforter or quilt or top.

Many people have discovered the ease of bedmaking with a European-style down comforter (eiderdown or duvet) that merely has to be shaken into place in the morning. (In addition to its labor-saving attributes, they are also terrific to snuggle under on cold winter nights!) The comforters are covered with a ''sheet case'' made from two sheets (matching or coordinating) sewn together with a long zipper running down one side for easy access and washing.

Building a modest wardrobe of sheets is the easiest, most fun and most affordable advantage of white sale reductions each January and July to add to your collection. Just as the ''layered look'' has swept the fashion world, it also works on beds with mix and match designer sheet patterns.

Sheets have also slipped off the bed and onto walls, windows, tables and furniture. They do provide an extraordinary expanse of seamless fabric; however, window treatments and tablecloths should always be lined for the extra body needed to hang properly.

In addition, sheet manufacturers recommend that sheets *not* be washed before use in decorating; laundering removes a layer of ink and much of the body. Carefully steam press out wrinkles and fold lines before cutting and sewing.

For the most handsome results in decorating with sheets, mix them with other fabrics and textures to avoid the look of an all-percale room. Sheets should be used for slipcovers or upholstery only on furniture that receives comparatively little use.

A wardrobe of colorful, luxurious bath towels will do great things for an old bathroom. Tired tile will fade into the background with vibrant towels to catch the eye. Having multiple sets of sheets and towels is not as extravagant as it may seem; they last much longer because of less frequent wear and washing.

Windows

When your immediate need is to get something, anything, on the bare windows of a new home, it's hard to sit down and design clever window treatments. That's why it's so easy to end up with the same pinch pleats or priscilla curtains that everyone else has on their windows.

Here are a few temporary or interim suggestions that will provide a modicum of light control and privacy—the real purpose of any window dressing—to tide you over until you're either inspired or compelled to do more.

• If double traverse rods sit at the windows, have pleated panels made out of good *lining material.* They will look like crisp white curtains hanging at the window. Then at a later date you can add drapery or side panels as desired. This works particularly well with open weave casements.

• Stitch up similar rod-pocket panels in drapery lining or muslin for sash rods, brass rods or wood poles. The fabric can always be recycled in future projects.

• Buy matchstick blinds or textured white roller shades for those windows facing the street or adjoining the neighbors.

• Bring your houseplants together temporarily and mass them in front of those windows that need more camouflage or privacy.

• Rummage through your closets for lovely old clothes, fabrics, scarves, tablecloths, quilts, carpets or textile hangings that could be temporarily ''on display'' at your windows until something more permanent can be worked out.

Window basics

The move to pare down, uncover, unclutter and generally simplify life has not left windows untouched. We've

Wood shutters left *au naturel* are an effective but uncluttered way of controlling light in this bedroom at right with a wall of adjoining windows.

A beautiful view by day can turn into a black void by night without a soft drapery to draw across the window, below.

come back to the basics of windows, focusing on light, ventilation and view. The challenge is to complement those qualities in as subtle and simple a manner as possible.

For example, the elegant and overstated look of heavy draperies laden with sheers, swags and jabots galore seems too ornate for most homes today—especially those with lower ceilings and smaller rooms. How refreshing instead to shir a sumptuous pair of straight hanging panels on a simple wood rod. A matchstick blind can be mounted behind fabric panels for light control. And the view, formerly obscured by layer on layer of fabric and drapery, is now beautifully framed.

Starting from scratch

Interior designers think of a window treatment *in terms of the room,* not just the window or the wall. They first decide whether the windows will serve more as *backgrounds* or as *accents.* The latter approach is desirable when the furniture is sparse and the room lacks character. In any case, the window decor *must* relate not only to the surrounding wall area, but also to the other furnishings viewed against it.

So step back when taking a fresh look at your windows. Pull down distracting hardware, rods, blinds, shades and curtains to get back to the unadorned window. Now it will be easier to visualize all kinds of possibilities that might have been mentally blocked by the old treatment.

Beg or borrow a metal measuring tape or folding carpenter's rule. Then, with pencil and paper at hand, carefully measure the height, width and depth of windows, moldings, rods, radiators, air conditioners or other obstructions. Write it all down.

Measure the wall elevation too and sketch the position of windows, doors and other openings on the wall. This is not only a valuable reference when shopping for home furnishings, but it's essential for the next step.

The fun begins. Place sheets of tracing paper over your basic room/wall sketches and begin to pencil in different window dressings. Try the hard-edge look of vertical blinds... floor-length side panels with a narrow-slat blind beneath... handkerchief panels pulled back in soft folds... wooden shutters or shutter frames with shirred fabric insets... cartridge-pleated panels that draw... a voluptuous balloon shade with a pleated heading... and that's just the beginning!

You don't have to be an artist to get a feeling for what might work in the room. You just have to know what you like.

Those ideas that don't quite work are quickly eliminated, freeing you to go in other directions. If you're stumped by problem areas, consider asking a professional interior designer to come over for a one or two-hour consultation. This could be an excellent investment and might also save you from making some expensive mistakes.

Color balance

Your new house may have come with draperies, blinds, carpeting or other decorative elements not of your choosing. And now they must all be coordinated with your own furnishings. Deciding what to change (if anything) and to what color is not as baffling as it may seem.

Your window materials will harmonize with the room if they are either:

1. The same color as the *walls,* or
2. The same color as the *major upholstery,* or
3. The *accent color* of the room (reserved for small occasional chairs, pillows and accessories).

If you want to keep the window treatment as is, consider painting the walls or slipcovering the upholstery, if necessary for color harmony.

A *printed fabric* at the windows can be a great way to pull the disparate elements of a room together. (This

The new narrow-slat blinds are a refreshing change from their Venetian ancestors. Here they unobtrusively filter the light on a wall of sliding glass doors, below. Photos: Dan Forer

Vertical blinds, above, are also capable of very precise light control. Because they have a rather hard-edge look, vertical blinds seem most compatible in rooms with plush textures, soft furniture and rich colors.

another original look

LouverDrape Verticals–100 more choices in texture & color.

Now you can enjoy LouverDrape Vertical Blinds with the rich texture of fabric. Select the soft subtle effect of Hopsack Prints!or the richness of'Suede, each with its own special look. Choose from 50 colors, each in practical room darkening opaque or delicate translucent louvers that glow like stained glass, 100 choices in all. Select a single color or mix and match to create an original striped effect. The outside surface offers a uniform appearance with a white, specially created heat reflecting surface of durable solid vinyl; reducing heat, cutting air-conditioning loads and saving energy. Additionally, unlike horizontal blinds, vertical louvers don't catch dust, making maintenance a breeze. LouverDrape, there is a difference. Send $1.00 for our 32-page "Vertical Imagination" brochure. LouverDrape Inc., 1100 Colorado Avenue,Department 40 , Santa Monica, California 90401. For more information circle 40 on the Reader's Service Card

LouverDrape

works best if everything else is plain.) The print design should take color cues from walls, carpet and upholstery. The more colors repeated in the print, the more integral a part of the room it will seem.

Rooms facing south or west receive maximum sunlight which is also warm in color and temperature. Occasionally a room receives so much harsh afternoon sun that it seems too warm. Tone it down with materials that carry an illusion of coolness—tile floors, crisp white fabrics and narrow-slat blinds, soft blues and greens with lots of wicker and rattan.

A room facing north or east receives a cool light, thus you might want to make the room feel warmer with heavier window hangings and natural materials such as wood and brick for walls.

The noble French pleat that has traditionally gathered draperies into precise folds is gradually giving way to softer, more natural tailoring. Lightweight fabrics are often smocked or shirred. Crisp medium-weight fabrics make handsome balloon shades or tailored Roman shades. Try fat cartridge or double box pleats for fabrics and treatments that need a bit more control. Even velvets and quilted drapery panels adapt neatly to being shirred on a fat, round rod.

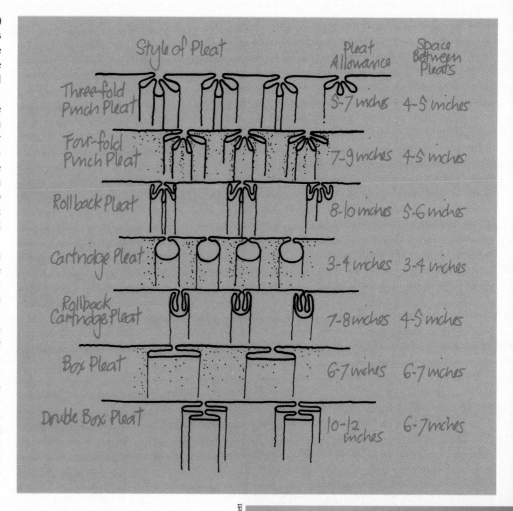

Style of Pleat	Pleat Allowance	Space Between Pleats
Three-fold Pinch Pleat	5-7 inches	4-5 inches
Four-fold Pinch Pleat	7-9 inches	4-5 inches
Rollback Pleat	8-10 inches	5-6 inches
Cartridge Pleat	3-4 inches	3-4 inches
Rollback Cartridge Pleat	7-8 inches	4-5 inches
Box Pleat	6-7 inches	6-7 inches
Double Box Pleat	10-12 inches	6-7 inches

DeLuca Brett

Dan Forer

Panels of fretwork, below, are an unusual and lovely way to filter the light (and disguise a poor view) in the bedroom.

Shirred fabric panels, above, add softness and texture to a room in a way that can't be matched by any other window treatment.

You <u>can</u> have beautiful windows.

You can do it…with a little help from Kirsch. Our full-color "Windows Beautiful"
shows you how…with 140 pages of ideas using Kirsch drapery hardware. Like the
elegant Vintage® traverse rod with Teflon-S® coating. Shown in antique gold. "Windows
Beautiful" and everything you need are at a fine store near you that carries Kirsch.
Or, to order book, send $1.95 plus 30¢ postage to Kirsch Co.,
Dept. GL-79, Sturgis, Michigan 49091.

Kirsch

Floor coverings

Ten tips on selecting a soft surface

Everette Short

There is nothing quite as luxurious as wall-to-wall carpeting in a room. There is probably nothing quite as expensive either!

Wall-to-wall carpeting adds elegance, warmth and softness; and it's probably the single most expensive item in any room. You can, however, achieve the same effect with area rugs (either a solid color cut from a roll of carpeting or with a room-sized carpet leaving a border of floor showing, or fitting exactly) and save the dollar or two a yard for installation wall-to-wall.

These soft floorcoverings have additional advantages, along with adding warmth to a room. Carpet laid wall-to-wall expands the size of a room. So if you have a warren of small rooms, or odd-sized rooms, wall-to-wall carpeting is another way of increasing its size.

Although carpeting is frequently chosen in a contrasting or darker color than the walls, choosing a similar tone as part of a monochromatic scheme will further increase its room-expanding qualities.

Carpeting also cuts down on the clatter of footsteps, deadening sounds within a room—one reason why it has so many devotees for the kitchen. It's also practical for that reason on stairs and heavily-trafficked halls. If you do carpet the stairs, choose a good quality carpet and buy a few extra feet so the carpet can be moved along after a few years when the edge of the stairs becomes worn.

Although the choice of carpet vs. hardwood floors or ceramic tiling is a very individual one for each room in your home, here are some tips that will help you make a happy choice.

Carpet (also called broadloom) most frequently comes in 12′ lengths. Although the store you buy from will measure, you can get a rough idea of the number of yards you need before you shop. If your room is over 12′ wide, the carpet will have to be pieced and there will probably be a good deal of waste. (When you figure, remember that there are nine square feet in a square yard.)

● Never save money by *not* buying padding. Unless you are buying very expensive wool carpet, you will probably be purchasing tufted carpet which accounts for well over 90% of production in this country. With that process there is no yarn in the back and you're walking only on the pile you see. Padding adds to the "bounce" of the carpet and prolongs its wear life.

● Put the better part of your carpet budget in the rooms that will get hard usage. If your living room is a front parlor, only for show, get a better grade in the family room or children's room and certainly on the stairs.

● Use area rugs to define activity centers within a room. Broadloom, cut to the right size and fringed, will define the conversation area in the living room, with another rug in the same or contrasting color setting off the dining table and chairs.

● Generally speaking, the tighter the twist of the yarn and the closer together the individual tufts in a row, the better

quality the carpet is. In shags, however, density is not an important factor.

● Use tight loops or twists in the heavy traffic areas. Often these carpets are considered "commercial" or "contract" grades. If they'll stand the wear in a hotel or office, they'll do the same in your home!

● Use carpet to carry out your color scheme. When choosing the grade for your halls and stairs, think how it will look from the open door of your living room, dining room etc.

● In areas of the country with high humidity and areas of your home with less than perfect ventilation such as the basement, kitchen and bathroom, choose carpet with backing that resists moisture and mildew. At the same time, be sure and pick a fiber that is synthetic, since the natural fibers are not mildew-proof.

● Mate carpet textures to your furniture style. A plush is perfect for very formal French styles of all periods, while a shag is preferred for casual or country periods. Early American or colonial will look handsome with a twist, a loop or a saxony, the term for a combination of plush and shag.

Mediterranean can take almost any carpet construction, provided it's in a rich color that will balance the dark-toned woods. The English periods, like Mediterranean, can take almost any carpet provided it balances with the dark woods of the period. As for modern and contemporary, choose a shag or a saxony, even a twist to carry out the proper mood.

Carpet fiber chart

Generic name	Characteristics	Suitable rooms
Wool	Luxurious, the standard which other fibers are measured against, high soil resistance, expensive	Any room
Nylon	Extremely strong, resistant to abrasion, excellent color retention, mildew-resistant	Any room
Acrylic	Most like wool in feel, very resilient and quite resistant to abrasion and soiling. Mildew-resistant.	Any room, including kitchens
Polyester	Soft "hand" and feel, brilliant colors, resilient, easily cleaned	Bedrooms and other low traffic areas
Olefin (polypropelene)	Very strong, most stain-resistant, low moisture absorbency, easy to clean	Especially good in kitchens, bathrooms

ARMSTRONG DESIGNER ☼ SOLARIAN®
THE ONLY NO-WAX FLOOR WITH THE RICHNESS OF INLAID COLOR.™

For the great new ease in living . . . The Great Room. A big, beautiful merger of kitchen-dining-family rooms. And the great floor for The Great Room . . . Cobble Square Designer Solarian, pattern 8922

INLAID COLOR:
A BEAUTIFUL DIFFERENCE
YOU CAN'T MISS.

Most vinyl floors have their colors and patterns just printed on. But Designer Solarian is different. And that difference is called Inlaid Color. It's Armstrong's exclusive process that builds up the color and pattern with thousands of varicolored vinyl granules. The result is a richness of color and a uniquely "crafted" look that no printed flooring can begin to match.

Inlaid Color begins with the precise placement of varicolored granules onto the backing . . .

gradually building up the design—color by color, shade by shade.

Once the pattern is complete, intense pressure and heat are applied— fusing it into a solid inlaid vinyl.

And when the Mirabond® wear surface is applied, the Inlaid Color is sealed with a lasting protection and shine.

ANOTHER BEAUTIFUL DIFFERENCE:
THE NO-WAX SHINE THAT
LASTS LONGER.

Most no-wax floors have ordinary vinyl surfaces which soon dull from scuffs and scratches. But Solarian has Armstrong's exclusive extra-durable Mirabond wear surface which—along with protecting the Inlaid Color and pattern—keeps its lustrous "like-new" look without waxing far longer than ordinary vinyl surfaces. And by eliminating the waxing chore, Mirabond makes Solarian the easiest of all Armstrong floors to care for. To keep it clean and shining, just sponge-mop with detergent, and rinse thoroughly. (If a reduction in gloss should occur in heavy-traffic areas, Armstrong Suncoat™ can be applied to help maintain the shine.)

ONCE 'N DONE™:
THE NEW EASY WAY TO
KEEP SOLARIAN FLOORS CLEAN.

The easiest way to keep any Solarian floor looking its best is with new Once 'n Done *No-Rinse* Cleaner. Developed especially for Solarian floors and available only at your Armstrong retailer, it saves you the chore of rinsing and leaves no dulling dirt-catching film.

To find your nearest Armstrong retailer, look in the Yellow Pages under "Floor Materials." Or use the coupon at right for retailer names and free booklet from Armstrong.

Floor design copyrighted by Armstrong

THERE ARE LOTS OF THINGS YOU SHOULD KNOW BEFORE YOU BUY A NEW FLOOR. AND THEY'RE ALL IN THIS FREE BOOKLET FROM ARMSTRONG.

If you're in the market for a new floor, you're ready to make a major investment for your home . . . one you expect to live with for a long time to come. So the time to learn all you can about all the features, functions, and options available in today's resilient floors is *before* you buy. And Armstrong's new consumer guide, "How to Buy Resilient Flooring," will give you all the help you need.

Whether you're planning to "do it yourself" or you prefer professional installation, this 20-page booklet offers all kinds of valuable tips to help make your shopping easier . . . and more fun. Things like . . .

- What to know before you begin shopping.
- How to select a flooring retailer.
- Questions to ask while shopping.
- What to look for in flooring features.
- A photo showcase of Armstrong's most popular floors.

There's an Armstrong floor just right for you . . . for your decor, your life-style, your budget. And one with the durability and maintenance features you expect. Let "How to Buy Resilient Flooring" help you find the floor you're looking for.

Send for your free copy plus names of your nearest Armstrong retailers today! Write Armstrong, Department 97FMH, Lancaster, Pa. 17604. Or circle 27 on the Reader's Service Card following the Index.

CREATORS OF ■ THE INDOOR WORLD®

For more information circle 27 on the Reader's Service Card following the Index.

Resilient flooring may be your answer...

Don't just think "kitchen" when you consider resilient flooring for your new home. Yes, these hard surface coverings are dandy for kitchens, but they're also perfect for foyers, dining rooms, family rooms ... every room in your home.

Some resilient types can only be installed above grade, but most can be used both above and below. Some come in tiles, while others are available in widths of 6 feet and 12 feet. All are perfect for the do-it-yourselfer, whether they're the type to be pressed on, stapled or adhesived.

The array of patterns available is breathtaking, mating with all periods of furnishings. Indeed, they are the perfect answer for all but the most formal homes.

Resilient flooring is, of course, an apt answer in kitchens, bathrooms and family rooms, but if you have a noise problem, keep carpeting in halls and stairs.

The no-wax flooring makes for easy maintenance, and some of these are cushioned to give almost the same comfort as carpet. Easy-care properties make resilient flooring a candidate for the family room with the seating area defined warmly with a rug. Consider it too for the bedroom, where, once again, the bedside sports a small throw rug. And, of course, by all means, use it in

the children's rooms where a hard surface for game playing or dancing is pretty much a "must."

There is a greater variety of design available in the sheet goods than the tiles and, of course, the sheet vinyl or asphalt gives an uninterrupted look to the floor, expanding the space.

Vinyl asbestos or solid vinyl tiles, on the other hand, lend themselves to quick solutions. Some tiles have adhesives on the back, while others need a special glue. Those with self-adhesive backs can be installed in just an hour or two. But if you feel like a designing woman (or man), you can take graph paper and create a super-graphic design in a combination of colors. With such a wide choice of designs to choose from—solid colors, simulated marble, stone, wood, brick, mosaic—it's possible to turn a very small area like a mudroom or a bath into something quite unique. The tiles are 12 inches square so it's easy to map out your grand design on graph paper with magic markers before you make your purchase.

Harold Davis

Look what's happened to attached pad carpeting!

It's in the living room right underneath your Queen Anne chair, or your antique love seat.

Once, the only place you wanted attached pad carpeting was in the basement. Or in the kitchen. But that was before VORACEL* Brand Urethane Backing.

Now you can have all the luxury of high-style, high-quality carpeting with the incredible benefits of urethane attached padding. For any room in your house.

VORACEL is a new, innovative concept in carpet padding. A concept that has revolutionized attached pad

carpeting. And it's created by Dow. The urethane experts.

Unlike traditional rubber or foam, the carpet fibers are tuft-locked right into the urethane padding. Not just glued on.

Carpet with VORACEL attached padding stands up to all kinds of wear—that other types of attached pads can't. Like kids. Furniture. Heavy traffic.

You get all the comfort a luxury carpet affords. With excellent resiliency and durability.

And VORACEL attached padding is moisture resistant. It won't absorb spills. And it won't mold, mildew or smell. A

great advantage over rubber or foam.

It won't shrink—no matter how often it's cleaned.

And so easy to install you can even do it yourself!

VORACEL* Brand Urethane Backing. It's the best thing that's happened to carpeting.

Available on these fine carpets: Aldon, Barwick, Galaxy and Trend.

 **Created by Dow**
Brand Urethane Backing

DOW CHEMICAL U.S.A.
*Trademark of The Chemical Company

...or perhaps a more permanent wood or ceramic tile floor

Hard floors can be either wood or made of natural materials such as brick, slate, stone terrazzo, marble or ceramic tiling.

All of them are expensive to install, are permanent, yet almost impervious to damage.

If you have bought a house with wood flooring, you may save a packet of money by just refinishing the floors. Sanders can be rented and the floors sealed afterwards with polyurethane. (Flip the page for more information on treating wood floors.) There are even hardwood tiles in six-inch squares, sold at Home Improvement Centers that you can lay yourself. They come with foam backs for cushioning, are available in several wood colors and have borders and threshholds that match for the perimeter of the room.

Other hard surface floorings have become more and more popular for indoor use as the casual look—baskets, plants, wicker furniture—becomes endemic, no matter what the climate.

Ceramic tiling, quarry tiles, brick, stone, slate, terrazzo and marble—all of these natural materials are practical for kitchen, bathroom, entryway, living room and dining room. They are, how-

ever, often used in conjunction with an area rug that is firmly secured to prevent slipping. Remember, these materials are dangerous when wet!

All of these materials are, however, reflectors of sound, and homemakers with many small appliances object to their use in the kitchen. They are, of course, also cold—an advantage or disadvantage, depending on where you live.

Advances have been made recently in ceramic tiling. They are available in a wide variety of designs and colors that can be used with all except the most formal furniture styles. The tiles comes in sheets, so it is no longer necessary to lay them one by one. Grouting, which is applied between the tiles after they have been laid, now comes in colors so it's possible to create interesting effects by setting off different areas within a room.

Ceramic tiling is installed over other tile, on plywood or other wood flooring that is smooth and clean. The adhesives are quick-setting, and the tools which are needed, like those for hardwood tiles, can be rented from a Home Improvement Center. All of these nonwood hard surface floorings need just a sweeping, never polish.

Free Information Center.
For products, planning, decorating and remodeling.

Many of the advertisers in the HomeBook are offering free full-color catalogs to HomeBook readers. Just turn to the back of the book and circle the catalogs you want on the postage-paid postcards. Drop your card in the mail, and we'll send back the catalogs you requested as soon as possible. Often as fast as three days of receiving your request. So that very quickly the information you need will be found right in your new mailbox.

More help from the HomeBook.

FOR 30 YEARS CONSUMERS HA VINYL FLOORIN EYES CLOSED.

It's really not anyone's fault.

It's just that over the years, vinyl floor manufacturers have shown people plenty of shiny floors in spotless, unlived-in rooms, and given them almost no information about vinyl floors themselves.

And so we at GAF—the makers of Gafstar® sheet vinyl and floor tiles—decided it was high time that someone opened people's eyes.

THERE'S A LOT TO LOOK FOR IN ADDITION TO LOOKS.

Before you decide on the fun stuff like color and design, there are a lot of other considerations to make. Like how long you want your vinyl floor to last. Unless you're either very fickle or very rich, you'll probably want it to be around for several years. So the first thing you should know is how well-armed a vinyl floor is against the assaults of everyday family life. Most Gafstar floors are topped

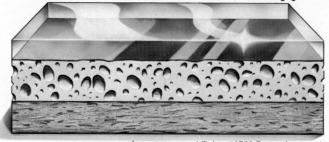

A cross section of Gafstar®6700 Series sheet vinyl.

with a tough, transparent wear-layer. There to provide an extra layer of protection between your floor and your family.

THE RIGHT FLOOR FOR THE RIGHT ROOM.

Different rooms demand different things from vinyl floor. An entrance room floor is greeted by a lot more foot steps than a sitting room floor.

A playroom floor has to put up with falling toys and noisy kids; a dining room floor, with massive furniture and a lot of spills.

And while it would be nice to think that all vinyl floors are perfect for all rooms, it simply isn't true.

So at GAF we specifically make certain floors to satisfy certain conditions. Some are amazingly resistant to abrasion; others to impact or indentation; and still others to liquids or sound resonance.

AMERICAN
E BEEN BUYING
G WITH THEIR

Gafstar®6700 Series sheet vinyl.

vinyl floors, there are certain things that have been — pardon the expression — swept under the rug. Contrary to what some people would like you to believe, all no-wax floors — even our own Gafstar® Brite Bond™ Floor Tile — require a degree of care. They should be mopped occasionally. And after a long while, you might want to apply a vinyl dressing to restore the floor to its original dazzle.

THE BEAUTIFUL PART.

Once you have looked into all there is to know about vinyl floors, you are finally ready to look at the designs themselves. This, of course, is largely a matter of personal taste. Just make sure that you expose yourself to a wealth of possibilities. At GAF we realize that there is no point in making great floors unless they're great-looking as well. So we've assembled an eye-boggling collection of colors and styles, representing every design point-of-view imaginable.

We hope we've answered some of your questions about vinyl flooring. In coming ads we'll try to answer more. Because the way we see it, the more we open your eyes about vinyl flooring, the more likely you'll be to look our way.

A VINYL FLOOR'S ULTIMATE TEST: THE KITCHEN.

No floor is abused like the kitchen floor. On it come the footsteps from the entrance hall, the toys from the playroom, the mud from the backyard and all kinds of potentially damaging household liquids. Which is why GAF makes a whole range of floors that are amazingly resistant to almost everything. They may cost a little more, but for the money you simply can't buy a better floor.

WHAT DOES NO-WAX FLOORING **REALLY** MEAN?

While there are many glowing things to be said about no-wax

GAF® **GAFSTAR**®
VINYL FLOORING
WE'RE OPENING PEOPLE'S EYES UP ABOUT VINYL FLOORING.

Webb AgPhoto

1   2

Kent Oppenheimer

Budget ways with floors

Although there's something to be said for beautiful floors, there's also something to be said about the budget. It can be stretched just so far in a new house.

Happily, there are inexpensive ways of handling floors that are stylish. Many of them won't last forever, but they will give you a breathing space until the bank account grows.

But be forewarned, the trade-off for money is time, and many of them will eat up your weekends for some time.

The easiest is to take broadloom you've used in your previous home, have it rebound as an area rug in one of your living areas, 1. Another carpet trick is to buy the large samples or remnants in your Home Improvement Center or at sale time in a furniture or department store. The pieces can be designed into a checkerboard pattern, with heavy-duty carpet tape on the back to keep the pieces from coming apart. (And, if you

like that look, there are carpet tiles which can be pressed right down on the floor.)

If you want to stick with your hardwood floors, there are several stylish ways to handle them. Wood, especially when laid in boards rather than parquet, can be painted with a high-gloss color. There are several brands made just for floors in a wide range of colors.

Hardwood floors can also be stained in different colors, as well as natural wood tones. The floor should, however, be sanded both before and after. And with both painting or staining, seal the floor to keep the color longer.

Perhaps the most chic look in hardwood floors today is bleaching, 2. With this process, the floor is first sanded to eliminate roughness. Then the bleach is applied with a long-handled brush—and keep your windows open to get rid of the fumes. After the bleaching, sand the

Harold Davis

Harold Davis

Darwin K. Davidson

E. Short

5

6

3

4

floor again and cover with polyurethane.

Another painting technique is stenciling. It's done on floors just as it's done on other furnishings, often on bleached floors as a border, 3, or if the whole floor is in bad shape, the entire area is covered, 4. It might even be simply the painting of a zebra on asphalt tile—instead of buying the endangered species! 6.

With the development of polyurethane finishes, which will last about a year under hard usage, it's possible to cover the floor with more unusual floor coverings.

There really isn't any reason why you can't wallpaper a floor, as well as a wall, and then seal it.

What's more, if you fall in love with a fabric, why not floor it? Either in the form of a fabric rug, 5, or just with glue, then sealed with polyurethane. There are endless possibilities.

137

Bigelow

Beauty you can believe in.

A SPERRY AND HUTCHINSON COMPANY

You've been through a lot. Now relax. And read about what's new in carpet for your home.

1.

[Th]ere's fabulous fashion [ne]ws in carpet now and [tec]hnology made it possible.

Bigelow technology brings you beautiful new soft carpet. The [ho]t, soft colors and never-before, [silky] soft textures work hard for you. [From] frosted highlights and subtle [ton]e-on-tone shadings to high-low [text]ures and subdued prints...any of [the]se looks work beautifully no [mat]ter what the period or style of [your] home.

2.

There's a new classification system for carpet called the Mark of Performance.™

It tells you what carpet is best for your family's needs. Only Bigelow has this system, and we have it on every Bigelow carpet. There are four traffic categories from I for seldom-used places like guest rooms to IV for stairs, hallways, playrooms, the heavy traffic areas. Select the right Bigelow traffic mark for each room and your carpets will look beautiful longer and save you money in the long run.

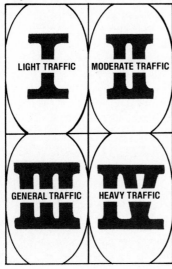

LIGHT TRAFFIC   MODERATE TRAFFIC

GENERAL TRAFFIC   HEAVY TRAFFIC

3.

The big news in carpet care is — you don't have to clean it as often. If it's a Bigelow!

Every Bigelow is treated with Scotchgard® Carpet Protector to resist soil and stain. So your Bigelow carpet will stay clean twice as long as an untreated carpet. And when you <u>do</u> clean, it's easier. In heavy traffic areas, Scotchgard is an absolute must...anywhere, it's a pleasure.

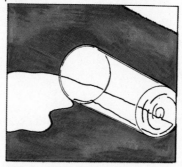

4.

A whole generation of new fibers is doing amazing things for carpet.

They absorb dyes with new clarity and richness...just look at the new Bigelows! Even that new luster comes from the way the fiber takes color. But fibers do more. They perk up when they're downtrodden. They hide soil. They almost refuse to wear out. That's because Bigelow is the leader in these latest techno-logical advances.

5.

New ideas in carpet are yours for the asking.

Bigelow incorporates all the fashion news you've been reading about and more in its new carpet collections. And Bigelow helps you decorate your new home beautifully with an up-to-the-minute guide called "Great Beginnings." It tells you everything you need to know about buying carpet wisely and how to live with it beautifully. After all, we're the experts, we've been making carpet for over 150 years. (Circle "Great Beginnings" on the reader service card.)

Bigelow-Sanford, Inc., P.O. Box 3089, Greenville, S.C. 29602

Great Beginnings

Your next smart move.

For more information circle 31 on the Reader's Service Card following the Index.

Ceilings

Look up for decorating design

3   James Brett

E. Short   1

2   Harold Davis

Next to walls, floors—and ceilings—are the largest areas in a room. Floors take hard thinking because they take hard use. But what about ceilings?

There are a dozen things you can do. Some cost more than others, some are easier than others. But all give a room a more finished look.

This bedroom, 1, for example, creates a cocoon when sheets are glued to the ceiling, as well as to the walls. Working with king-sized sheets eliminates the problem of matching seams, but, yes, it does take more than one person to put up.

Or fabric can be shirred, 2, and run on drapery rods. Then they're easily removed for cleaning. A third fabric treatment is to create a tent effect with shirred fabric, or fabric attached to the perimeter of the walls, ballooning down from the center of the ceiling.

If you're lucky enough to have a room with an old-fashioned tray ceiling, play it up, either by refinishing the wood or by covering it with wallpaper.

Or if you have moldings along the ceiling, or around a chandelier, paint them a different color for interest. And if you don't have moldings—but want

Hedrich-Blessing

4

6

5   Hickey-Robertson

Kent Oppenheimer

2 photos: Harold Davis

2 photos: Les Turnau

10

7 11

12

them—they're available in heavy rag paper. Put them up with small finishing nails to carry out your period room scheme, 3.

Wallpaper on the ceiling can balance the color in a room, 4, or it can be the same as the walls, creating a cocoon as fabric does, 5.

That old standby, paint, can be used either formally or informally. In a youngster's room, hobgoblins can be painted, 6. In a powder room, 7, the sky's the limit!

Another friendly fake is the polyurethane beam, designed to turn a square cube of a room into a Tudor mansion. The beams are featherlight, despite their weighty effect, 8.

Lumber can be used in other ways on ceilings. Here, they radiate around a dining table below. They're really stained moldings that surround painted stucco, 10.

Of course objects of all sorts can be attached to the ceiling...for wit, via an umbrella in a youngster's room, 11; for elegance, via a painting in a very contemporary living room, 12; for style, via fabric covering a light fixture, 13; or just to reflect upon...mirrors, 14.

2 photos: Harold Davis

9 14

8 13

Ernest Silva

Furnishings

How to find your style

You're an individual. Your family is unique. And you're lucky enough to live at a time when your home can reflect your personal style. Unlike your ancestors, you're not forced to live with one furniture style. Designs from traditional to contemporary; from formal to casual crowd the stores, waiting for you to say: "That's me."

Ironically, the very wealth of choices can make choosing difficult. Perhaps that's how the eclectic style was born. The eclectic room brings together Aunt Edith's patchwork quilt, an African mask, a Haitian cotton-covered modular sofa, a Shaker rocker—each element representing a different side of your family's nature, a particular interest, a personal point of view.

The key to success here is harmony; the disparate elements must have something in common. The objects described above, for instance are all from different times and places, yet they all share a rustic simplicity

The eclectic style is also casual, as in this sunny living room that mixes white-washed brick walls, bleached floors and low seating. Casual is simple, casual is eclectic, with its roots in many countries. It can combine with the nostalgia of turn-of-the-century Eastlake, with the Art Deco of the twenties or it can be the country look of French Provincial, the rustic earthiness of Mediterranean or English Jacobean. But whatever the derivation the decor is casual...relaxed.

At the other end of the spectrum is this paneled English living room with a handsome Chesterfield sofa. Its hallmark is formality, as well as comfort. Stepping inside it is going back to a more peaceful period, shutting today away. All of the French periods and many of the English and American and Italian ones are formal. If you choose to live graciously in this way, be prepared to spend more time caring for your home.

Which suits you best ... casual or formal? This chart will help you select the one that best suits your life-style.

Ernest Silva

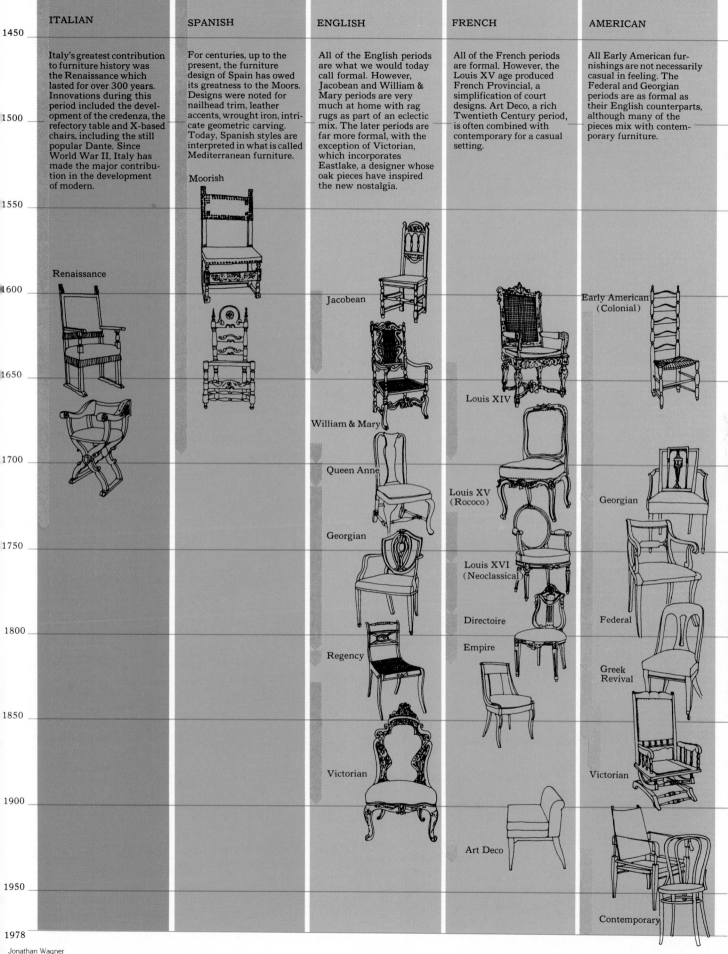

| 1450 | **ITALIAN** | **SPANISH** | **ENGLISH** | **FRENCH** | **AMERICAN** |

Italy's greatest contribution to furniture history was the Renaissance which lasted for over 300 years. Innovations during this period included the development of the credenza, the refectory table and X-based chairs, including the still popular Dante. Since World War II, Italy has made the major contribution in the development of modern.

For centuries, up to the present, the furniture design of Spain has owed its greatness to the Moors. Designs were noted for nailhead trim, leather accents, wrought iron, intricate geometric carving. Today, Spanish styles are interpreted in what is called Mediterranean furniture.

All of the English periods are what we would today call formal. However, Jacobean and William & Mary periods are very much at home with rag rugs as part of an eclectic mix. The later periods are far more formal, with the exception of Victorian, which incorporates Eastlake, a designer whose oak pieces have inspired the new nostalgia.

All of the French periods are formal. However, the Louis XV age produced French Provincial, a simplification of court designs. Art Deco, a rich Twentieth Century period, is often combined with contemporary for a casual setting.

All Early American furnishings are not necessarily casual in feeling. The Federal and Georgian periods are as formal as their English counterparts, although many of the pieces mix with contemporary furniture.

1500

1550 — Moorish

Renaissance

Jacobean

Early American (Colonial)

1600

Louis XIV

1650

William & Mary

Queen Anne

1700

Louis XV (Rococo)

Georgian

Georgian

Louis XVI (Neoclassical)

1750

Directoire

Federal

Regency

Empire

1800

Greek Revival

1850

Victorian

Art Deco

Victorian

1900

Contemporary

1950

1978

143

Terms you'll meet while furniture shopping

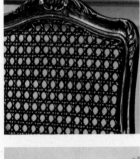

Acrylic—A man-made fiber used to make velvets and wool-look upholstery fabrics. Acrylics are easy to clean, take color well and resist fading. Also a rigid thermoplastic material used to make plastic casegoods. Attached molded pillowback—Sofa or chair cushions, which look like loose pillows, but can't be removed.

Batik—A fabric printed using the wax resist method. Real batik, often from Indonesia, is printed by hand, but machine-printed imitations, usually of cotton, are widely available.

Bentwood—Furniture made of wood that has been bent into curved forms after being softened by steam.

Bleached—A wood finish created by removing the wood's natural color to make the surface more uniform and to minimize graining.

Breuer chair—A cantilevered chair made of cane, chrome and wood, designed by 20th century architect and designer Marcel Breuer. Copies of his original design are widely available.

Burl—A wartlike growth in the bole or root of a tree. Burl is characterized by a pattern of "eyes"—actually undeveloped buds—and is used to make decorative veneers.

C.O.M.—Abbreviation for Customer's Own Material. Better grades of furniture are often sold C.O.M., allowing the customer to cover the piece in the fabric of her choice.

Campaign furniture—Furniture modeled on the portable furniture used by British Army officers in the field. Units were strengthened with metal edges and corners to withstand rough treatment.

Cane—Reedlike material obtained from palms or grasses, and used to make woven chair backs and seats, and to cover case furniture. On inexpensive furniture, a plastic substitute is sometimes used.

Canvas—A heavy cotton or linen fabric, similar to duck and sailcloth, currently popular for upholstery and available in many colors.

Case goods—The furniture industry's term for all non-upholstered furniture—tables, desks, chests—and particularly those pieces used for storage.

Chesterfield sofa—A heavily upholstered sofa with high, roll-over arms. The back and sides are often tufted.

Chintz—A thin cotton fabric, often printed, which is treated to give it a glazed or polished appearance.

Chipboard—A material in panel form, made by mixing wood chips with resins and binding agents and subjecting it to great heat and pressure. Panels are used as backings on cabinets and drawers and as cores for veneered furniture. Also called fiberboard, particle board and composition board.

Chrome—Plated metal, often tubular, covered with a thin layer of chromium, and used as trim and supports for contemporary furniture. The quality of chrome-plated furniture depends largely on the thickness of the chromium layer.

Custom-order—Furniture made to a customer's personal specifications, as opposed to stock furniture which must be purchased as it comes off the assembly line.

Distressed—A wood surface that has been gouged, scratched or spattered to make it look antique or rustic.

Étagère—A tall, freestanding, usually backless, set of shelves used to display books and brick-a-brac.

Fabric grade—A letter or number, appearing on the furniture tag, which indicates the price per yard of the upholstery fabrics available to cover that piece. The higher numbers and letters indicate higher-cost fabrics, but not necessarily greater durability, since certain costly fabrics are delicate.

Grain—The distinctive pattern of a particular wood, formed by a tree's growth rings and cell arrangement.

Hand-screened—Fabric or wallpaper, printed by hand, using silk-screens. In this process each color in a pattern is applied using a different screen, set in a wood frame. The screen is laid on the cloth or paper and a roller is used to apply color. Then, the next screen is laid down and the process is repeated until all the colors in the pattern have been printed.

Hardwood—Wood from deciduous trees—i.e., trees that lose their leaves each year. Common examples are oak, birch, maple and cherry.

Knock-down furniture—The furniture industry's term for furniture that the customer assembles herself. K-D furniture is usually less expensive and lighter in scale than assembled furniture.

No home should be without one.

Before you decorate, take this quiz.

Knowing your style makes decorating easy.

Turn your home into a French castle.

What is your living room saying about you?

Don't just furnish your bedroom. Decorate it.

Looking for a dining table? We can help.

Preplan your family room so it's adaptable.

There's more to decorating than furniture.

This is Thomasville's "Good ideas for furnishing your home."

And whether you're decorating your home or redecorating it, you'll find it very helpful.

It's a 350-page full-color decorating guide that'll show you how to plan rooms. Select window, wall, and floor treatments. And it'll take you "window-shopping" through the entire Thomasville line, helping you choose living room, dining room, and bedroom furniture in any major style. Or accent pieces that'll complement the style you already have.

So before you get anything for your home, get "Good ideas for furnishing your home."

An $8.50 value, you save $4.50 by sending $4 to Thomasville Furniture, Dept. 97TMH, Thomasville, N.C. 27360.

Thomasville®

FROM THE INDOOR WORLD® OF Armstrong

145

Sometimes called "life-style," "carry-away" or "self-assemble."

Kiln-dried—Lumber which has been dried under controlled conditions in a heated oven. Kiln-dried lumber is less subject than air-dried wood to warping, and is therefore used to make quality furniture frames.

Laminate—The process of gluing or bonding layers of material together. Also, a plastic product used like a veneer to cover furniture and counters.

Lawson sofa—A simple classic sofa with roll arms that are usually mid-height between the seat and the top of the back.

Leather—A natural hide, obtained most often from steers, which is used to make durable upholstery fabric and table-top finishes.

Loose pillowback—A casual sofa or chair style characterized by removable back cushions.

Modular furniture—Case goods and upholstery pieces sold in individual units that can be joined together to make larger units. Modulars are currently popular because they are easy to transport and can be combined in a variety of ways. Modular case goods are also called bunching units; upholstered pieces are sometimes called sectionals or pit groups.

Muslin—A plain-weave, bleached or unbleached cotton used as the under cover on upholstered furniture. Some decorators advise clients to buy upholstered furniture in muslin so that slip-covers can be changed seasonally.

Nylon—The strongest synthetic upholstery fabric.

Olefin—A man-made fiber with exceptional strength, soil resistance and abrasion resistance.

Open stock—Furniture that can be purchased separately or with matching pieces, as the customer chooses.

Peacock chair—A tall, wicker chair with high fan-shaped back, that originated in the Victorian era. Most peacock chairs are made in the Orient.

Plywood—A wood product created by joining thin veneers to a core. The veneers are laid so the grain of one layer runs perpendicular to the grain of the adjoining layer, increasing the strength and warp resistance.

Polyester—A cotton-like synthetic fiber with good wear-resistance and cleanability characteristics.

Quilting—Two layers of fabric filled with thin padding, which are joined together by stitching. Quilted fabrics are currently popular for upholstery. The most common styles are outline quilting (usually quite costly), in which the stitching follows a print fabric's design; channel quilting, in which parallel lines of stitching create puffed rows; and box quilting in which stitching forms squares.

Rattan—The stems of a palm species found in the Far East, which are cut into various thicknesses and woven into furniture. The best rattan furniture has smoothly finished ends.

Reproduction—A piece of furniture that copies exactly the materials and workmanship of an antique.

Softwood—Wood from evergreen trees such as pine, spruce, fir, cedar and redwood.

Soil-resistant finish—A stain-repellent chemical applied to fabric to help keep it clean.

Solid—Wood furniture in which all exposed parts are made of the wood indicated on the label—without veneer. Concealed parts—e.g., drawer backs and sides—can be made of another material.

T-cushion—A chair seat cushion which is roughly shaped like a T.

Tufting—An upholstery technique in which the cover fabric and padding are joined in a geometric pattern by tying them together. Self-covered buttons are usually added.

Tuxedo sofa—A simple sofa style in which the slightly flared arms are the same height as the back.

Veneer—A thin layer of wood that is applied over a core of solid wood or particle board to decorate furniture. Veneering allows manufacturers to offer costly, exotic woods at affordable prices.

Vinyl—A soft, leather-like plastic product used to make simulated leather, patent-look and suede-look upholstery fabrics.

Wicker—A generic term used to describe any furniture woven of rattan, thin strips of wood or twigs.

For free help in a hurry, turn to the back of the book.

Many of the advertisers in the HomeBook are offering free full-color catalogs with detailed product information and decorating ideas.

Refer to the back of the book to find descriptions of the free catalogs, along with postpaid cards for ordering them.

You send the card, and we'll send you the catalogs fast. Often it'll be mailed within three days after we get your request.

More help from the HomeBook.

Tips on furniture selection

Shopping for upholstery

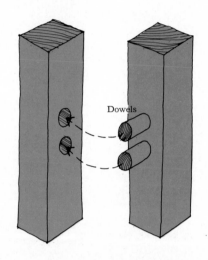

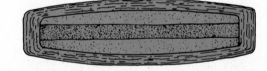

Dowels

You're ready to shop for upholstered furniture. You've heard this is a tricky proposition and, in a way, it is: Upholstery is made up of a number of components, the most important of which—the frame, springing and padding—can't be seen. How then can you determine quality.

If you're an inexperienced shopper, your best guarantee is to buy brand names from reputable stores, where experienced salespeople can guide you. A trained salesperson will be able to answer questions about the frame materials (kiln-dried hardwood is best), how it's put together (preferably with dowels, never with nails) and about springing.

In addition to asking questions, it's a good idea to examine the piece carefully and perform a few tests yourself.

Start by sitting down. It may seem obvious, but shoppers often forget that upholstered furniture, like shoes, must "fit" comfortably.

As you sit, examine the workmanship. Chances are good that if externals—the fabric, stitching, detailing—are well-crafted, the piece is of good quality throughout.

Test the joints of the frame by jiggling the arms. They shouldn't budge. As you sit, observe the front of the deck (the area on which the seat cushion rests). It should give uniformly under your weight, without sagging in the middle.

Now, stand up and lift the seat cushion. In a well-made piece, the deck will be covered in a fabric that closely matches the color of the upholstery fabric.

At the same time, look to see if the cushions have zippers. These are inserted to provide a better fit, not as you may think to make covers removable. (In fact, manufacturers caution that cleaning zippered covers separately may lead to uneven shrinking or fading.)

Cushions, whether filled with feathers and down or synthetic foam and batting, should feel free of lumps.

Now, check the fabric quality. This is best done by holding a swatch up to the light. If you can see through it, it probably won't hold up to daily use. Look, too, at how the fabric has been applied. Its grain should run straight and true to the lines of the piece. Patterns should match at seams. Skirts should hang straight and be even around the bottom.

Check the welting, if any, to make sure it's firmly sewn on, with no narrowing or widening at any point. Tug gently at any buttons to make sure they're secured.

Run your hand over any exposed wood. It should feel smooth to the touch, and the finish should be even and free of drips and thin spots.

The traits described apply to traditionally crafted upholstery—still the most popular kind. However, thanks to technological breakthroughs, new methods of construction are constantly evolving. Some furniture is sold unassembled; some is made of fabric-wrapped, molded foam; some of durable plastic covered with batting and fabric. These new, simpler constructions are often easier to understand and shop for, but even these should be checked for stability in use, good-quality fabrics and smooth, flawless finishes.

Shopping for bedding

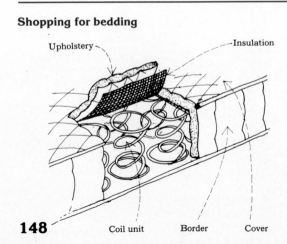

Upholstery

Insulation

Coil unit   Border   Cover

Buying a mattress and box spring is akin to buying upholstery, since most of the important construction features are concealed from view. The temptation is to select the prettiest ticking fabric and leave it at that. But, since most mattresses have a life-span of some 14 years, it's important to look beyond the pretty fabric and find out what you're getting in terms of comfort and wearability.

Conventional mattresses (not including waterbeds) come in two types: foam and coil spring. Because of its simplicity, foam—literally a slab of latex covered with fabric—is easier to judge and less expensive.

As with upholstered furniture, it's a good idea to buy a brand-name coil-spring mattress from a reputable dealer. If you do, you may have access to cutaway models of mattresses which should help you make your selection.

Coil-spring mattresses consist of steel coils—anywhere from 180 to 1,000 depending on the size of the mattress and its construction. (Bear in mind, however, that a higher number of coils does not necessarily indicate a better-quality mattress.)

The coils are topped by a synthetic fiber that prevents the upholstery from working down into the coils. On top of the fiber is a layer of foam padding to which the ticking fabric is quilted.

The best way to judge a bed is to lie down on it full-length. Although you may feel foolish, it's important to assume your normal sleeping position to test the bed's performance. If you share a bed with your spouse, it's a good idea for both of you to test it.

Check to see if the mattress has handles. (These are to facilitate turning, an important feature of mattress care.) Stitching should be smooth and free of pulls and the surface of the mattress should not feel bumpy.

Unless you own a fairly new box spring it should be replaced when you replace your mattress. The box spring is the foundation of the mattress; if it sags, the mattress will sag, too.

What size bed should you buy? This is very much a matter of personal taste, but you might keep in mind that the larger your bed, the more your linens will cost. You may feel, however, that this is outweighed by your need for comfort, particularly if you're tall. In fact, anyone over 5′ 10″ will probably be most comfortable on a bed that is at least 80 inches long as opposed to the standard 75. That means buying a king (76″ X 80″), a queen (60″ X 80″) or an extra-long twin (38″ X 80″).

Shopping for case goods

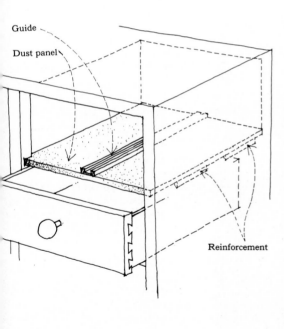

Guide
Dust panel
Reinforcement

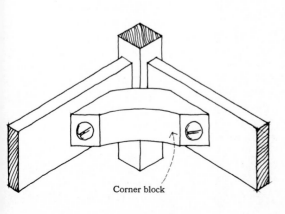

Corner block

Tables, chests, buffets, china closets—in the furniture industry, these and other non-upholstered items are known as case goods. Unlike upholstery, the construction features of most case goods are accessible and easy to examine if you know how. The three important factors to study are the materials, the construction methods and the finish.

These days, a case's interior core may be constructed of plywood, particle board or solid wood. Although the first two don't have the romantic connotations of wood, they are widely used, even in the finest furniture, because of their high resistance to warpage and their relatively low cost.

Over this foundation goes the surfacing material: it may be beautifully grained wood veneers; washable, scratch-resistant plastic laminate or even a paper-thin simulated wood surface created through a photoengraving process.

Sometimes case goods are made of solid wood throughout. For instance, much Scandinavian Modern and Early American furniture is made this way. When you see the word solid, it indicates that the visible parts of the item are made of the wood named on the label. Other parts, however, such as backs and drawer sides may be made of other materials.

Regardless of the materials used, certain construction features are desirable. Look for them. Drawers and doors, for instance should be well-fitted with edges that align with the edges of the case. To test, open and close them. Drawers should glide smoothly, separated by dust panels, and doors should open without catching or squeaking.

When buying a table, don't look at the top alone, take a peek underneath, too. In quality construction, corners where the legs join the top are reinforced with triangular blocks of wood screwed in place. These keep the table steady. In another test for stability, grasp the table top and jiggle it. It should not move.

Shopping for side chairs is much like shopping for upholstered chairs, and trying them out for comfort and strength is a must. Do this by sitting down and moving from side to side, then back and forth. Then, examine the underside, looking for the triangular reinforcing blocks described above. Check to see that stretchers and side rails are snugly joined to the legs.

If the piece has a wood finish—solid or veneered—it should be free of bubbles, streaks and runs. There should be no drips of varnish or stain on the insides of drawers or in crevices. Even distressed surfaces—those that are gouged and nicked to make them look old—should be stained and varnished clearly and evenly.

Surfaces finished with laminates should be free of bulges and hairline cracks. Check along edges and at corners to make sure the laminate is adhering firmly to the case. The same check should be made on wood-veneered furniture.

Finally, examine the interiors and backs of chests and cabinets and the undersides of tables. The finish should feel smooth and free of splinters and flaws. All inside and back surfaces should be finished in some way—at least varnished or painted—to protect against warpage and cracking. In the finest pieces, the backs will be finished almost as nicely as the front. This is important if you plan to place the piece in the middle of the room.

149

Jessie Walker

Putting in your personality

They're just like fingerprints...individual and uniquely your own. They're the accessories in your home. Some may be prized heirlooms, others dime-store finds, but whether they're inexpensive or priceless, where you put them and how you arrange them helps to make your home different from the one just down the block.

Whatever you collect, whatever you love, whatever your pastime, your interests, all are part of the accessory game. A beach bum? Then fill shelves with shells, perhaps spray-painted in silvery hues. A gardener? Then one perfect blossom in a dime-store flask. You say you are a clothes horse? Then hang pairs of gloves on hooks, or perhaps hats, ropes of beads, belts. Fishermen can hang flies, or show a collection on a tabletop, while wine lovers can build a narrow shelf and line up their favorite empties—not to mention a screen created with a montage of favorite labels. And along with the ubiquitous travel posters, gourmet travelers can frame or mount menus of memorable meals.

Not too many years ago, when everyone's home was traditionally English or French, there were rules for accessorizing, as well as for everything else. But with today's less formal, more maidless living, accessorizing etiquette has changed. Family photographs can be placed in the living room as well as in family quarters, and the creamer from Aunt Fanny's silver tea set can become the container for your field flowers.

So clean out your drawers and closets and turn the insides out. Skiis and ski poles are wonderfully graphic on walls. Ditto a bicycle, hung securely in an entryway. And don't think of shelves as just places to put books. A trayful of your collectibles can slide right in, photos can be propped up, scarves can hang down.

Just remember that the accessories in your home shouldn't clash with your life-style. Clean, contemporary living usually calls for clear, uncluttered surfaces while formal French and English welcomes wonderful groupings in and on tables.

Free Room Service!
It's all yours with the Ethan Allen Treasury.

Whether you're settling into 6 rooms or 16, here's all the decorating help you'll need. The Ethan Allen Treasury. It's free at your nearest Ethan Allen Gallery. Nearly 400 pages of inspiring ideas for decorating your new home <u>your</u> way—whether it's traditional, contemporary or a happy mixture.

Browsing through the Treasury will give you an idea of the wide collection of furnishings available at Ethan Allen. Everything—from four-poster beds to modular seating to that perfect brass candlestick—is displayed in homelike room settings to make it easier to see how everything might look in your new home. If you already know Ethan Allen, a visit to your new neighborhood Gallery will be like visiting an old friend. And some new friends, our interior designers, are waiting to help you decorate your new house.

The Ethan Allen Treasury. Free at your Ethan Allen Gallery. (No purchase necessary) You'll find your nearest Gallery in the Yellow Pages under "Furniture—Retail." If you can't come in, mail $7.50 plus your name and address to: Ethan Allen, Box 1066, Danbury, Connecticut 06810.

Ethan Allen Galleries © 1978 Ethan Allen, Inc.

Come on over to our house.
Look us up in the Yellow Pages.

Jessie Walker

E. Short   Harold Davis

China cabinets, both open and closed, are the traditional garb for dining room accessories. But the collection of plates or figures or dinner bells can just as easily rest on a series of shelves painted or papered to match the walls. A handsome collection of candlesticks, a plethora of paperweights or a series of saucers are also dining accessories.

If gourmet cooking is your hobby, or if your kitchen is a small one, don't restrict the tools of your art to the galley. A wall full of wooden spoons or a series of pegs for gaily-colored enamel pans can add to the enjoyment of entertaining, as well as freeing valuable storage space. The only taboos as far as art on the walls is to limit yourself to scenes that won't offend sensitive stomachs. Prints of dogs holding ducks in their mouths may be art, but they're best kept on living room or library walls.

The dining table itself is another place to display your collectibles. But if your yen is for small objects, place them on a tray that's easily moved out of the way when it's time to set for supper. Do consider this spot a highlight in your home that can show off an arrangement of boxes, miniature plants, small sculpture, gourds, plants or whatever you fancy. Put some of the pieces on lucite or painted blocks for varying heights and you even have a centerpiece.

Family rooms

The games you play are fair game for accessorizing the family room. Backgammon, chess and checkerboards are bold graphic wall decor, either on shelves or hooks. The checkers and chessmen, too, can be held in glass brandy snifters from the dime store.

For cardplayers, antique sets found at flea markets in box frames make marvelous montages. Or place family photos in quick frames, changing them from time to time as a moving display. Magazines and phonograph records can be heaped in baskets of the type that's used for firewood. Or place a picket fence in a corner and heap floor pillows inside it. Another corner can balance the room via a profusion of plants in pots to show off your collection of African violets or bromeliads.

Bedrooms

Bedrooms are boring and there's no need. The trick is to think big and balance the bulk of the bed and the dressers. On the walls, a rug of a quilt hung on window hardware or modern PVC plumbing. It's what you hang, not where that counts. Antique apparel, Indian blankets and pretty parasols are possibilities.

Or create a row of cubbies right over your bed and around the room, like the ones found in old-fashioned desks. Paint the outside the color of the walls and the inside a contrasting color so your collections will stand out. What collections? Jewelry that ordinarily stays in drawers now draped on pegs, petite piles of handkerchiefs, perfume bottles, silk flowers. If your bedroom doubles as an office, then cubbies are where you'll cluster pens and pencils.

Baskets are an inexpensive and attractive way to organize bedrooms. Tray shapes and closed boxes can comfort, holding a multitude of makeup needs on a dresser top, easy to look at and equally easy to keep clean.

152

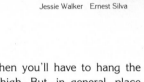

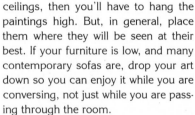

Phillip MacMillan James

Jessie Walker   Ernest Silva

Living rooms

This is the most formal, public area in your home. It's where you appear in your best dress and most carefully applied makeup. So it takes your most careful accessorizing. If your home is traditional, you'll stick to the rule book and place sterling, crystal and antiques on tables and oils and prints on the walls. If you're more informal and contemporary in your feeling, you'll feel freer to mix and match. If budget is a problem, think of several large accessories grouped together on a table rather than bits scattered about. A small Chinese chest next to a handsome glass ashtray and a terracotta planter on a large coffee table says more in impact than the three items placed separately elsewhere in your home.

For the walls, one large painting, perhaps hung off-center over your sofa, is better than a grouping of insignificant small ones and gives more excitement and style. And don't go by that old-fashioned rule book in deciding where to hang your wall art. If your house has more than the conventional eight-foot ceilings, then you'll have to hang the paintings high. But, in general, place them where they will be seen at their best. If your furniture is low, and many contemporary sofas are, drop your art down so you can enjoy it while you are conversing, not just while you are passing through the room.

Children's rooms

Children's rooms don't need accessories. Their lives are in full view, via open storage shelves that hold their books and games and hobbies. Let children's possessions become the natural focal point of your accessory hunt. Like the family room, their interests and hobbies come first.

This is the place for their own artwork. Simple moldings from the lumberyard arranged in rows become the guide rules between which you can slip in finger paintings, celebrity photos, school play programs . . . whatever they like.

When children are older, let them make their own wall art. A gluepot is all you need to form collages of corsages and bits of fabrics for girls, postage stamps and coins for boys. All held together in a wood frame that's been sprayed the color of the floor or the bedspread.

Other areas

Entryways are where you welcome your guests. Usually the floor space and the wall space is limited, broken by doors to other rooms. Use the space there to express yourself—showing interests and hobbies. Travelers can mount keys from hotel rooms or coins on felt and gourmets might frame favorite recipes, while gardeners take prints of flowers from books.

Stairs, too, can take graphics, while those leading to the basement or garage can be fitted with pegboard and hung with tools of the trade.

Hallways and landings lend themselves to floor-to-ceiling accessorizing. If there's room, shelves for books are a natural placement. If not, photos, prints, objects of all types can be hung on nails to make travel from room to room a more interesting journey.

153

Room arrangement

Here's how you put it all together

Start by putting your ideas on paper. Just pretend the ceilings are missing and look down on your rooms from above. For no matter how beautifully rooms are decorated, unless they suit the way you and your family want to live, you'll be working for them, but they won't work for you.

Take a look at the next two pages. Graph paper and what's called templates for the various pieces of furniture that may be on your list of what-to-buy for your home.

You'll need a measuring stick and pencil, and then go to work marking down the sizes of each room. Figure ¼ inch to a foot on the graph paper and draw an outline of the room on the boxes. Indicate doors, windows, electric outlets, fireplaces and built-ins. Then mark the way the doors swing so you won't be putting furniture in their way.

Now it's time to play paper dolls. Using the arrangement guidelines in this section, choose the pieces of furniture needed for each room and start to push the templates around. You can, by the way, cut them out, or by tracing, use them again and again.

Every room should have a center of interest, a focal point. If there's a fireplace, that's what it will be. If you're planning the family or living room, it might be the conversation group. But it may be a spectacular window view or treatment or a wall of built-ins. Whatever the case, it's usually the largest mass in a room that the eye is immediately attracted to.

When you have an arrangement that you think might work, put in dotted lines for the traffic patterns, using the table here as a guide. For living and family rooms, try to keep the seating areas away from "through" traffic that might disrupt conversations, and the telephone away from conversation or stereo. In the dining room, plan for the credenza or cart near the kitchen door to ease serving and meal removal. In other words, walk your activities list through the floor plan to make sure that the traffic patterns work for you.

Another thing you can learn from your floor plan is how successful your proposed color scheme will be. After the templates are all in place and you've checked the traffic pattern, pencil in your area rug (so you'll know what size to buy) and then lightly color the wall lines and floor and furniture. Add small dots for lamps and pillows too. This will help you balance the colors in a room. For example, if you're planning on blue walls and a green sofa with several yellow upholstered chairs, you'll want to use an area rug in greens and yellows under the conversation group to unify the grouping.

At the same time, watch your lighting. Every chair should have a lamp to light it, unless it's a very formal room that functions as a parlor. Every chair or sofa should also have a table within arm's reach.

Make more than one floor plan. This is the most important step in decorating your home, and from it flows your list of purchases. Place the most important pieces in the plan first, then the others. Ask your family to help. They may have ideas you never thought of!

After you have the perfect floor plan, put it away for a day or so. Then, take it out and restudy it. There may be changes you can make that you've never thought of.

Once the floor plan has *your* approval, you have the skeleton on which your decorating purchases will be made. Take a page of a lined pad for each room and rule vertical lines as shown. Attach each page to a manila envelope or staple a folder together. On the outside, mark your furniture, window, flooring etc. purchases with all the information in the proper columns. Inside the envelope or folder keep tear sheets of room ideas you've collected from magazines, swatches and color chips. Gather the envelopes together, along with a measuring tape, on each of your shopping expeditions.

As you make purchases, file bills of sale and care information within the same folder. Should you want to lodge a complaint or find out how to clean a particular possession, you'll have a complete dossier on your home...all in one place. You may want to keep them in an inexpensive cardboard filing drawer.

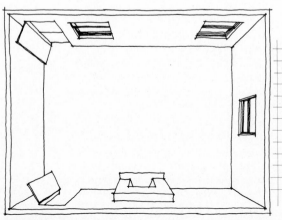
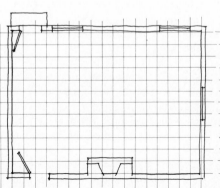
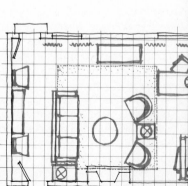

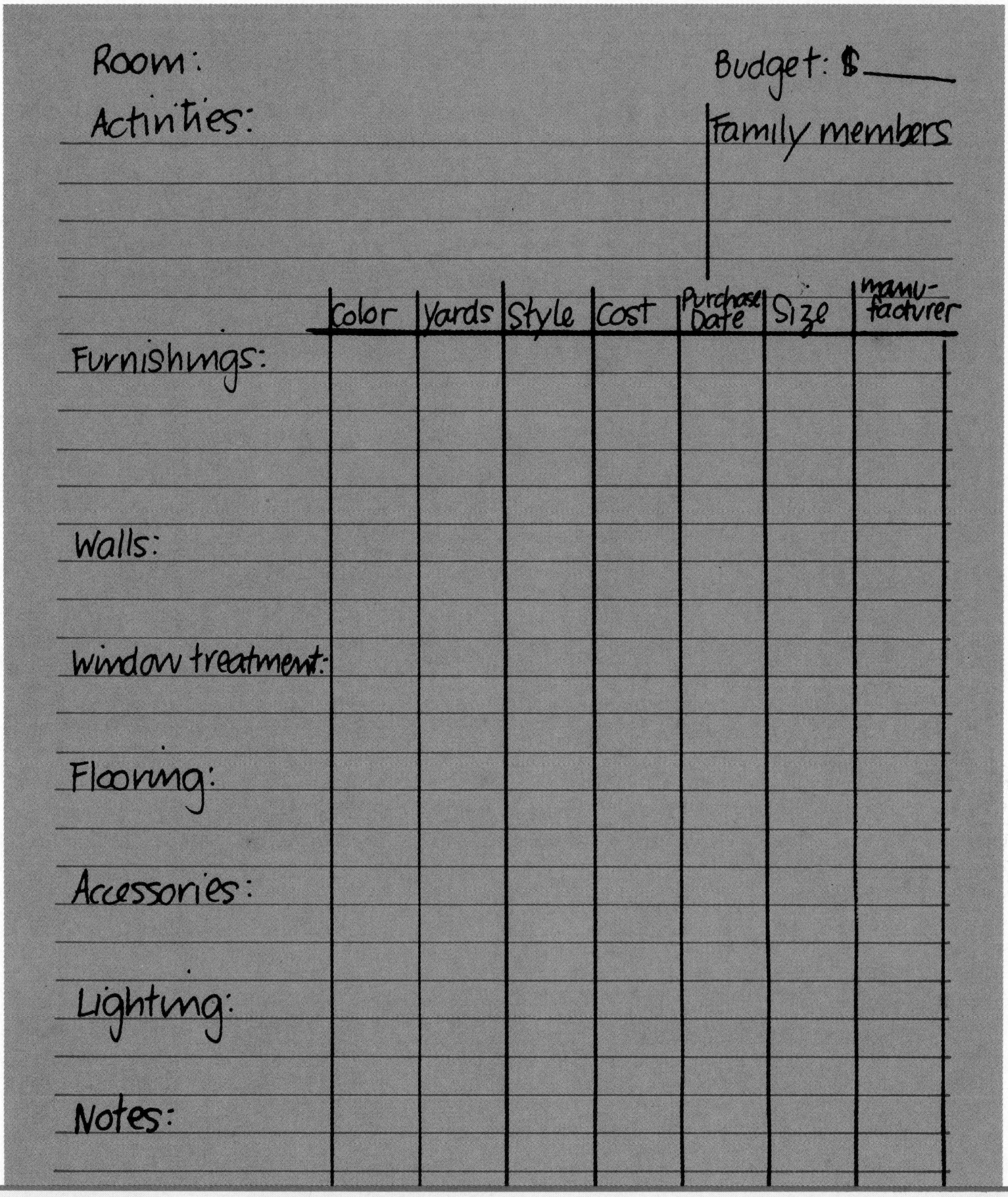

Room:

Activities:

Budget: $_____

Family members

	Color	Yards	Style	Cost	Purchase Date	Size	manu-facturer
Furnishings:							
Walls:							
Window treatment:							
Flooring:							
Accessories:							
Lighting:							
Notes:							

SPACE ALLOWANCES	MAJOR TRAFFIC PATH	3 FT TO 4 FT
	MINOR TRAFFIC PATH	1½ FT TO 2 FT
	DOORS TO ROOMS	3 FT
	FRONT DOOR OF HOUSE	4 FT
LIVING ROOM	SPACE BETWEEN SOFA OR CHAIR AND COFFEE TABLE	1 FT TO 1½ FT
	SPACE FOR FEET IN FRONT OF CHAIR OR SOFA	1½ FT TO 2½ FT
	SEATING SPACE AT DESK OR PIANO	3 FT
DINING ROOM	ROOM AT TABLE FOR EACH ADULT	20 INCHES TO 2 FT
	SPACE TO GET INTO DINING CHAIR	2 FT TO 3 FT
	SERVING SPACE BEHIND CHAIR	2 FT TO 3 FT
	SPACE FOR PUSHED-IN CHAIR AT DINING TABLE	1½ to 2 FT
SLEEPING AREA	SPACE FOR BEDMAKING	1½ to 2 FT
	SPACE IN FRONT OF CLOSET	3 FT
	SPACE IN FRONT OF CHEST	3 FT TO 4 FT
	SPACE FOR DRESSING	3 FT TO 4 FT
	SPACE FOR GETTING IN AND OUT OF BED	2½ FT

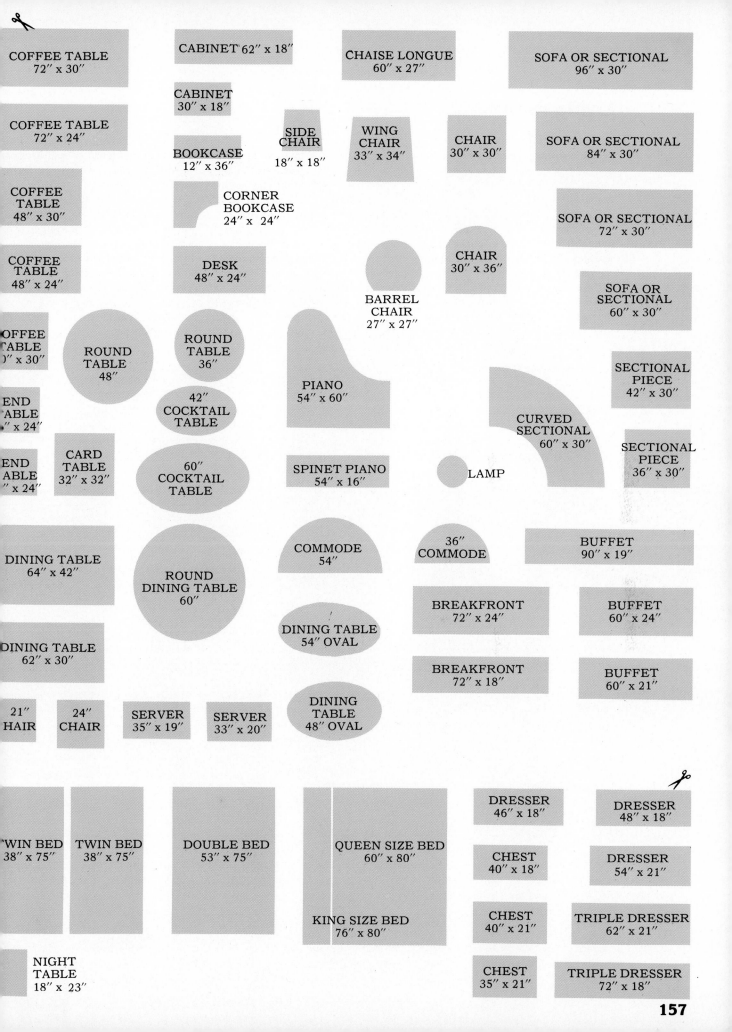

COFFEE TABLE
72″ x 30″

CABINET 62″ x 18″

CHAISE LONGUE
60″ x 27″

SOFA OR SECTIONAL
96″ x 30″

COFFEE TABLE
72″ x 24″

CABINET
30″ x 18″

BOOKCASE
12″ x 36″

SIDE
CHAIR
18″ x 18″

WING
CHAIR
33″ x 34″

CHAIR
30″ x 30″

SOFA OR SECTIONAL
84″ x 30″

COFFEE
TABLE
48″ x 30″

CORNER
BOOKCASE
24″ x 24″

SOFA OR SECTIONAL
72″ x 30″

COFFEE
TABLE
48″ x 24″

DESK
48″ x 24″

CHAIR
30″ x 36″

SOFA OR
SECTIONAL
60″ x 30″

BARREL
CHAIR
27″ x 27″

OFFEE
TABLE
0″ x 30″

ROUND
TABLE
48″

ROUND
TABLE
36″

SECTIONAL
PIECE
42″ x 30″

END
ABLE
″ x 24″

42″
COCKTAIL
TABLE

PIANO
54″ x 60″

CURVED
SECTIONAL
60″ x 30″

END
ABLE
″ x 24″

CARD
TABLE
32″ x 32″

60″
COCKTAIL
TABLE

SPINET PIANO
54″ x 16″

LAMP

SECTIONAL
PIECE
36″ x 30″

DINING TABLE
64″ x 42″

ROUND
DINING TABLE
60″

COMMODE
54″

36″
COMMODE

BUFFET
90″ x 19″

BREAKFRONT
72″ x 24″

BUFFET
60″ x 24″

DINING TABLE
62″ x 30″

DINING TABLE
54″ OVAL

BREAKFRONT
72″ x 18″

BUFFET
60″ x 21″

21″
HAIR

24″
CHAIR

SERVER
35″ x 19″

SERVER
33″ x 20″

DINING
TABLE
48″ OVAL

DRESSER
46″ x 18″

DRESSER
48″ x 18″

WIN BED
38″ x 75″

TWIN BED
38″ x 75″

DOUBLE BED
53″ x 75″

QUEEN SIZE BED
60″ x 80″

CHEST
40″ x 18″

DRESSER
54″ x 21″

CHEST
40″ x 21″

TRIPLE DRESSER
62″ x 21″

KING SIZE BED
76″ x 80″

NIGHT
TABLE
18″ x 23″

CHEST
35″ x 21″

TRIPLE DRESSER
72″ x 18″

157

Living room

The list of activities and the number of people who use it will determine how and with what you furnish the living room... and every other room in your home.

The living room is usually the most complex and difficult space in the home to furnish, because it is a "public" area and should reflect the interest of all the members in your family.

Make your list of activities and the materials needed to perform them with the help of the list on this page. Be sure to include the needs of guests, should you entertain in the living room.

Now begin your tally of furniture needs. You can, of course, keep storage functions in another room. For example, if you plan to set up a comfortable reading corner, you needn't put all the books you own in it.

If your living room only functions as such and you also have a dining room, family room and guest room, you are indeed blessed! Most families have to double up and make the living room perform as two or three rooms in their home. If that's the case in yours, you'll have to pick furnishings that perform more than one function—and a color scheme that makes your room seem larger than it really is.

Arrange your furniture to suit the activities that are most important to you and your family. If conversation and entertaining are your forte, then make the seating group the focal point. If, however, you use your living room quite privately, set up several groupings... one for reading, and another as a music corner. This is an ideal example of form following function.

Living Room Functions:

Reading
Playing music
Watching television
Entertaining
Overnight guests

Office work
Sewing and other crafts
Playing with children
Snacking
Dining

Good Furniture Choices:

Chairs and sofas that open into beds
Tables behind desks that double for dining
End tables with doors for storage of dining and entertaining needs
Nests of end tables
Modular sofas on wheels
Movable cart as an end table
End tables with shelves for books
Drop-leaf end tables
Ottomans and footstools with storage space
Drop-leaf tables that extend for dining, crafts, sewing
Coffee tables with stools stored underneath
Coffee tables with storage space for bottles
Tables with changeable heights
Bookcases with desk doors
Chairs that stack
Armoires that hold tv or stereo
Fold-up butler's tables
Mobile server tables
Swivel chairs

Dining room

Traditionally, the dining room provides a comfortable and peaceful place for meals. The dining table is in the center of the room surrounded by chairs with serving pieces, such as credenzas and china cabinets against the walls.

The luxury of a room that's used just for mealtimes is one that few can now afford, so the dining room has become a double or triple function room with totally different conformations.

The dining table need no longer be placed in the center of the room. Instead, there can be a long, narrow table against a wall, with chairs on either side.

Or, built-in banquettes.

The dining room can function as a quiet reading area off the kitchen, or as an office or library, a sewing or guest room—all secondary focal points in the area.

In some homes, the dining room can become a separate room, via folding doors, and function as a library or child's room with the mealtime functions given over to the kitchen, living room or even the entryway of the house.

Traffic patterns and serving space between walls and table are of great importance in the dining area or room.

It's wisest to "walk" a meal through your graph paper room arrangement all the way from setting the table to clearing it, as a way of making sure that your dinnerware is stored in a convenient spot and serving pieces are handily placed by the kitchen.

And make sure that the entrance between the kitchen and the dining area isn't blocked by furniture so you can get through it easily when your hands are full or you're carrying a tray. One reason, by the way, why swinging or folding doors are the preferred treatment on kitchens.

Dining Room Functions:

Family meals
Entertaining
Homework
Office work
Guest room
Sewing room
Greenhouse
Play area for children
Card playing
Studying
Reading

Good Furniture Choices:

Gateleg table
Harvest table
Stacking chairs
Modular bookcases with fold-up table
Modular upholstery
Server on wheels
Etagere
Space-expanding mirror
Space-expanding glass-topped table
Hanging shelves
Butlers' tray table
Glass-doored chests
Chests of drawers
Highboy
China cabinet
Semanier (Seven-drawered chest)

Bedroom

Bedrooms used to be occupied only at night and in the morning for sleeping and dressing functions. But no more. They now serve office and eating and reading functions, putting them on a twenty-four-hour-a-day schedule.

Since this is a very private area of the house, it's a place to experiment with color and design. It is, however, a room that must take certain furniture specifics: bed(s), mirror and chests or dressers, all of which are very large objects.

Beds should be placed away from the light and from drafts. Until recently, they had always been put on the long, unbroken wall of the bedroom, but now some beds have been designed to stand free so the walls can be used for the placement of chests or a small reading area with a chair and table, or a desk and chair.

If the bed is freestanding in the middle of the room, a sofa table can be used behind it for a lamp and books and refreshments. If the more conventional placement is used, make sure that there is a table surface at either side of the bed, as well as a proper light on either side or hung over the bed.

If the bedroom is shared, each person should have their own area. The chest of drawers, topped by a mirror, should be near the appropriate bed or side of the bed and near the closet where clothes are hung. This avoids a traffic jam in the morning and, once again, it's wise to walk the morning routine on a floor plan before moving furniture into its permanent place.

Of course if you live in an older house, the bedroom will give you plenty of room for sleeping and dressing furnishings and additional amenities such as pier mirrors, armoires and loveseats with tables.

Bedroom Functions:

Sleeping
Dressing
Watching T.V.
Eating (and/or snacking)

Listening to music
Sewing
Office or homework
Entertaining

Good Furniture Choices:

Headboard with shelf space and lights
Bed on casters
End tables with doors or drawers
Chest that doubles as footboard/bench
Armoire with built-in mirror and drawers
Modular bookcases with drop-leaf desk
Table with ottoman storage beneath
Chairs that match those in other rooms
Beds with drawer storage below
Drop-leaf tables
Tables that attach to walls and drop down
Pier mirror
Modular units with vanity/desk
Corner bed table
Trunks for storage and writing surfaces
Stacking floor pillows
Comfortable swivel chair

Family room

The family room is a peculiarly American invention. It replaces the traditional European family kitchen, although it's still frequently placed near the kitchen, especially when there are small children. Ideally, it's near the kitchen and away from the bedrooms, because this is where all the noisemaking, all the snacking, all the roof-raising is done.

You'll arrange the room into several areas. Perhaps one for television watching, another for playing cards, and a third for just plain conversation. You'll decorate the room with resilient floor-ing, plus an area rug; wallcoverings that are scrubbable; a ceiling that has been acoustically tiled; and furniture that can stand a lot of wear and tear.

Durability is obviously the key to purchasing, and flexibility is the key to the floor plan. With smooth-surface flooring and as much furniture as possible on wheels or easy to carry about, the family room is one of rather constant change as well as of great informality.

This is the room where built-in storage is most desirable to hold hobby and game-playing paraphernalia, sports equipment, entertaining necessities, musical instruments, records and tapes. Built-ins not only provide storage, but in this room, via window seats or room dividers, additional seating space as well.

Although the family room is a public area, like the living room, its furnishings can be very informal. This is the place to use spray-painted, hand-me-down furniture, rugs cut from wall-to-wall carpeting from your former home and less expensive knockdown, carry-home pieces.

Family Room Functions:

Conversations--adults
Conversations--children
Children's play room
Listening to music
Playing musical instruments
Playing cards, games
Watching television
Club meeting room
Hobby and crafts center
Snacking
Occasional Sleeping
Greenhouse
Occasional Mealtime
Reading

Good Furniture Choices:

Wall of modular pieces with doors, shelves, possibly pull-out table, desk
Card table with extension leaves on wheels
Stools
Cart on wheels
Floor pillows
Coffee table with storage space
Table with changeable height
Modular, movable upholstery
Extension table
Portable bar
Display cabinet with movable shelves
Etageres with movable shelves
Bunching or nesting tables
End tables with shelves or drawers
Server with shelves on wheels
Convertible sofa bed

Children's rooms

This is another room in your home that's in use twenty-four hours of the day. Functions that are shared by the bedroom, family room, dining room and living room are all found in this one place. Add the occasional sleep-over friend and you add the function of a guest room.

Like the family room, a child's room should have durable furnishings, not because they should be used forever, but because they'll receive lots of wear and tear.

Unlike living rooms, which tend to look unappetizing when the furniture is arranged around the four walls of the room, this is the ideal solution for a child's room. No matter what the age, children need plenty of floor space for playing games, using toys on wheels or learning the newest dance step. So combine the smoothness of resilient flooring with an area rug near their bed, and leave the room's center free.

As for furniture, use the wall space by building up, rather than crowding out the floor. (And if it's a shared bedroom you might, by the way, give the youngsters your larger master bedroom and bath.) Provide open shelves for youngsters and a combination of closed and open storage for the older ones. Try double-decker beds in a shared room, or a trundle bed for a visiting friend. You might even attach a table to a wall, rather than taking up permanent space with it, so it's only used when the finger-painting set or jigsaw puzzle comes out.

Shared bedrooms are more difficult to arrange. Use different colors that are compatible for each child, and separate the sleeping quarters from the desk or play area of the room, if you possibly can.

And, most important of all, let your youngster share in the decorating and they'll enjoy their new home doubly.

Child's Room Functions:

Sleeping
Eating
Homework
Playing
Dancing
Entertaining
Listening to Music
Reading
Guest room

Good Furniture Choices:

Trundle beds
Chairs that open into beds
Desk/vanities
Headboards with shelf space
Chests that double as benches
Swivel chairs on wheels
Modular chests with bookcases above
Semaniers (slim, seven-drawer chests)
Tables that nest
Corner bed tables
Dictionary stand
Floor pillows
Armoire for clothes storage
Fold-up table and chairs
Easel

Double duty: study/guest room/sewing room

Every room in the home performs more than one function, but sometimes it's necessary to make them do triple and quadruple duty. Some functions go together easily—like listening to music and reading—while others don't mesh at all.

Try to separate functions by the amount of concentration they need and the frequency they're performed to find the right room to put the activity in.

If, for example, you rarely have overnight guests, they could easily be lodged in the living room on a convertible sofa, with a screen put up for privacy and a luggage rack, paper chest of drawers and hangers in a nearby closet. If, however, guesting runs to week-long visits, there may be a better room that will please Aunt Matilda.

Sewing rooms and libraries and music rooms are other "spare rooms" that have been demoted to "area" as the size of houses shrinks. All of them need a fair amount of quietude for concentration and a fair amount of storage space. Which room you put the activities in is a very individual decision that is dependent on your family's interests and size.

Guest Room Furnishings:

- Bed or convertible sofa
- Drawer space or chest
- Closet space or hat rack
- Luggage rack
- Good lighting
- Screen for privacy
- Access to bathroom

Sewing Room Furnishings:

- Expandable table for cutting
- Modular storage for patterns, materials, sewing accessories
- Table for sewing machine
- Bench
- Good lighting
- Closet space for ironing board, dummy, etc.

Library/Music Room/Office Furnishings:

- Modular bookcases with open and closed storage space
- Desk with drawers
- File cabinet
- Game table
- Comfortable chairs
- Stacking or fold-up chairs
- Book stand
- Telephone access
- Music stand

Entrances, exits and connections

The foyer or entryway to your home should set the decorating mood. It's a way of welcoming guests and establishing your own individuality. Front entrances need good lighting, a place to put down packages and mail, as well as a closet nearby. A bench or chair (to help in taking overshoes on or off) plus a mirror are other gracious notes.

The foyer, if it's reasonably near the kitchen, can also be the place to set a buffet for guests or a Thanksgiving dinner via a gateleg table that can be expanded.

The color scheme of the foyer should be harmonious with the hall or stairs, or rooms that open off it. If the foyer is dark, use white or a light color that will expand and brighten the area.

Back doors used primarily by family and friends have the same needs. Good lighting, a place to store overcoats, and more importantly a box or shelf to line up boots is a must, if you live in a cold climate. Add a place to put packages on their way to the kitchen.

Halls and landings are the highways of your home. And like auto highways, plan on rest stops! If your halls are more than three feet wide, you may have room for valuable storage space via a built-in or store-bought bookcase, an étagère or even a set of small chairs that stands outside your living room and can be brought inside to accommodate additional guests.

Landings can even function as complete rooms. Perhaps yours can take a convertible sofa for an overnight guest or a traditional hope chest that will store linens outside the bathroom as well as sewing necessities. Add a tall mirror and you can move your portable sewing machine there when the other rooms in your home are occupied.

The trick is to examine every square foot of space, and then decorate it to serve you and your family.

Entryway Functions:

Storage of outer clothing
Entertaining of guests
Storage of out-of-season apparel
Home office

Entryway Furnishings:

Mirror and console table
Gateleg table
Built-in Banquette seating
Hat rack
Bench
Desk and chair
Good lighting

Back Door Functions:

Storage of outer clothing
Storage for out-of-season apparel
Pantry
Laundry area
Home office

Back Door Furnishings:

Built-in box for boots and seating
Shelf for packages
Laundry equipment
Storage for outdoor toys, games
Storage for out-of-season equipment
Desk and chair
Shelves for pantry

Stairs and Landings:

Storage of books, accessories, etc
Music or reading room
Guest room
Sewing room
Dining area
Workshop
Storage of linen, toys, etc.

Stairs and Landings:

Bookcases or étagères
Extra seating
Convertible sofa
Screen for privacy
Chest for storage
Bench
Desk and chair
Extension dining table

Books on How to Give Your Home the Tender Loving Care that Increases
Both PLEASURE and PROFIT!

See how easily you can be a wiz at home facelifts . . .
old-age prevention . . . rejuvenation . . . first aid . . .
major overhauling . . . individualization . . .
space-stretching . . . room-adding . . . burglar-proofing . . .
beautification . . . and tax reduction!

The House and Home
KITCHEN PLANNING GUIDE
Editors of The Housing Press (formerly House and Home). Your kitchen! Tiny or immense, it's the hub of your home. What it will cost (plus its adjacent facilities) to build or remodel depends on how you plan! Here are the facts, layouts, guidance, and pictures (over 500 photos, diagrams, charts, and tables) showing you ideas, design principles, techniques, and calculations to help you to plan right and to save you from errors, disappointment, and needless spending. $18.95

HOME LANDSCAPE
The Art of Home Landscaping. Revised, enlarged ed. Garrett Eckbo. Let this famous landscape architect's famous book (heavily revised) show you all about those "extra rooms" for living you can create out of doors—to fit every need, taste, type and size of lot, terrain problem—and budget! Its 100% practical guidance shows you easy, sure methods for blending beauty and utility. With 468 photos and other illustrations to help you visualize! $13.95

MORE FIRST AID FOR THE AILING HOUSE
Money-saving Ways to Improve Your House and Property. Robert C. Whitman. Robert Scharff, ed. Patch it, paint it, repair it, de-pest it, preserve it. The nation's longest-running syndicated do-it-yourself columnist tackles your thorniest house-and-grounds questions and gives you 1-2-3 answers to emergency and long-term fix-it, protect-it, improve-it problems—*without* recourse to slow, costly—often unnecessary—service calls. Illus. $15.95

YOU CAN GET YOUR REAL ESTATE TAXES REDUCED
Ronald E. Gettel. You're almost certainly paying much more than you should in real estate taxes. But how much more? 20%? 30%? 66%? This well-known real estate appraiser's guide shows you how to check out, challenge, and have your assessment changed—*without* filing an appeal. Remember, only the uninformed are overpaying. This book reveals many ways to get your real estate and property taxes lowered (some of them unknown even to professionals!). $15.95

BURGLARPROOF
A Complete Guide to Home Security. James E. Keogh and John Koster. Today, *every* neighborhood is wide open to break-ins and robberies. People are spending thousands to make their homes secure. But you can find out how to safeguard your family, your house, and everything in it for only $9.95! Lively, easy-to-follow, proven security techniques—knowing how a thief thinks, how to spot one beforehand, what makes your home "easy pickings," what you must do and *not* do to stop thieves cold, how to use the law—make this book a priceless possession! $9.95

HOW TO FARM YOUR BACKYARD
THE MULCH-ORGANIC WAY
Max Alth. Now you can read (and see!) all about today's easy, low-cost, *natural* way to farm your backyard for your table's bounty! If you have even one lazy bone in your body, you'll love the author's simple way to grow the most luscious vegetables, berries, and fruits you've ever tasted—without drudgery and without fertilizers, chemicals, and poisons. While mulch-organic farming is far from new, the method shown here is nothing short of magic! Illus. $9.95

FINISHING TOUCHES
Handmade, Inexpensive Ways to Make a House a Home. Jack Kramer. You really like your home. But something's missing—those personal finishing touches that make it *your* home and nobody else's. If you simply won't settle for an assembly-line look—no matter how "little" it may cost that way—here's just the book to show you (with 50 working, start-to-finish construction drawings) how you can stamp every room in your house with *your* character and taste! Plus 79 photos. $14.95

YOUR HOME IS MONEY
Managing Your Home for Profit. Editors of Consumer Guide®. Buying, selling, maintaining, managing, or renting a home? Whatever the transaction, especially today when real estate values are soaring, it's likely to be an extremely important one. How you can benefit financially from your property, including ways of making money without selling it, is what this book's all about. How to profit from prepaying the mortgage, refinancing, improving, adding—every step is explained and evaluated by the people at *Consumer's Guide.* Illus. $10.95

HOME EMERGENCY REPAIR BOOK
XyZYx Information Corporation. From now on there will be hundreds of electrical, plumbing, mechanical, cleaning, health, and other emergency jobs around your home that will never again seem complicated to you. Because this book gives you the right words and pictures to show you properly and exactly how they're done! Using techniques developed for Air Force mechanics, you'll save incredible amounts of time and money fixing it and doing it yourself! Illus. Paper, $6.95

HOMEOWNERS' ENCYCLOPEDIA OF HOUSE CONSTRUCTION
Morris Krieger. Before you call in a contractor, make sure *you* understand what's involved, the good and *the better* ways of handling a project, how much it should cost, what the inconveniences are, and whether you could do some jobs yourself. With this book in hand you probably *will* decide to use your increased skills with electrical and hot-water systems, foundations, plastering, septic tanks, wall framing, and much more! 350 illus. $19.95

MULTIPLY YOUR LIVING SPACE
How to Put an Addition on Your Home at a Cost You Can Afford. Dan Browne. How would you like, for instance, to build a simple 4000-square-foot extension, including a full bath, for $11.50 a square foot instead of $42? This remarkable "teaching book" not only shows you (100% clear how-to artwork) every step the inexperienced worker should take, but also where you can pick up a lot of your material (stone, wood, slate) for nothing or nearly nothing! $12.95

HOW TO FIX IT
Morton J. Schultz. Even real experts welcome this Schultz bestseller! With its 600 fully captioned photos and detailed text on every fix-it project imaginable, it pays for itself over and over, year after year. Nothing that needs fixing around the house is left out. It's perfect for every large and small job—simple, complex, next-to-impossible, and impossible—whether you've ever held a screwdriver or not! $11.00

A Threesome to Crown Your Collection!

The McGraw-Hill
HOME IMPROVEMENT LIBRARY
Over 1000 pages! Over 600 illustrations! Only $19.95
(You save over $17.00 over separate prices!)

IMPROVEMENTS THAT INCREASE THE VALUE OF YOUR HOUSE. *Hubbard C. Cobb.* Some improvements add value to your house. Some just cost you money! Knowing the difference—and *why*—and how to go about getting the work done right (either by someone else or yourself) is this book's job and it does it superbly!

THE COMPLETE BOOK OF HOME REMODELING. *Robert Scharff.* Your needs change, your tastes do too! Now, see how easily you can modify your home to meet the changing activities and patterns of your family's life. From basement to attic, every room and closet, every area both inside and outside, can be remodeled, added to, modernized, or created whole with this book's complete guidance.

HOW TO BE A FIX-IT GENIUS USING 7 SIMPLE TOOLS. *J. Stockwell and H. Holtje.* All thumbs? A dolt when a doorknob loosens? Never mind. If you own a hammer, a saw, a screwdriver, and 4 other inexpensive, simple tools, you're a fix-it genius with this amazing book at your (or your spouse's) elbow!

For more information circle 32 on the Reader's Service Card following the Index.

165

Decorating with color

How to save space and money with color

Color is power. Color is magic. Color is money. Want to make a room smaller? Use color and save the cost of an architect. Want to raise your ceilings? Color can do it. It can also make your furniture look less shabby, your walls further apart. It can make your cool bedroom warmer and more inviting, your dining area bigger.

Color is the most magical of all the decorating tools at your command. Here's how to use it:

How to warm or cool a room

Some colors are warm, others are cool. The warm hues are the yellows, the reds and the oranges. The cool ones are blue, green and violet. Take a room facing north and decorate it in reds or yellows. Suddenly, the room looks warmer and more inviting. Contrariwise, a blue, green or violet room will cool down a southern exposure.

The cool colors do more than just change the emotional temperature of a room. They also appear to retreat from the eye. That means that they appear to make a room larger, while the warm ones advance and invite, making a room seem smaller.

The cool, restful colors are generally chosen for areas like bedrooms where relaxation is important. Or perhaps a formal living room rather than an informal one where conviviality is more important.

Children's rooms are often decorated in reds or yellows, especially if they face north, as a way of energizing; and the same can be said of kitchens.

How to raise or lower ceilings

The wizardry of color can make your rooms look taller or bring down the ceiling of your house. Along with the color itself, there is its intensity . . . the shading from light to dark. Put a dark color on the ceiling, as in this cozy bedroom, and it seems to be lower than it was before. Still too high? Then bring the color down a foot or two on the walls and the ceiling appears even lower.

Light colors, or white, will make a room seem higher as will the light hues of colors. (And another noncolor decorating tip to raise the apparent roof is to put tall furnishings such as bookcases and skinny floor-to-ceiling paintings in a room to make its ceilings seem higher.)

Changing a room's dimensions

Color can make a long, narrow room seem squarer, a square room longer and narrower.

How? Don't paint or paper all the walls in the same color. If you're aiming for that long, narrow look, make two of the four walls a different, darker color or a different value of the same one. Or, if your aim is for a perfect square, then paint the smaller, side walls a ripe, warm color so they'll advance into the room, making the four walls seem of a similar size.

Room too large? Then use dark, deep values of colors—wine and brick rather than pink, sapphire and copen blue rather than sky blue. The more intense the colors seem to be, the more room they seem to need. The deep, dark tones close in space.

So obviously choose the pastels or the pale tones of colors if you wish to expand the walls, and add white as a noncolor that also increases spaces.

Unify a room

If you're faced with a problem room—perhaps odd-shaped windows, too many doors, or just too many jogs or strange beams, color will do the decorating job for you. Covering walls, upholstered furniture, windows and flooring in the same color for what is called a monochromatic color scheme unifies a room. Nothing stands out, nothing attracts the eye, and what remains is the brightness or conviviality of a warm color or the restful kindness of a cool one.

If, on the other hand, you wish to divide a room, color is far simpler to use than another wall, a screen or a barricade of furnishings, mid-room. One part of a room can be green, via a green wall, area rug and upholstery. The other part of the room can be defined with blues on wall, flooring and other furnishings.

That monochromatic color scheme can hide more than architectural defects. It can also hide a sofa that needs recovering. Once again, if a green sofa is placed against a green wall, what you will see is the effect of the color, not the shape and condition! The sofa will just blend into the background like a "wall flower."

Light-colored furnishings look larger and much more important if they are against dark walls than against light ones. Their outlines and shapes stand out more prominently—as do their defects. Of course, if you have new and beautiful furniture, choose a different color on the wall to show it off; but if you'd like to put your decorating dollars into something else, keep as little contrast as possible between the walls and furniture.

Texture and light

These are the tricks you play with color. But light and space play tricks on it. For example, light affects color and colors look different in sunlight than they do in incandescent or even candlelight. So make sure that you're looking at all the swatches and samples of fabric and rug and paint colors in the same light, and, if possible, in the room they'll be used in.

Texture also affects the way we perceive color. A red ceramic tile seems much livelier and brighter than the exact shade of red in velvet. So compensate for the texture difference in your color scheming.

Colors get bolder and brighter as the space you give them increases. A tiny blue paint chip will look much brighter when you cover a wall with it. The bigger the space, the bolder the color. It's better to err on the side of virtue than end up with floors or walls that vibrate when you look at them.

Lastly, remember that furniture has "color" too. Along with walls and floors and sofas, wood adds to the color feeling of a room. Dark woods, like mahogany and walnut, make a room more somber, while the new pale pines and ash pieces add a lightening note to a living room. Chrome and brass, as well as glass pieces and pastel-painted woods, are the room expanders.

Everette Short

The easy way to find your color scheme

But how do you choose a color scheme? It's really quite easy...but first you have to fall in love!

Fall in love with a painting, fall in love with wallpaper, a rug...and take your color scheme from it. Anything with a pattern—upholstery fabric, vinyl flooring, even an elegant toile lamp is a good place to start.

Not too many years ago there were definite rules about what colors went in what room of the home. Never red in the bedroom, never blue in a child's room. But no more. Color, whatever color you fancy, can go in any room of your home.

If you're unsure of how a color or a wallcovering will look, use it first in a private area of your home—the master bedroom or bath—before you apply it liberally to the living or dining room.

Now take that favorite upholstery fabric or painting and start your color scheming. Since walls are the largest area in your room, they should be decorated in the most neutral color of the pattern. The ceiling and floor are the next largest space for color in the room, so they should, ideally (and most safely) be the next brightest color from your sample, unless you're juggling as described on the previous page.

Then comes the window and upholstery fabrics and last the throw pillows

Ernest Silva

and accessories which become the bright little accent colors in the room.

In general, no more than three colors should be used for the large areas—walls, floors and upholstery color—although the colors can be repeated elsewhere in the room. Leave the pattern-on-pattern mix and the five-and-six-color rooms to the experts, who've had years of practice.

Historically, pale colors tend to be used in formal and period rooms, as shown in this living room, while the bright primaries are associated with a more contemporary look.

The color scheme in this living room was based on the elegant rug design.

Cream colors the walls, as well as the major part of the rug. But the blue in the design was repeated in draperies and upholstery, while the raspberry is an accent for the pull-up chair and throw pillows. The use of two rugs rather than wall-to-wall carpet makes the room look smaller, but it neatly serves to divide the dining from the living room function.

If your color scheme seems to lack this kind of contrast, then find contrast in texture rather than color. A monochromatic scheme, just about the easiest thing to do, gains excitement from the slick look of vinyl or ceramic flooring, chrome and glass surfaces as contrasted with the nubby feel of carpeting

and tweedy upholstery fabrics.

You can also achieve contrast and excitement in the different shapes of furnishings—alternating rounds of coffee and end tables with the straight lines of sofas and bookcases.

The informal sitting room shown (facing page) takes its plan from the sunflower fabric that's used on the chair and screens. Walls and floor are white, to expand the size of the room, while a small area rug in the same black, white and gold defines the conversation area. But even though every object in the room is one of these three colors, there's excitement in the style, thanks to different shapes and textures.

The secrets of finding storage space and fitting it out efficiently

No one seems to have enough storage space—even though when you moved you "really cleaned things out." So here you are in your new house with not enough storage space. How do you tackle the problem? where do you start to look? Like so many things, it all depends...on what you need to store, where you want to store it, and where the spare space (there *is* some, somewhere) can be found. The way to start is room by room, and...

If your problem is bulk storage, or storage of things you don't use or need every day, the places to look are the basement, the garage and (if you have one) the attic.

These are the easiest places to find storage room, of course, and the solutions are fairly obvious. Just a few hints:

In the attic (if you're lucky enough to have one) you can simply hang clothes poles from the roof rafters and string out the clothes. You can store heavier objects on the floor—but nothing too heavy; ceiling joists are not typically sized to carry heavy loads. Warning No. 2: You're not going to be going up there too often, so you do have to worry about the possibility of a roof leak developing, or rain blowing in the gable vents during a strong summer storm, or the moths or squirrels getting in. And remember an attic can get awfully hot. In short, don't store anything like your very best fur coat up there.

In the garage and the basement you simply have to do some figuring about where you can mount or install a big storage cabinet or storage wall. The basement should have plenty of space—but look for a space that shows no signs of water leakage and raise the lowest shelf off the floor (every basement *eventually* gets water in it). And not too close to the furnace, for obvious reasons. If the garage is sized for a full-sized car and you drive a compact, you can put a storage cabinet ahead of the nose of the car (but fasten a 4x4 piece of wood to the floor to block the front wheels as soon as the rear bumper

Jo Voigt

James Brett

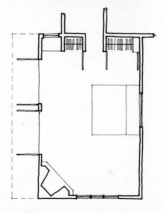

clears the door so you don't keep hitting the cabinet). And don't make it permanent—maybe you'll win a gas guzzler on a quiz show.

The secret to efficient storage: organize. You can't just "pile stuff in." Fasten a rack to the wall (you can even nail a board to cinder block or concrete walls with concrete nails and a great deal of difficulty) and hang the garden tools and wheelbarrow and extra hose and extra tires and skis. A piece of plywood similarly nailed to the wall can be fitted out with nails or hooks to hang all your tools. Your lumber yard will have a variety of storage cabinets and tool racks you can buy.

In the bedroom: "double-deck" the closets, slice off a wall-length closet, look under the bed and under the eaves.

The first place to look for more closet space is in the closets. Most closets are built with the rod about 70 inches off the floor with a shelf above. In a man's closet, by removing the shelf and hanging two rods—one 85 inches and one 46 inches off the floor—you can double the hanging space. It takes some getting used to (you hang the suits and jackets you use most often on the lower rod) but it works.

In women's closets, dresses are too long for this doubling up technique—but in these days of slacks and jackets, you can hang one high rod, having room under the jackets and the like for an extra dresser (you can buy an unpainted one).

Stores are filled these days with ways to "fit out" the closet—hanging bags that store a score of sweaters, or a dozen pairs of shoes. The usual shelf above the hanging rod in a woman's closet shouldn't be bulk storage—it's a good place to fit cubbyholes for stockings and sweaters and pocketbooks and jewelry boxes.

If you've made the closets as efficient as possible, another good place to look is under the bed. If you sleep in grandfather's heirloom bed you can't use this technique. But in the children's rooms at least, you can buy or make a "captain's bed" with drawers underneath. (Shelves under the bed is a design trick used in boats that goes back hundreds of years.) And, if there's room at the

foot of the bed, a "foot locker" makes as much sense in a home as it did in the army. An inexpensive camp trunk painted in cheerful colors will do for the children's room. "Compartmentalize" it with hardboard dividers and you've got convenient bins for underclothes, socks, handkerchiefs, and just about everything but dresses and Sunday suits.

To solve the problem forever and a day, it's not hard to add an entire storage wall—if the bedroom is big enough. Check all four walls—is there a space where you can give up two feet of room length or width? Then you or your friendly local carpenter can simply frame out hanging sliding doors, and fit out all kinds of hanging space, shelves and cubby holes, and a dresser or two behind the doors (and since they are behind the doors, you can use inexpensive unpainted furniture). If there's a window in the way, simply frame around it and make a window seat. And maybe

Jo Voigt

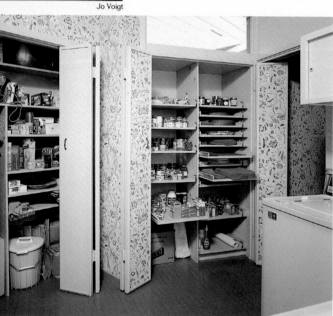

Kark Riek

one section ought to be given over to shelves—for books and ship models. If you work at home you can even build in a filing cabinet.

In many older houses, second-story bedrooms are built up under the rafters, with knee walls where the ceiling gets too low. Guess what's behind those knee walls? Empty space. You can simply remove the drywall and fit shelves and bins in that space.

Ernest Silva

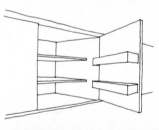

The kitchen—look up and look under, make the cabinets more efficient, add a wall of shelves for food or dishes.

The first attack is to make the best use of the cabinet space you've got. Most kitchen cabinets have adjustable shelves—adjust them. There's no sense storing soup cans on a shelf high enough for the giant box of Whammo Crunchies.

The bigger problem (and opportunity) is those under-counter cabinets—which are always too deep. Instead of getting down on your knees and reaching back for that can in the back, consider fitting under-counter space with pull-out drawers. You may also buy rotating "Lazy Susan" shelves.

Another space-maker is to trim the front five or six inches off the shelves and build shallow bins on the inside of the door—so when the door is swung open, frequently needed items come to hand—while the space "way back under" is used to store things you don't need everyday like the Thanksgiving turkey roasting pan and the case of dog food you bought on sale. (You can also store the giant cans of pink lemonade back there—let the kids dig them out.) Another good use for under-counter space—a wine rack.

Again, "fit out" the space under the sink—the sink drain hangs through

Robert Perron

171

Ernest Silva

STORAGE

there but you can build bins around it to hold the cleansers and polishes.

The most useful (and probably under-used) storage device in kitchens is the hook, a five-to-twenty five-cent item that solves a multitude of storage problems. If your pots and frying pans are at least halfway respectable looking, don't store them away—hang them from the walls and/or ceiling around the stove. You can even hang them over the stove—they get greasy pretty quickly, but just toss them in the dishwasher. (A caution: if you use screw-in hooks, you have to find a stud or the ceiling joist to screw them in—but you can also buy hooks with butterfly nuts so you can hang all but the heaviest from the drywall.) You can also hang your favorite bread baskets, the colander, the

sieves, and even a hanging pot of ivy or Christmas cactus, which do well in the warm, moist atmosphere of a kitchen.

Another place to look for hanging space—over the refrigerator. Good place to hang baskets.

Really need more cabinet space? Look for a wall or section of wall where you can give up a little depth and frame out some shelves. A foot is deep enough—you can build a wall of shelves to hold dishes and glasses and pans; or put some doors on and store food in there. If you have a free spirit and really enjoy the kitchen as a workplace, you could build a very shallow set of shelves (say five inches deep, using 1x6s) and *display* cans and bottles of herbs and boxes as a wall decoration—if Andy Warhol can sell paintings of Campbell's soup cans you can display the real thing.

The bathroom: Another space to fit out like a ship's cabin.

If you've bought an older house with a clawfoot tub and lots of space, you're lucky. It's tough to find space in newer houses with smaller bathrooms. Where to look:

1. The under-sink cabinet.
As in the kitchen, this cabinet with its drain is usually under-used. The best solution is to build in a series of small drawers—one for makeup, one for first-aid equipment, one for the hair dryer, a bigger one for clean washcloths and towels.

2. Over the sink.
You can build in a high cabinet—perhaps with a light underneath to illuminate the mirror. Keep it shallow—or you'll bump your head every time you bend over to shave or wash your face.

3. In the stud space.
The photo shows a 3½"-deep cabinet and a towel rack built by simply cutting

Joe Clayton

away the drywall between two studs. The cabinet has a plywood door, simple shelves nailed to the studs. The towel rods are half-inch aluminum rods set into drilled holes in the studs.

4. Of course you can buy any number (in any size) of excellent cabinets with mirror and lights built in.

Other places to look for storage: under the stairs...

In many older homes, the space under the stairs was simply boxed in. You can fit a low closet or a series of shelves in this space.

...in an extra-wide hall. Again especially in older houses, the halls are wider. The photo shows a 4-foot-wide hall with 30-inch-high, 14-inch-deep storage space faced with sliding doors, with an 8-inch-deep set of bookshelves above.

... in the living room. The idea of cabinet space with bookshelves above is an obvious one: no end of handsome "storage walls"—with space for books and record player and art objects and storage space with doors available on the market. They can be built against the wall or stand free as a divider—perhaps between the living room seating area and the dining space.

If you need space and you need a new coffee table—you can buy or build a box or chest-like table with drawers (rather like fitting drawers under the bed). Such a space is suitable for storing extra blankets and sheets for weekend guests.

...in the laundry room. Don't forget the space above the washer and dryer. A wall-hung cabinet makes a fine space to store the detergents—and a good place for soiled laundry and/or the laundry fresh from the dryer (let the children come get their own when they need it).

And—after this, if you *still* don't have enough room—it's tag sale time!

An investigation of new systems to make your home safer

There are two threats to your new house—fire and burglary. There's no way to create 100 percent security for you and your family—but it makes sense (and you'll feel better) if you think it out.

Fires and burglaries make news in almost every suburb and small town—but there's no sense getting uptight about it. The vast majority of families *do* manage to get through their lives without having their house burn down or being burglarized. The statistics on fire tend not to emphasize that the vast majority of lives lost in fires are lost in urban housing—and while this is a serious problem that must be solved, it is not a problem related to your new house. Nonetheless, it just plain makes sense to check out your new house from the point of fire safety and security—and if you find some areas of concern, to do something about them.

The first step towards fire safety is to make a thorough check through your new house.

Go room by room and look high and low for evidence of anything that might be a fire hazard. For example:

Check at least the wiring you can see. Often, older houses are short on electrical outlets. In setting up your lamps and appliances in the new house, have you had to resort to multiple plugs and extension cords? If so, straighten it out—outlets are meant to take *one* plug, one lamp, one appliance; a spider of wires leading from one outlet can cause an overload and overheating back there in the wall. If necessary, have your local electrician install extra wall outlets—it's not an expensive job and it's worth it. Too many extension cords tacked along the baseboard is a sure sign you need more outlets.

The kitchen is an important place to check—with the array of electric appliances we surround ourselves with these days, you may want to have the electrician install a strip of wall plugs along the wall over the counter, so you can plug in at a number of convenient locations. Caution: if you plug in an electric oven, a toaster, and the frying pan all at once, you'll be putting a heavy load on the circuit; tell the electrician how you plan to use the wall strip so he can determine whether you'll need a whole new circuit tied back to the circuit breaker and entry panel.

The bathroom is another spot where electrical loads are increasing—with the new hair dryers and the like. No "spiders" of multiple plugs in here! And make sure the outlets are nowhere near the water everyone splashes around a bathroom.

If you come across any frayed or cracked wires on this inspection tour, replace them now.

Check the attic, the basement, the garage. The attics of many older houses are a prime fire hazard. Take a flashlight and check it out. It can get awfully hot up there on summer days—so clear out those carefully stored magazines the previous owner was saving for posterity. All paper . . . out. The bird's nest in the gable-end vent . . . out. Anything combustible . . . out.

In the basement and garage: first throw out the boxes and packing material left from the move. And previous owners tend to leave shelves full of old paint cans, alcohol, kerosene and the rags that go with them—clear them out. There's no good place to store gasoline for the lawn mower—but surely not in the basement or the attached garage. The furnace: you should have it checked and serviced—just for the sake of efficiency and lower fuel bills. But tell the serviceman you've just moved in and ask him to check it out carefully while he's at it. And don't wait until cold weather sets in and every serviceman in town has more work than he knows what to do with. While he's there, make sure you know how to turn off the furnace when it "makes a funny noise"; and ask him how to check whether you're out of fuel (if it's an oil furnace), how to reset the furnace motor if it cuts out (they do, unaccountably, from time to time), how to check the water level (if you have a hot-water or—there still are some—a steam system). A furnace is not nearly as complicated as an automobile—it makes sense to have a rudimentary knowledge of how it works and how to run it. (But if that's just not your style, don't worry—fuel company servicemen tend to be almost as prompt and helpful as telephone company servicemen.)

Fireplaces: especially in older houses, make a good visual check of the fireplace and its chimney. If the mortar has cracked or is falling out from between any of the bricks, or if there are any loose bricks, call in a mason to look things over. (And do it *before* you build your first roaring fire and start worrying about the wall getting hot!)

If you need new andirons or a new grate to hold the logs, buy a quality product. "Wobbly" andirons can fail to hold the logs securely—and a log that has burned in half and rolls out of the fireplace can stir you into frantic action.

About leaving a fire burning when you turn in: If you're fresh from a city apartment and new to fireplaces, you probably just won't be able to go to sleep until the fire burns down—and you might even try putting the fire out with the kitchen kettle (it makes a big mess!). A fire that has pretty well burned down can be left—but *make sure* the logs are firmly seated on the grate or andirons and *be sure* to close the screen so sparks can't fly out onto the rug.

It may seem "overdoing it" to have a fire drill—but it's not.

If your new house is single-story, the problem is of course simplified. The rule for everyone should simply be to open their window and get out. But . . . part of your family fire drill must be a check that the window (and the storm window beyond) can really be opened. In many older houses, windows can be painted stuck, or jammed during the humid summer months. In two-story houses, with the bedrooms upstairs, the problem is more difficult. The main idea is to give the children an alternative route if the stair is on fire. You can purchase rope ladders that any reasonably agile child or adult can throw out the window and climb down. Athletic boys (not all boys) may be able to manage climbing down a knotted rope from their bedroom window. Needless to say, both ladder and rope must be securely fastened and neatly stowed; and—again—the window must open easily. In many fire situations, such athletics may not be required—indeed, may be needlessly dangerous. Train your children to follow your instructions.

Then, of course, you must plan for the less agile—the very young child, any elderly in the house, and yourselves, if you're not in the shape you once were. Again, the principle is to find two alternative routes to safety—at least one of them will be away from the fire.

Try to impress on everyone to get out—not stop for valuables. Try to impress upon them to stay low—to crawl from bed to place of safety. Heat and gasses collect at the ceiling, and there is often breathable air down close to the floor when the air a few feet higher (where your head would be if you stood up) could render you unconscious.

Assign a meeting space for all family members after they have "bailed out"—too many fathers have gone back into a burning house to look for children who have already made their way to safety.

About calling the fire department: the rule is get out of the house and call from a neighbor's. Obviously, this rule can be tempered by common sense: if the fire has just begun at a far end of the house and everyone else is out of the house, you might choose to make the call faster from your own phone, *if it's near an exit door.* A must rule (do it now, as you read this): Write the number of your fire department (and you might as well add the numbers of the police, the doctor(s), and the local ambulance service) on a tag and fix it to the wall near the phone or phones. You don't want to have to find the phone book in the midst of an emergency.

What about fire extinguishers? Do they make sense around a house? The answer is sometimes . . .

Many homeowner's guides don't talk much about fire extinguishers—the rule is you should get out of the house and make the call to the fire department without waiting to fight the fire yourself. But, again, you might wish to temper this very good rule with a little common sense. If you are a reasonably calm person, and the oven catches fire from the pork roast or pecan pie bubbling over, you might consider putting it out yourself with a kitchen extinguisher. Most fire departments will urge homeowners to have one or two small CO_2 extinguishers in the kitchen for minor emergencies. If you purchase an extinguisher, be sure you know how to use it—it won't do any good if you don't know where the release pin and the trigger are. You can get a lesson at your local firehouse—and most fire departments can arrange to have your extinguisher checked and refilled periodically.

But even if you do have an extinguisher on hand, if the fire frightens you, get out and call the fire department.

The next best safeguard to your own common sense: smoke detectors.

In recent years, smoke detectors available at modest cost have come on the market and been extensively promoted. They are a sensible and affordable precaution—ranging in cost from about $25 to $100 per unit. There are two kinds:

1. Ionization detectors work on batteries or house power, sense the gases emitted by a fire and (more slowly) smoke.
2. Photoelectric devices, powered by house current, sound off when particles of smoke disrupt a beam of light within the detector housing.

Both emit shrill alarms, enough to wake the soundest sleeper. The best locations: at the head of the stairs to the second floor, in hallways near the bedrooms, perhaps in the children's bedroom area and down by your workshop. The units come with complete installation instructions—and your local fire department will be willing to give you advice. At any rate, any unit you buy should carry an Underwriters' Laboratories (UL) or Factory Mutual (FM) label.

If you are especially concerned about fire, you can have a more sophisticated system installed by professionals.

In addition to smoke detectors, powered by both house current (which could fail in a fire) and batteries, professionals can install heat sensors—which sound the alarm when the temperature at the sensor either reaches a certain point (usually 180 to 200 degrees) or rises at an abnormal rate (say 10 to 15 degrees per minute). Such home security systems can also be set up to detect break-ins, which brings us to the other form of home security . . .

Protection against break-in and burglary: you can have anything from a super-sensitive system to some simple locks (all applied, of course, with common sense).

Burglar-alarm systems can be as elaborate as you choose—with switches or contacts on every door and window that sound an alarm when any of them is opened, foil tape on the glass window panes that detect when any of them is broken, infrared or photoelectric cells that detect a person walking through "the beam," and central control panels (which can even be wired into the police department or a private service) to control the system. Such systems are expensive—running to a thousand dollars or more—but for some families are worth it.

Simpler burglar alarm systems are available for do-it-yourself installation from many manufacturers. Check your local hardware store, the Yellow Pages, the major merchandisers.

For most families, however, a check on how well the house can be locked up is sufficient protection. Get good deadbolt locks for all the doors, so that your door can't be opened with the skillful application of a plastic card. A secondary lock on windows is also a sound (and inexpensive) investment—the thumb-set locks on most double-hung sash pull out with modest effort on a crowbar. Your local hardware store will have a variety of such "double-check" locks for your doors and windows. They're worth looking over.

And—as in many areas of homeownership—a little common sense may be the best protection of all.

You've read these rules a hundred times: when you leave the house lock up. If you're going away overnight, leave an upstairs light on (or buy a timer that switches on a lamp or two at dusk). If you're going on vacation, stop the mail, the newspaper, the milk delivery. All are sure signals to thieves (and sometimes young vandals) that the house is vacant. Ask the police to check out the house from time to time.

At any rate, once you've taken sensible precautions against fire and break-in, relax about it all. Your new house is meant to be a source of pleasure, not constant concern.

Your home outside your door

1 2

3 4

...greenhouses and gazebos, decks, patios and pools, lawns and plantings

Your new house is getting straightened out, most of the boxes are emptied and gone, you've done the first round of fixing up—and it's time to start thinking about indoor-outdoor living. The Californians—with their beautiful climate—started it all, but these days everyone from Maine to the state of Washington, and all points south, can add to the pleasure of their new house with carefully planned outdoor living spaces.

And make no mistake—a deck or patio or greenhouse or any other outdoor space needs to be thought of as living space, and needs to be carefully planned; as carefully planned as any other addition to the house. Let's start with decks and patios:

Your first question: where do you want the outdoor space? Most common answer: outside the living room, so you and your guests can move outside, perhaps through a sliding glass door. But think.... One of the most pleasant outdoor experiences is eating out under the trees—so you should consider an outdoor living space outside the dining room or just outside the kitchen (at any rate, a space close to the kitchen). Another possibility: a private outdoor space outside the master bedroom, ideal for sunning and a lovely space to spend a warm summer evening.

Sometimes, if your house is L-shaped or U-shaped, you can plan a patio so it opens from and serves a number of rooms, tucked in out of the breeze, as shown in photo 1.

More often, of course, the deck or patio must be extended off one room. Photo 2 shows a deck three to four feet off the ground and opening through a sliding glass door to the kitchen. This would be a pleasant space for breakfast and dinner alike—framed by the house and evergreen plantings, protected from the summer sun by a huge shade tree, overlooking a handsome garden and brick walk leading on to the rest of the yard. These owners have elected not to fence their deck—which is an exceedingly handsome solution but perhaps "nervous-making" if you have small children or accident-prone friends. The furniture is simple and clearly able to take a little rain from time to time.

Photo 3 shows a handsome deck off a one-story house—sited just outside the dining room. It has a table for outdoor dining—and a frame of low benches that acts as a fence and provides a larger seating area when friends drop in. Here,

Hedrich-Blessing   **5**

Jonathan Wagner   **6**   **7**   Ezra Stoller

broad steps lead down to grade.

These three handsome decks make an important point—it is very nice to have your outdoor space on the same level as the floors of the house. Somehow, even a step down tends to isolate or separate the inside room from the outside room—having both at just the same height is much more pleasant.

Sometimes—if your floor level is close to the ground, as in many houses with crawl spaces—you can have both a deck and a patio. One successful example is shown in photo 4. In this split-level house, a broad deck has been added off the family room, where it is convenient for both entertaining and dining; and broad steps lead down from the deck to an on-grade patio with its own furniture and wide bench. Tiny evergreens around the patio will, in ten years, form a green wall creating a most interesting octagonal outdoor room.

The easiest and cheapest solution of

all, of course, is possible when your house opens directly to grade—so you can simply open the door and step onto your patio. Photo 5 shows a modest, easy-to-build, and exceedingly handsome patio outside the family room of a split-level house. The dining area is defined by the concrete floor and trellis overhead; and this space is extended by the brick paving and informal benches into the garden and yard beyond. This patio offers, within its small space, a number of choices—sitting or stretching out; sun or shade. It is framed by the low benches and the simple planning into what is, in effect, a real outdoor living / dining space.

A more "romantic" patio is shown in photo 6. This little patio is sheltered in an L between the living room and bedroom of a house—opening to the living room through a standard door, opening to the bedroom through double French doors. When these doors are open, the

bedroom simply expands into the outdoors. There is a tiny garden for summer color and winter evergreen, brick paving, and a low bench atop the stone wall that defines the edge between the patio and the lawn.

Some construction ideas: Make sure you know how big you want your deck or patio to be. Try putting some furniture out on the lawn before you start construction and see how it "feels." Big is not necessarily better—a small deck or patio off the bedroom suggests even to the children that it is "your space."

As to materials: local advice is best. For decks, redwood is always good. So is cedar. Fir or pine needs occasional treatment with rot preventive. If you build it yourself, use aluminum or galvanized nails so you won't have a thousand tiny rust spots. Patios of course can be paved with stone, or brick, or cement patio blocks (which come in a variety of colors), slate or bluestone;

8 9

10 11

even—if raised a bit off the ground—of wood.

You can buy plans for a variety of decks and patios from the newsstand—or simply consult your local contractor or architect. The construction rules vary with locality, and with the conditions on your site—too skimpy a base under your patio will cause it to become uneven the first winter; too skimpy a foundation under a deck four feet off the ground can be disastrous.

And don't forget your local regulations—as with any addition, you'll have to stay within side and rear-lot restrictions, meet your local building codes.

About "furnishing" your outdoor room: Even if you have a brown thumb, it's easy to grow annuals in big pots or those sawed-off beer kegs all the lumberyards are selling. They look wonderful on a patio.

Try to convince yourself to buy quality outdoor furniture. It is tough to buy a

$75 chair for the patio when you can get one of those aluminum-and-nylon folding chairs at the discount store for about $10. But it's worth it—in comfort, in long life, and in design.

Outdoor lighting is a job for your local electrician. You'll need waterproof (rainproof) fixtures and connections. Don't just tack a spotlight on the side of the house—it gives too harsh a light. What you want is a softer, diffused light coming from more than one direction—you're not, remember, on stage. One idea (if you can get your electrician to do it): mount a light up in a tree, so the light is diffused down through the leaves. Put the wire on the far side of the tree and your guests will think you're a magician.

A final word for those lucky enough to have large lots: A little patio (again, think outdoor room) well away from the house at a spot of special interest—as in photo 7—is a lovely addition to your way of living . . .

Greenhouses are becoming more popular every year—for the very good reason that they are fun to live with.

Many avid gardeners have built, with one or another connection to their house, what we would consider "a proper greenhouse"—with its curved and peaked glass roof, opening panes at the ridge to vent the summer heat, and business-like planting benches (8, 9). Such avid gardeners will need no advice from a book like this.

But if you simply enjoy the greenery and color of plants, consider transforming one wall of your kitchen or dining room (maybe even the living room) into a wall of lovely plants—set on the floor, resting on shelves, hanging from the framing of the ceiling overhead (9).

At modest cost, a greenhouse addition can be simply framed into an opening in the wall—perhaps where a sliding

Cantina.

SPANISH BOLD!
From Tropitone.

Hedrich-Blessing

12

Lisanti

Hedrich-Blessing

13 14

door is located now. A wide variety of stock greenhouse sections—in aluminum or steel—can be purchased from local suppliers. Perhaps more elegant is to frame out your greenhouse in wood as shown in photo 11. This addition to the living room is in effect an oversized bay window—with the posts and beams equal in finish to the living room wall, and the glass nicely let into the wood. Note the glass-to-glass joint where the glass wall meets the overhead glass—a handsome detail that takes a lot of care, a good sealant, and a little luck...but worth it!

Some cautions: obviously such a wall needs to face the sun—facing southeast through south to southwest is about as far as you ought to push it. (A north-facing wall, to be obvious about it, would get very little sun and, at least in colder climates, present an enormous heat loss.) Even with double glazing, which is in vogue these energy-conserving days,

there will be heat loss through a greenhouse wall. But if you really want such a room, you can look at it this way: all day all through the winter solar heat will be pouring *in* through the glass wall. It's still a net loss of heat, but then you have all those flowers all winter...

Given the heat loss involved, try and be sure that your heating system is up to the extra load—and there will be an extra load on cold and windy winter nights. A small supplementary heater in or near the greenhouse may be needed if you live in a harsh climate. (If you're really into energy conservation, any of the good books on solar heating will show you how you can *store* heat that pours in through the wall on sunny days.)

Again, obviously: opening a major opening in a wall to add on your greenhouse must be done carefully. Unless you know your construction, better call in a contractor or architect for advice on spanning the opening, building the

foundation for the greenhouse, and tying the greenhouse framing—whether metal or wood—into the house.

You'll be using a lot of water in the greenhouse—you may want the plumber to run in a new water line. At any rate, remember water will be dripping onto the floor, so choose a floor that can take it.

Another treat to give yourself if you really enjoy living outdoors: a gazebo.

If you have a large enough lot you can have a gazebo—and if you love eating outdoors or sitting on a summer evening listening to the crickets, an outdoor room like this is a wonderful addition. The formality of the 19th-century gazebo—usually set at the end of a formal garden, octagonal, with a pointed roof—has given way (as most formality has) to contemporary schemes like the ones shown above (12, 13, 14).

Free Information Center.
For products, planning, decorating and remodeling.

Many of the advertisers in the HomeBook are offering free full-color catalogs to HomeBook readers. Just turn to the back of the book and circle the catalogs you want on the postage-paid postcards.

Drop your card in the mail, and we'll send back the catalogs you requested as soon as possible. Often as fast as three days of receiving your request. So that very quickly the information you need will be found right in your new mailbox.

More help from the HomeBook.

Around a pool built at the edge of a drop-off, a wooden deck supported on poles creates a stunning tree-house view.

Left and below: two curvilinear shapes.

Swimming Pool Institute

Swimming pools are now within the reach of the average homeowner

Once a plaything of the wealthy, a pool can be had today for about the cost of a new car.

Not long ago, pools were made of either reinforced poured concrete or concrete sprayed (technically, united) over wire mesh. Concrete pools are still extremely popular. They are the most expensive (usually $10,000 and up), the longest lasting (it's tough to be tougher than concrete) and the highest style (with Gunite, you can have any shape you want, including those curvilinear shapes shown in several of the pictures).

At the low-cost end are the extremely popular above-ground pools—some with sheet metal walls and vinyl liner, some of wood with vinyl liner. The latter, which come in sizes up to 20' x 40', can—with a little thought and care—be integrated into a raised deck to avoid the

"beached whale" look that marks so many installations of above-ground pools.

In between as costs go, is the in-ground vinyl liner pool. A host of contractors and manufacturers offer a host of such pools—you can get pools with aluminum walls, steel walls, fiber glass walls and wood walls. A hole a bit larger than the final pool is dug four feet deep. The wall panels are set in place, fastened to each other and braced with metal brackets. The bottom of the pool is usually smooth sand. (If a diving well is wanted, the backhoe operator simply scoops out another four feet at the "deep end" and the contour of the well is finished in sand carefully troweled on.) A vinyl liner—in effect a huge plastic bag—is smoothed into place over the pool floor and walls, clamped over the top of the pool walls by the coping of the pool. Then the necessary electrical work (specifically, careful grounding of all metal in or associated with the pool—such as underwater lights, the support braces, and ladders) is done just below ground level, and the excavation outside the pool walls is backfilled.

This type of pool—which costs between $5,000 and $10,000 depending on size and quality—is becoming increasingly popular not just because of its cost, but because of speedy installations—with a little luck, not much over a week from first shovelful of excavation to first dive.

You'll need to check out local regulations on setbacks from property lines; distance from any surface body of water, septic tank or sewerage system; water lines or well; and the approved method of disposing of backwash water from the pool. Many municipalities, many insurance companies, and perhaps your own sense of concern will require fencing to prevent small children and animals from tumbling in when the pool is unattended. (Fences can be unsightly—with a little thought you can often integrate a fence into the lines of the house, or into shrubbery, so that your pool doesn't look like a prison yard.)

When budgeting for a pool, you'll need to consider some extras. The pool contract will include the pool itself, excavation (unless you hit rock), and the pump and filter equipment—but typically steps into the pool, an underwater light, a pool heater or solar blanket (which can extend the season several weeks at each end), and cleaning equipment are extras. Wiring of the pool pump, the light, and the necessary grounding is seldom included in the contract because of the great variation in cost depending on pool location—and it can cost $500 or more. Most pools come with little or no deck or terrace around the pool, so you'll have to budget for the deck and for the outdoor furniture you're sure to want on the deck. You may want a phone out by the pool to save those frantic dashes into the house. Finally, check on property taxes—in most municipalities, above-ground pools are not taxed, in-ground pools are taxed as an addition to the house. It can add up—check it out!

But enough of the cautions and costs. Pools today, once you have faced up to the initial costs (which can usually be tacked onto the mortgage) are relatively easy to clean and maintain, and come with astonishingly lengthy guarantees. And—if you enjoy swimming and sunning—what could be nicer. A pool is a social center for you and the children, a source of very good exercise, and—if well planned—a beautiful thing to overlook from your kitchen and breakfast room.

You Can Build This Covered Patio Yourself...
In Less Than Three Weekends!

What you're looking at is one of the quickest and easiest ways to improve the value and liveability of your home.

It's a do-it-yourself patio cover built with Filon Sunbreak, one of the newest and most exciting of our fiberglass reinforced building panels for 1979.

As you can see, "Sunbreak" looks like custom installed lath-work. The big differences are that Sunbreak goes up in about half the time, it is

light, yet amazingly strong, rot proof and shatter proof. And, of course, it lets in the light...but not the rain.

Your nearby Filon dealer has free plans for this patio, and other exciting projects. All buildable with simple hand tools. If you don't have the address of your nearest Filon dealer handy, just write us and we'll send it to you. After all, fair is fair.

Build It With...
FILON DIVISION OF VISTRON CORPORATION

12333 SOUTH VAN NESS AVENUE, HAWTHORNE, CALIFORNIA 90250

For more information circle 33 on the Reader's Service Card following the Index.

Growing and caring for lawns

There are two good reasons for caring for the greenery and flowers around your new house—or growing some if your new property is on the bare side.

One is simple enjoyment—it just plain makes you feel better to arrive at a house framed by a handsome green lawn and trees. Flowers and vegetables are the frosting—adding color and a hobby activity that many homeowners find deeply rewarding.

The other good reason is a financial one. A recent survey of realtors across the country indicated that a thick, green lawn would add an average of $1,400 to the price of a $45–50,000 house and attractive trees, shrubs and flowers would add an additional $1,500 to the value.

Some of the basic rules for planting and care of lawns, flowers, vegetables, and trees and shrubs are given here—but you can get more detailed information from free booklets on each of those subjects offered by O.M. Scott & Sons, Marysville, Ohio 43040. And of course there are hundreds of fine books on the subject.

To begin with lawns: Fall is the best time.

Most of us think of spring as the gardening season—but for lawns, the most important season is not the spring, but late summer to mid-fall. Dollar for dollar, and in terms of the time you'll have to invest, work done in those months will give you the best return.

The reason: Nutrients in the soil are exhausted during the summer, and replacing them with fertilizer at this time of year helps the grass liven up, grow strongly during the fall, and be in good shape for the winter's rest. Seeding in the early fall is the best time because the conditions are just right for germination—the soil still warm; the air warm during the day and cooler at night; with a good chance of reasonable rainfall.

If the lawn of your new house has a lot of weeds or coarse grasses, the fall is a good time to lay them low—by applying weed control to the lawn. But take note: You can't undertake weed control and seed new grass in the same season. Weed controls and grass seed are not compatible.

The best advice: If your lawn is very sparse of good grasses, do your seeding in the fall and postpone controlling the weeds until spring. But if there's a fair amount of desirable grasses, it's better to eliminate the weeds now, build up the grass, then overseed (reseed) in the spring.

In any event, with lower temperatures and the sun lower in the sky, you should reduce your lawnmower's cutting height by about ½ inch. This shorter cut will improve growth, and if you water during the fall whenever there is not enough rainfall (your lawn needs ½ inch of water twice a week) you'll have your lawn in great shape by winter, ready to give you a real treat as soon as it warms up again in the spring.

Early spring is the second key period

Your first job is a cleanup—you should rake up the leaves you missed in the fall, and the twigs and debris left by winter storms. Next step is a good mowing, to clear off an inch or so of brown blades and let the sunshine reach into the base of the plant. And then fertilize. Spring is a good time to reseed thin and bare areas—you'll need to loosen up the top layer of soil in any bare spots by using a power rake. When you reseed, keep the surface moist **all the time** until the seedlings are clearly established. Use a special starter fertilizer on new grass areas—it provides the extra punch tender seedlings need.

The rest of the season is easier: Late spring is time for another application of fertilizer. If you have problems with dandelions or other weeds, now is the time to get them. Pick a day when the dandelions are still in bloom, wet them down, and apply weed control. Face up to it—if you don't they'll be worse next year; almost all such non-grass weeds are perennial.

Summer? This is survival time. You'll want to watch your lawn and help it where it needs help—by application, as needed, of insect control, weed control, and water, water, water.

The soil needs to be kept moist 3 to 4 inches deep. If nature has failed you, water ½ inch every third day.

...flowers

You don't have to make a full-time hobby out of growing flowers to have handsome color around.

Start with annuals; they're easy to buy, easy to plant, and easy to maintain. And start with transplants—plants which have been started at the nursery or garden store. You can of course start with seeds—but save that for a year or so until your thumb is greener.

The best place to get advice on what flowers to grow is your local nursery. The people there will know what grows successfully in your part of the country, will help you plan a garden that will provide a display of color through the seasons—first frost-resistant flowers for the spring, then hardy summer flowers, finally a last burst of color in the fall. Where to plant? You'll want color out front to set off your new house—and a garden out back to enjoy as you work in the kitchen or sit in your living room or on your terrace. Most annuals grow best in full sun, so if your garden area gets sun only part of the day, or gets sun filtered down through the trees, be sure to ask for flowers that can flourish in partial shade.

After careful selection of plants, the critical step is preparation of the bed. You'll need to turn over the soil with a spade or fork down a good six to eight inches, pulverizing any clumps as you go. If the soil is too heavy—too clay-like—you'll need to spread three to four inches of peat moss or compost over the bed and blend it in. After raking and smoothing, an application of special fertilizer for flowers is called for. Then transplant your flowers into the garden—spaced as your supplier will suggest. From then on, you'll need to water during periods when it doesn't rain (flowers want at least an inch a week) and tend to the weeds.

And that, for starters, is it. Later, when you're settled into your new house and have more time, you can start thinking about roses...and perennials.

...vegetables

Growing a bit of your own food seems to be an increasingly popular family activity. The truth is that it probably doesn't save you much money—your "crops" come in the same time that tomatoes and corn and zucchini hit the stores from local farms. But somehow or other, your own vegetables (especially tomatoes!) always taste better.

How to start? You'll need a place that gets sun almost all day—the more the better. And start small—you'll get better results from a smaller garden carefully tended than a big garden that's gotten out of hand. To prepare a garden, you'll need to strip off the grass or weeds, cultivate the soil 6 to 8 inches deep (a power tiller is probably called for unless you like heavy labor), rake smooth and pulverize, and get some fertilizer (this time, special vegetable garden fertilizer) into the soil.

What to plant and how to plant it requires some planning. Again, your local garden supply or nursery is probably the best source of advice. Obviously, gardening rules are different in most states than they are in the South, along the Gulf Coast, or in California. You'll get the best advice on when to plant from a local expert.

What can you grow? The most popular homegrowns are tomatoes, snap beans, onions, cucumbers, peppers, radishes, lettuce, carrots, corn, beets, cabbage, squash and peas. If you're willing to plant and wait a few years, you can even have artichokes. And if you've got the space (they take a lot) you can grow melons.

How big a garden? A plot 10' x 26' can supply a family of four—so scale down from there.

If the prospect of your own fresh vegetables tickles your fancy, you might want to get a good book on the subject—they'll provide a variety of garden plans—with details on the right spacings between rows and between plants to help you on the way to success.

...shrubs and trees

You're lucky if the house you've just moved into has mature trees and shrubs. They add a great deal to your property—and planting new shrubs and trees can add up in cost pretty quickly.

A good starting place, if your plot is a bit bare, is plantings around the foundation. These shrubs and low plants help "tie the house to the ground," covering the concrete of the foundation, softening the corners. Another common "starter planting" is to edge and define the walkway to the house—the beginning of a gradually evolving plan of decorative landscaping out front. Out back, if you have no trees to provide shade on a summer day, you might want to get one started. You might also consider a hedge or row of tall shrubs along the side lot-lines—they define your property but, importantly, are "friendly fences...

If you live in the northern part of the country, you'll probably want to think first of evergreens—plants that will provide spots or bands of green all through the long, hard, gray-and-brown winter. If your primary problem is shade, you'll choose a deciduous tree—a tree that sheds its leaves in the fall. If it is carefully sited, within relatively few years you'll have the shade you want—on the patio or to keep the house cool—with the bonus of that special spring freshness of new leaves, the fall kaleidoscope of color, and—once the leaves have fallen—the benefit of winter sun reaching your windows when its heat is welcome.

Planting shrubs is relatively simple—and the secret is to "dig a 25-dollar hole for a 10-dollar plant." Your nursery man will show you how to plant your first shrubs—ask him, and follow his advice.

A final tip if you have the space on your land: You'll often see small evergreens or other plants on sale for five dollars or so. You might consider picking up a dozen or so and planting them in a back corner of the property for transplanting later.

Index

For free help in a hurry, turn to the back of the book.

Many of the advertisers in the HomeBook are offering free full-color catalogs with detailed product information and decorating ideas.

Refer to the back of the book to find descriptions of the free catalogs, along with postpaid cards for ordering them.

You send the card, and we'll send you the catalogs fast. Often it'll be mailed within three days after we get your request.

More help from the HomeBook.

Free catalogs listed on the following pages.

For detailed product
information, and
help in planning, decorating
and remodeling.
To help you get
your new home
homier.
Send the card today to get
your information faster.
Often it'll be mailed
within three days after
we get your request.

More help from the HomeBook.

Free Catalogs To Help You

In Your Planning, Decorating and Remodeling

Many of the advertisers in The HomeBook are offering free, full-color catalogs to HomeBook readers. These catalogs are illustrated and described on this and the following two pages.

To receive the catalogs you want, just turn to the cards at the back of the book and circle the appropriate numbers. Drop your postage-paid card in the mail and we'll send back the catalogs as soon as possible. Often as fast as three days after receiving your request. So that very quickly the information you need will be found right in your new mailbox.

Georgia-Pacific Corp.

This 30-page booklet contains colorful remodeling ideas and directions for installing plywood paneling, gypsum wallboard and mouldings, and includes helpful hints for framing non-bearing partitions. To help you achieve professional results, there are tips on great do-it-yourself projects, decorating with color and style. **Circle No. 24 on Reader Service Card.**

See advertisement page 31, 113.

Quaker Maid

Quaker Maid's Cabinet Specification and Accessory Guide provides informative pages of facts, drawings and photos, many in full color. A valuable aid for "Kitchen Planners," the guide covers everything from door styles and storage features to construction details and cabinet sizes. **Circle No. 11 on Reader Service Card.**

See advertisement page 35.

Tappan

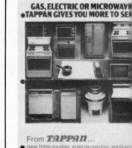

New 16-page brochure illustra the full line of Tappan ma appliances. Includes gas and elec ranges, microwave ovens, d washers, refrigerators, trash c pactors, disposers and range ho **Circle No. 12 on Reader Ser Card.**

See advertisement page 37.

Panasonic Company

Provides you with all the information you want and need to know about the Panasonic line of quality microwave ovens – from the exciting Genius model to their space-saving compact. It's all here in one colorful but simple format that easily tells you about each oven and its features. **Circle No. 13 on Reader Service Card.**

See advertisement page 41.

American Standard, Inc.

Full-color, 34-page brochure illustrates most residential plumbing fixtures and fittings available from American-Standard. Booklet is filled with suggested room arrangements and color ideas. Catalog numbers and dimensional detail make planning easy. Products range from a 32-inch deep soaking bath to money and water-saving toilets and faucets. **Circle No. 14 on Reader Service Card.**

See advertisement page 51.

Kohler Company

KOHLER ELEGANCE. Forty pages of colorful bath and kitchen ideas for your home, including whirlpool baths, environmental enclosures, bathtubs, shower coves, toilets, bidets, lavatories, kitchen sinks, water-saving faucets and showerheads, and many more. Booklet assists with product selection, color coordination and decorating ideas. **Circle No. 15 on Reader Service Card.**

See advertisement page 53.

Howmet Aluminum Corporation

This free full-color, 24-page helpful patio planning guide shows a wide variety of woodgrain Skylight patio cover styles and installations. The booklet introduces a new Skylight Room™ patio enclosure that increases your recreational space for about half the cost of conventional construction. **Circle No. 16 on Reader Service Card.**

See advertisement page 69.

Thermograte Enterprises, Inc.

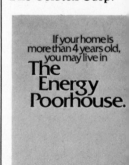

This 20-page booklet includes s articles as: "Yes…It Pays to B Wood!"; "Fireplace Heaters Wood Stoves" and "The Hottest ternate Energy Product of the Ye **Circle No. 17.**

A brochure on a new wood burr appliance, which combines highly efficient, Tubular Heat changer with a durable triple-construction Fireplace/Stove. C cle No. 18 on the Reader Ser Card.

See advertisement page 85.

Carrier Corporation

For this 4 color Booklet, "How to Keep Your Family Comfortable at Today's Costs" Circle number 19. It tells you all about family comfort and the options to consider, why it pays to work with an expert, and how Carrier technology confronts the cost of energy. Or call your Carrier dealer. He's in the yellow pages. **Circle number 19 on Readers Service Card.**

See advertisement page 87.

Alcoa Building Products, Inc.

A brochure outlining the complete Alcoa Building Products System line. Includes information on: siding, gutters and downspouts, soffit and fasciae, insulated windows, ventilating systems, shutters, railing and trim. **Circle No. 20 on Reader Service Card.**

See advertisement page 89.

Owens-Corning Fiberglas Corporation

This brochure provides you with information regarding insulation and energy conservation. It explains R-Valves, types of insulation, where to install it, how to install it and how much to install. Energy conservation tips covered include ventilation and moisture control, caulking and weatherstripping. **Circle No. 21 on Reader Service Card.**

See advertisement pages 94 & 95.

The Celotex Corp.

The Celotex Corporation offers four-page folder which explains benefits of insulating your h when you re-side. The folder why Celotex Thermax® Insula board is the most efficient insulat sheathing that you can buy on market today! **Circle No. 22 Reader Service Card.**

See advertisement page 97.

The Homefoamers

Our 8-page booklet "Almost All About Home Insulating" discusses conduction, convection and radiation and how it relates to home insulation. Additionally, the three most common types of home insulation are discussed . . . foam, fiberglass, and rock wool. **Circle No. 23 on Reader Service Card.**

See advertisement page 99.

Champion Building Products

A complete 26-page catalog that illustrates the versatility of wall paneling. Included is information on how to buy prefinished paneling, how to choose the proper paneling, problem walls, and installation. Additionally, a tear out Color Guide is provided to help determine which color backgrounds best suit your own color scheme. **Circle No. 25 on Reader Service Card.**

See advertisement page 115.

Masonite Corporation

Complete line of Masonite brand paneling covering full design and price spectrum is shown in colorful brochure. Included ,are elegant woodgrains, textured and smoothgrains, and panels that simulate brick, cork, stone and stucco. **Circle No. 26 on Reader Service Card.**

See advertisement page 59.

Kirsch Company

Most authoritative book on window treatments yet! 140 pages of decorating advice. Room setting photos in color; examples of most popular types of treatments; styles suitable for various rooms; ideas for common and problem windows; how-to for measuring and sewing basic treatments. Kirsch must be contacted directly for this catalog.

See advertisement page 125.

rmstrong Cork Company

CONSUMER GUIDE. Colorful age illustrated booklet gives ful advice on shopping for mod- vinyl floors. Information pro- d on no-wax surfaces, cushion- installation and upkeep, plus to decorate. Tells what to ask the salesperson, shows newest designs and colors. Free. Armstrong Cork Company, Dept. P.I., P.O. Box 3001, Lancaster, Pa. 17604. **Circle No. 27 on Reader Service Card.**

advertisement pages 128 & 129.

GAF Corporation

GAF offers a beautiful full-color, ten panel brochure completely describing the benefits of its new SVS™ GAFSTAR® 6700 Series sheet vinyl flooring line. Included are decorating ideas showcased in room settings which include living rooms, bathrooms, kitchens, dens and family rooms. The wide range of 28 colors are graphically illustrated in color swatches. Send for this invaluable decorating guide for fresh new ideas. **Circle No. 29 on Reader Service Card.**

See advertisement pages 134 & 135.

Dow Chemical U.S.A.

This booklet give you six reasons why VORACEL Attached Urethane Backing protects your carpet investment . . . keeps your carpet looking beautiful. It's comfortable . . . durable . . . locks fibers in place . . . moisture resistant . . . easy-to-install . . . and easy-to-move. **Circle No. 30 on Reader Service Card.**

See advertisement page 131.

gelow-Sanford, Inc.

omprehensive 28-page booklet ll color, covering the essentials home decorating with carpet. vides professional advice on r schemes, explores color inten- furniture and carpet styles, pat- terns and textures to help you make good decorating decisions plus how to choose the right carpet for each room in your home.

Circle No. 31 on Reader Service Card.

advertisement pages 138 & 139.

Thomasville Furniture Industries, Inc.

Thomasville has "Good Ideas For Furnishing Your Home," a 350-page, full-color decorating guide. It'll show you how to plan rooms. Select window, wall and floor treatments. And it'll take you "window-shopping" through the entire Thomasville furniture line. So before you decorate (or redecorate) send for your copy of this colorful book. Thomasville must be contacted directly.

See advertisement page 145.

Ethan Allen, Inc.

Just what your new house needs! The Ethan Allen Treasury. Big (nearly 400 pages), beautiful (nearly 300 color photos), and yours, *free*, when you visit Ethan Allen Gallery. The Treasury will give you a wealth of ideas on furnishing every room in your home. If you can't come in for your Treasury, contact Ethan Allen directly.

See advertisement page 151.

Turn page for more catalog descriptions.

Read the descriptions of the helpful catalogs you can get.

Then circle your choices on the postcards in back.

McGraw-Hill Book Company

Descriptive brochures on a wide selection of books to help you give your home loving care that increases both pleasure and profit. Books that help you become a wiz at home facelifts...old-age prevention...first aid...major overhauling...space-stretching...room-adding...burglar-proofing...and *tax reduction!* **Circle No. 32 on Reader Service Card.**

See advertisement page 165.

Filon

Whatever you build in your new home — a patio cover, a carport cover, a fence, a room divider, a greenhouse, or whatever — build it economically; build it with soft, safe light fiberglass; built it with color; build it to last. Build it with Filon! This free brochure helps you select the right Filon fiberglass reinforced panel for any job and the right color for any decor. **Circle No. 33 on Reader Service Card.**

See advertisement page 183.

Montgomery Ward & Company

Montgomery Ward offers 30 individual brochures — plus their current sales catalog — on a wide variety of products for the home. Examples include — microwaves, lawn mowers, washer/dryers, paint, and kitchen cabinets. **Contact your nearest Montgomery Ward location or circle No. 34 on Reader Service Card.**

See advertisement page 17.

National Home Improvement Coun

This 8-page pamphlet gives y series of steps to follow in plan your home improvement pro Included are ideas and informa on the selection of the contra detailing specifications, the ro the lending institutions, wha look for in a contract and prac tips on working with a contra **Circle No. 35 on the Reader S ice Card.**

See advertisement page 23.

GAF Corporation

A brief brochure describing the problem-free, fire-resistant, wind-resistant advantages of GAF-Timberline "look like wood" shingles. For the look of wood but not the problems — choose Timberline asphalt shingles. **Circle No. 36 on Reader Service Card.**

See advertisement pages 66 & 67.

Heatilator Fireplace

FIREPLACE IDEAS — A beautiful 12-page, full color brochure showing numerous fireplace ideas along with a complete selection of fireplace models. It also shows step-by-step installation ideas for those do-it-yourselfers. This brochure is chock-full of ideas.

Circle No. 37 on Reader Service Card.

See advertisement pages 71 & 83.

Weyerhaeuser Co.

"Go Wild with the Wood Weyerhaeuser" contains 18 dec ing ideas with paneling. Ideas clude wood grains and decora prints that look like the fi wallpaper. The easily installed 4 panels cover walls rapidly. paneling provides years of be with little upkeep. Weyerhae P.O. Box 1188, Chesapeake, 23324. **Circle No. 38 on Re Service Card.**

See advertisement page 117.

Kenney Manufacturing Co.

WINDOW DECORATING — now in a brand new edition, the most helpful book ever published on this subject has over 100 pages of beautiful window treatments plus how-to ideas galore — from making your own drapes to selecting drapery hardware, woven woods and roll-ups. Normally costs $1.95, but readers of the McGraw-Hill Home Book get it FREE. For name of nearest Kenney dealer, plus your free book, circle No. 39 on the Reader Service Card.

See advertisement page 121.

LouverDrape Inc.

This award winning 32 page color brochure is designed to show the various applications of vertical blinds in homes and offices. A wide variety of textures and colors are shown and it is pointed out that in addition to being attractive vertical blinds are also practical. They reject summer heat to help keep room cooler and lower air conditioning costs. And, they do not collect dust. **Circle No. 40 on Reader Service Card.**

See advertisement page 123.

Tropitone Furniture Company, Inc.

A full color, 48-page brochure illustrating Tropitone's seven lines of exciting outdoor aluminum frame furniture. Patio and pool settings are amply illustrated to give the buyer an idea of the 18 different colors available in both frame and lacings. Send $3 to Tropitone Furniture Co., P.O. Box 3197, Sarasota, FL 33578.

See advertisement page 179.

FREE Planning and Estimatin Guide

Here's a quick and easy reference guide to help you figure the amount of paint, wallpaper, paneling and carpeting you'll need for your home.

Included are easy-to-use formulas showing how to estimate square footage... ways to save on purchases... how much time for each job... hints on decorating.

Check the special box on Card No. 1 to receive your free estimating guide.

a. On Card No. 1, circle the key numbers corresponding to the number under each catalog you would like to receive at this time.

b. Clearly print your name and address.

c. At a later date, you may use cards 2, 3, 4 to request catalogs and other information not previously requested.

NOTE: All cards must be used prior to 6/30/80.

1

For the catalogs you wish to receive, circle the corresponding numbers below. There is no charge for this service.

10	11	12	13	14	15	16	17	18	19	20	21	22
23	25	26	27	29	30	31	32	33	34	35	36	37
38	39	40

Name

Address

City

State   Zip

We would appreciate your comments regarding The HomeBook

☐ Also send my FREE PLANNING GUIDE.
Card must be received by June 30, 1980.

V

2

For the catalogs you wish to receive, circle the corresponding numbers below. There is no charge for this service.

10	11	12	13	14	15	16	17	18	19	20	21	22
23	25	26	27	29	30	31	32	33	34	35	36	37
38	39	40

Name

Address

City

State   Zip

Card must be received by June 30, 1980.

V

3

For the catalogs you wish to receive, circle the corresponding numbers below. There is no charge for this service.

10	11	12	13	14	15	16	17	18	19	20	21	22
23	25	26	27	29	30	31	32	33	34	35	36	37
38	39	40

Name

Address

City

State   Zip

Card must be received by June 30, 1980.

V

4

For the catalogs you wish to receive, circle the corresponding numbers below. There is no charge for this service.

10	11	12	13	14	15	16	17	18	19	20	21	22
23	25	26	27	29	30	31	32	33	34	35	36	37
38	39	40

Name

Address

City

State   Zip

Card must be received by June 30, 1980.

V

BUSINESS REPLY CARD

FIRST CLASS PERMIT NO. 42 HIGHTSTOWN, NJ

Postage will be paid by

McGraw-Hill HomeBook
P.O. Box 409
Hightstown, NJ 08520

NO POSTAGE
NECESSARY
IF MAILED
IN THE
UNITED STATES

BUSINESS REPLY CARD

FIRST CLASS PERMIT NO. 42 HIGHTSTOWN, NJ

Postage will be paid by

McGraw-Hill HomeBook
P.O. Box 409
Hightstown, NJ 08520

NO POSTAGE
NECESSARY
IF MAILED
IN THE
UNITED STATES

BUSINESS REPLY CARD

FIRST CLASS PERMIT NO. 42 HIGHTSTOWN, NJ

Postage will be paid by

McGraw-Hill HomeBook
P.O. Box 409
Hightstown, NJ 08520

NO POSTAGE
NECESSARY
IF MAILED
IN THE
UNITED STATES

BUSINESS REPLY CARD

FIRST CLASS PERMIT NO. 42 HIGHTSTOWN, NJ

Postage will be paid by

McGraw-Hill HomeBook
P.O. Box 409
Hightstown, NJ 08520

NO POSTAGE
NECESSARY
IF MAILED
IN THE
UNITED STATES